EIGHT DECISIVE BOOKS
OF ANTIQUITY

Eight Decisive Books
of Antiquity

by

FREDERICK RUSSELL HOARE

Essay Index Reprint Series

BOOKS FOR LIBRARIES PRESS
FREEPORT, NEW YORK

Copyright 1952 by Sheed & Ward, Inc.

Reprinted 1969 by arrangement

ACKNOWLEDGEMENT

The extract from *Mother India*
is here reproduced by kind
permission of Jonathan Cape Ltd.

STANDARD BOOK NUMBER:
8369-1414-7

LIBRARY OF CONGRESS CATALOG CARD NUMBER:
73-99638

PRINTED IN THE UNITED STATES OF AMERICA

TO MY OLD SIXTH FORM AT THE
ORATORY SCHOOL
WHO WERE COMPELLED TO LISTEN TO MUCH OF THIS BOOK
IN ITS RUDIMENTARY STAGES
THIS FIRST PART OF IT IN ITS FINISHED FORM
IS DEDICATED IN REPARATION

CONTENTS

PREFACE

WHAT may the author of a book like this reasonably be expected to have read? Not, whatever the specialist reader may say, all the latest specialist publications in the specialist's own field, for that would mean (what he is apt to forget) all the specialist publications in twenty-four other fields also. Nor is this reading to be ruled out solely on the ground that no life would be long enough for it unless it were entirely given to the book from youth upwards. Even if it were so given, such reading would not be desirable unless the author, having accomplished it, gave himself time to forget most of it before putting pen to paper, for in no other way would he be able to see the wood for the trees. But if he gave himself time enough for that, by that time another set of the latest specialist publications would be in existence, which he would be told he should have read, and he would have to begin all over again.

By all means let the critic say that, if such is the case, a book like the present should not be written; but if he allows that it may be written at all, let him not make the impossible demand that it should consist of eight up-to-date specialized monographs—impossible for the physical reasons just given, and even more radically impossible because the very *raison d'être* of a book like this demands that it remain from first to last an essay. An essay I would define as a literary composition, whether long or short, on any subject, from theology to art and from history to mathematics, that is chiefly concerned, not to present the subject-matter but to develop an idea through the medium of the subject-matter, and derives its unity from that development. The present work, at any rate, is modelled upon that definition.

But when all this is said, the fact remains that it would be

1*

both folly and an impertinence to rest content to base a book
like this solely on the reading of bygone years. There are, it is
true, fashions in scholarship that have their little day and
fortunate is the Rip van Winkle who sleeps while they come and
go. But research does often bring permanent alterations in the
landscape and then those who disregard it may easily find
themselves, as the saying goes, barking up the wrong tree. At
least sufficient acquaintance with recent scholarship is necessary
to give the writer confidence in ignoring the rest of it. How this
is to be acquired without acquiring far too much presents a
problem like a paradox of Zeno, to which, when a life has been
crowded and what is left of it is short, the old reply is still the
best : *solvitur ambulando*.

I will only add two things. First, this book, such as it is, has
no dependence on any other book except in such ways as can
be, and have been, indicated in footnotes. In the second place,
I have been very fortunate in the fact that, when I have asked
the learned for help, it has been given most generously; and
there are three scholars to whom I owe special acknowledg-
ment.

The dates adopted in Chapter I (on Hammurabi's Laws) have
been supplied to me most generously by one of the first authorities on the subject, Mr. Sidney Smith, of the British Museum,
who has given also a general endorsement to those I have
adopted for early Egyptian history in Chapter II. Monsignor
J. M. T. Barton, D.D., has been good enough at my request
to read through and comment on Chapter III (on the Torah),
on which I was particularly anxious for a sound judgement to be
passed. I have very good reason to be grateful to him but I
must make it clear that he has not thereby made himself
responsible for all the statements contained in it. Chapter IV
was read through, most kindly, by Sir C. M. Bowra, the
author of *Tradition and Design in the Iliad,* who made a number
of criticisms of which I have gratefully taken advantage. In
particular, he pointed out a fatal flaw in my theory of Homer's
Achaeans, as originally set out. This led me to make modifications in it which, without changing its essential character,
made it (I cannot but think) much more convincing. But I wish
to say most emphatically that my use of Professor Bowra's

criticisms is my own, and does not make him in any way responsible for the chapter as it now stands or for any part of it. It would ill become me to repay his kindness to one who had no claim on it by fathering on him speculations with which he might reasonably not wish his name to be associated. At the same time I have a real debt that I must acknowledge and real gratitude I must express.

INTRODUCTION
DECISION BY BOOKS

INTRODUCTION

DECISION BY BOOKS

I

IN June, 1851, when the Great Exhibition was displaying the triumphs of a generation of peace, Sir Edward Creasy wrote an apologetic preface to a book designed to show that battles had sometimes exercised a decisive influence on the course of history. The apologies were needless. From that day to this, *Fifteen Decisive Battles of the World* has found readers. Imitators have added their tribute and the book is now definitely a classic.

And rightly so, for it provided and still provides a standpoint from which the world's history can be viewed with a new understanding; it plots a series of focal points around which familiar facts may be grouped with a fresh significance. Something like an outline of European history could be made to emerge from a course of lectures on the decisiveness of Creasy's battles, with perhaps three or four others added; and the outline would bear comparison for richness of content with many a more pretentious portraiture claiming to reveal the true lineaments and contours of history by stripping them of the accoutrements of war.

The title of my book, therefore, should not be taken as a disparagement either of Creasy or of Creasy's thesis. On the contrary, my aim is to re-read history on the general plan suggested by Creasy, substituting, however, a set of factors of a different kind. Books, not battles, are to be my landmarks; the force of ideas rather than the force of arms is to figure as the instrument of decision in the successive crises of history.

3

It is a legitimate transposition, for ultimately the course of history is ruled by mind. What, after all, in the last resort makes Creasy's battles decisive? It is not the killing or maiming of so many thousand men; a tidal wave could do that much, and history never hear of it. It is not the destruction of one organized force by another, nor even the substitution of one dynasty or one race for another as the rulers of a land; the triumphs of the Moguls and of Tamerlaine are not in Creasy's list. With hardly an exception Creasy's battles are decisive in history because the military decision led to the preservation or the spread or the extinction, as an effective historical force for the time being, of some set of ideas or ideals.

We cannot always simplify the issue to the extent of saying, if the political system or cultural tradition inspired by these ideas was that of the victors it survived or spread but if it was that of the conquered it was eclipsed; for "captive Greece led captive her savage conqueror". We can, however, say that the building or preservation or extension of civilizations or societies inspired by these things of the mind not infrequently depends on, even though it may affect to despise, the military security or political prestige won in the first instance by the sword and destructible by the sword. It is a commonplace among historians of all schools of thought that the ruthlessly enforced *pax Romana* with its framework of military roads and frontiers was a considerable factor in the spread of the Catholic Church itself during its first centuries.

It would appear, in fact, that the historical decisiveness of battles is in some sense complementary to that of books, with the battles taking their importance from the books rather than the books from the battles. The statement that the battle of Marathon was of the first importance because it enabled the books of Homer to survive as the mould of Greek genius, and those of Sophocles and Plato to be written as the expression of it, is far nearer the truth than the statement that the books of Homer are important because they inspired the Greeks to fight the Persians at Marathon and those of Sophocles and Plato because their genius caused Marathon to be remembered. To use a military analogy, the battles are related to the books whose writing they made possible somewhat as the ammunition wagons are related to the high explosive shells that they carry from the dumps to the guns.

This is an assertion the acceptance of which is demanded by the idealist and inevitable for the determinist. If we believe intensely that God is Spirit and that man, in virtue of his rational mind, partakes of the same Spirit, we shall insist, in season and out of season, that mind, though it may be limited in its operations by the material at its disposal, has naturally dominion over matter and can never be wholly immersed in it except by its own perverse choice. If we are Marxists, professing belief in a series of historical phases whose succession is determined strictly by economic factors, we shall nevertheless be conceiving that succession after the pattern of Hegel's dialectic, which presupposes mental activity, and endeavour through an intellectual understanding of this pattern to identify ourselves with the historical process and actively promote it. Moreover, we shall look to the intellect of a Lenin or a Stalin to teach us how the Marxist idea is to be applied to our particular circumstances of time and place.

If we belong to the older school of historical determinism represented in England by Buckle,[1] then, even if we hold with him that religion and morals are but "the fabric of a vision, which leaves not a rack behind", we shall at least have to admit with him that "the discoveries of genius" remain and "influence the most distant posterity". "The changes in every civilized people", he says, "are in their aggregate dependent . . . above all on the extent to which the knowledge [possessed by their ablest men] is diffused and the freedom with which it pervades all classes of society."

It is true that Buckle held that outside Europe this mental activity was so little operative that civilization depended almost entirely on physical causes. But when he, with like-minded historians of our own day, cites Egyptian civilization as the product of geographical factors alone, he is betrayed by his own illustrations. For, as Acton put it,[2] "the original inhabitants of the valley of the Nile were not better off or more civilized than their neighbours in the deserts of Libya and Arabia. It

---

[1] *The History of Civilisation in England*, 1857.
[2] *Historical Essays and Studies* : "Mr. Buckle's Philosophy of History".

was by the intelligence of the remarkable people who settled there that Egypt became the richest granary of the ancient world". The physical character of the Nile valley may have set the material problems to be solved by the creators of Egyptian civilization and imposed limits upon their constructional achievements; but it does not account for the fact that the earliest inhabitants of the valley made no approach to a solution while a batch of immigrant strangers grasped the problems and solved them. Still less does it account for the religious and political purposes to which they turned the colossal achievements of their genius. There is, indeed, good archaeological opinion in support of the view that these immigrants came of the same people who, under the name of Sumerians, were confronted with the similar and yet technically very different problems set by the river-system of Mesopotamia and solved them equally successfully, setting the stamp of their peculiar genius upon this solution also.

It is as when topographical conditions restrict architects to (say) brick as a building material. The materials will then confine building operations to a certain range of constructional forms, but differences in the minds of the architects will bring it about that the peak of building achievement is in one case a mud-brick hovel, in another a Babylonian ziggurat and in a third Santa Sophia. Moreover, the architect who built Santa Sophia would certainly have been capable of thinking out a very different but equally grand design if he had been confronted with the task of building in ferro-concrete or in stone.

II

If the case is thus with economic construction, far more will the pre-eminence of mind assert itself in the political construction that is the central activity with which history is concerned. For this activity, which creates the settings for the achievement of pure thought, culture and religion, is itself the expression of thought, culture and religion, so that ultimately the whole pattern of history is shaped by mind or by institutions that are in the main the product of mind.

Even Behaviourists and others who regard all mental activity as an illusion (and no doubt hold the terminology used here to be unscientific) may be disposed to agree that the "illusion" of mental activity is generated in a peculiar degree in the processes of economic and, still more, of political construction. If so, the assertions made in this chapter as to the close association of books with some crucial transitions in history will have a certain truth for them also. And if they cannot interpret the influence of books in terms of self-determination and intellectual freedom, since they deem these things to be illusions, they may at least find it interesting to relate it to their own illusion of mental activity as Behaviourist psychologists.

To return to the main argument regarding the mental element in political construction, it is true that there are institutions political in character in the shaping of which conscious intellectual activity seems scarcely traceable—the immemorial social organization of the pastoral nomads, for example. But neither these institutions nor the peoples cast in their mould are, considered simply in themselves, the proper material of history. For history is not merely something quite different from geography; it is also something much more than ethnology. That is a science that does indeed describe the social habits and fabrics of human communities but is most at home among those that do not change and is thus more akin to the studies of the naturalist than to the art of the historian. The time-factor enters as little into its most characteristic descriptions as it does into an account of a colony of ants; and the ethnologist has done a perfect work if his picture of a community at one period will serve in all essentials as an account of it a millennium later.

The people of whom this is true do indeed figure in history, but ordinarily as a background of barbarism and occasionally as a deflecting or destroying force. Contacts such as these are not woven into the fabric of history unless the creative minds of the historical peoples convert them to their own rational ends or are frustrated by them in the pursuit of those ends. Even when, as sometimes happens, the incoming barbarians figure in history as a stimulating force, as when they bring new blood and new vigour into a decaying but cultured society, they will not modify constructively the essential character of that culture and impress their own stamp upon it until its stamp has been first put upon themselves. Their own minds must be educated and stimulated by the minds of the indigenous people in proportion as their bodies and their bodily energies have invigorated and disciplined its physical stock.

In other words, history as distinct from ethnology comes into existence only when the physical setting of human societies, with their racial ingredients and corresponding temperaments and aptitudes, are utilized by purposeful men and women as the raw material of intelligent social construction. It is this shaping of matter by spirit which creates purposefully organized community life, that prerequisite of civilization. It is that same shaping by the spirit which differentiates political systems, generates and characterizes cultures and, in these processes, brings about significant events, the only proper subject of historical narrative.

By "significant events" in this connection I mean events that are, in the first place, unique, in that they are not merely elements in recurring cycles, like the annual passage of the earth through the point at which it comes nearest to the sun or the annual celebration of a king's birthday. In the second place, to be historically significant events must be public, either of their own nature or because they affect the private lives of public persons in such a way as to have their repercussions in public affairs. Finally, they must convey a meaning worth conveying, because it springs from intelligent public purposes. The peoples who bring these events to pass are historical peoples because their actions are intelligible and interesting to other peoples.

III

The formation of minds by mind, then, is required before an historical people can come into existence. But this formation may proceed along two quite different lines and the outcome will be two very different types of historical peoples. The states of history have not as a rule been the product of conscious political planning; the exceptions are relatively few and mostly of comparatively recent origin. Changes in the constitutional form of established states have, of course, been innumerable;

but it is a comparatively rare thing for a state to be founded and constructed in accordance with a design drawn up on the principles of some political philosophy, in the sense that (say) a dam is projected and built in accordance with a design drawn up on the principles of structural engineering; nor have states often submitted to being completely remoulded on any such plan.

For the ground-plan of life in political communities has not been regarded by the bulk of mankind, even of reflective mankind, as something that needs to be invented. Men have usually taken for granted the basic purposes for which they live together in states. They have similarly accepted without much questioning those primary and traditional groupings in families, villages, towns and vocational associations in which the everyday working relations between the citizens of states are framed. They have, moreover, instinctively recognized certain essential mutual moral obligations as the standard of behaviour binding on members of any human society and only requiring to be made more particular and precise to serve to regulate also behaviour in any particular specialized group. All these fundamentals of life in political communities have ordinarily been taken for granted even by the most radical innovators, and most revolutions of the past have had for their aim the expulsion of the usurpers of novel powers and, for their slogan, "Back to the good old ways ! "

For this reason it would be wrong to conceive the part played by mental activity in the political formation even of the historical peoples as normally or primarily a process whereby speculative thinkers plan a state *in vacuo* and practical politicians embody the design in actual institutions. The human mind has more than one way of moulding human activities and its most effective and enduring way is not through lectures or blueprints, but through the shape it imposes in virtue of its own inherent characteristics upon the actions of every human being who uses his mind when he acts.

For reason has its own laws and the rational moral judgement has its own laws; and these laws constitute the natural behaviour pattern of men in so far as they are acting in a distinctively human way and particularly in so far as they are acting in a distinctively social and political way. For the need to live politically is one of the first dictates of human reason. As Aristotle said more than two thousand years ago, man is a political animal. He has only to follow the natural bent of his mind and conscience to find himself constructing, or rather maintaining, a very tolerable state-form.

So it comes about that the largest and most enduring states of history have owed little to political speculation; men found themselves living in certain political relations with one another and continued so to live. This has indeed been the secret of the stability of these states. In this respect they stand in sharp contrast to what we may call the experimental states, which have been founded, or at least refounded, under the inspiration of men who have thought of politics in abstract terms and held it possible to write new schemes upon human nature as upon a blank sheet.

IV

It is necessary, however, to avoid the error of confusing these stable states of history with the communities that have no history, which were described in the last section. Even when we have added that the stable states of antiquity tended to conform to a particular geographical, as well as to a political pattern, so that they were commonly associated with the basins of the great rivers, while the experimental states have belonged more often to the towns upon the trade routes or on the little coastal plains—even then we shall be far from having surrendered their political history to the physiographer and the ethnologist.

For not only do the reactions of men in communities to their physical environment and the extent to which they master it or, alternatively, are mastered by it, depend (as has already been said) almost entirely upon the quality and vigour of their minds; but even their acceptance of the political behaviour pattern imposed upon them by the pattern of the human mind may be (and normally is) itself a conscious and deliberate act of the mind. Men knowingly and purposefully follow what they naturally know and purpose. The behaviour pattern of a colony of bees is imposed upon it by the physiological and sensitive structures of the different types of its inhabitants and, marvellously rational though it is in its essential nature, is followed wholly irrationally by all the bees. But since human nature is rational as well as sensitive and physiological, it is as natural for men to fulfil the behaviour pattern of their lives consciously and reflectively, that is to say, fully rationally, as it is for the bees to fulfil it unconsciously and by automatic reflexes.

This is none the less true because part of men's behaviour is non-rational; nor is it inconsistent with the fact that their minds, working consciously and reflectively, nevertheless manifest certain uniformities in their conclusions and products, for there are certain uniformities in human nature.

It is normal, therefore, even in the stable communities of history—Egypt, China and the like—that men should be conscious of the rational pattern of their behaviour as a community and should express their thoughts in words, should display the reason for what they do naturally, should rectify by reason what irregularities in nature have distorted and should use reason to perpetuate what weaker natures might let slip. In contrast with these stable communities of history, the communities that have no history follow their customs blindly and unreflectively. They may, indeed, be conscious of them as facts in a way that bees are not; but they are not conscious of them as having a knowable plan or purpose.

For this very reason, the unreflective communities are the less natural of the two types. They are further from the human norm and even from the communities of early man. The specimens of them studied by travellers and anthropologists have little that is either natural or primitive about them, if by natural we mean (as we should) conforming to the standards of undebased human nature and if by primitive we mean belonging to the earliest ages. These contemporary "primitives" have long been recognized by the more discerning anthropologists to be peoples in a late and decayed phase, whose customs, perpetuated by blind imitation, have become for the most part meaningless even to themselves and have sometimes outlasted the conditions that originally gave them both meaning and utility.

Such communities are the remote descendants of peoples who once thought about their lives and were ordering them rationally even when they lived them regularly. Either because their environment became, with a change of climate, too exacting or because, in an enervating climate, their mental energies drained away, they sank to the conditions of slaves of their surroundings and ended by obeying irrationally conventions that had once been commended by the intellect.

What I have termed the stable states of history are, then, to be distinguished as sharply on the one hand from the peoples that have no history as from the experimental states on the other. Indeed, the former distinction is the deeper of the two. For both the stable and the experimental states of history are in the last resort governed consciously by the mind and those that have no history are not, and the gulf between rational life and the irrational is the deepest in the natural order. Nevertheless, for the purposes of our present enquiry, the distinction between the two types of historical states, in respect of their mental formation, is of more immediate relevance. Though naturally no rigid line of demarcation can be drawn between the two types and it would be difficult to find any state conforming to either type to the complete exclusion of the other, nevertheless we shall find this classification illustrated again and again in the course of this book.

For the moment it will be enough to note that the distinction between the stable and the experimental states corresponds, broadly speaking, to the distinction between formation by precept and exhortation and formation by deductive logic. The stable states, just because their members take the fundamental rightness of political society for granted, tend to be content with the formulation of particular precepts of the moral law or of a code of positive law. (By positive law is meant regulations made and enforced by the state at some particular time and place in view of the circumstances of the moment.) In the experimental states, in which very little is taken for granted, political thinking becomes speculative and asks ultimate questions, and thinkers formulate universal propositions (true or false) about human nature and political society. From these generalizations, purporting to be true for every place and period, inferences are drawn, by means of deductive logic, which similarly claim for themselves universal applicability.

It is true that these principles and these inferences are seldom successfully applied in the community where they happen to be first formulated but, by way of compensation, their political effectiveness is unaffected by the passage of time. They have only to be preserved in writing to be capable of being disinterred centuries later and of forming minds in periods and in regions undreamed of by those who formulated them. Indeed, they all too often convert these minds into instruments of political construction in which all the ages of human experience count for nothing.

I should, of course, be grossly oversimplifying the variety of operations by which the human intellect moulds states and civilizations if I asserted that they could all be classified under these two types. It would not even be true to say that they could be completely described as participating in these two types in varying proportions. As we proceed with this book we shall find cases in which the formative influence should be described as the work of the political imagination rather than of political intelligence, and others in which the influence has not been directly political at all but has flowed from some masterpiece of theology, literature or science.

Nevertheless, the broad distinction I have been making between formation by precepts and formation by first principles should serve a useful purpose. The two types of mental operations it distinguishes are certainly fundamental from the standpoint of logic and psychology. They have, at the same time, a significant relation to two types of political community. They can even be helpful up to a certain point in suggesting chronological dividing lines in our list of decisive books.

v

Since, then, ideas and intellectual systems play in these various ways so pre-eminent a part in history, books can hardly be denied pre-eminence among history's decisive factors. It is true that ideas and books are not inseparable. Not only the precepts and ritual formularies that constitute the formative tradition of the peoples without a history, but even abstract ideas of the simpler kind with the simpler logical deductions from them, are capable of propagation without the aid of books, and even of transmission from one generation to another. But further than this unwritten ideas will not go. Folk-dances (to take an analogy from music) are perpetuated for centuries without a written score and the latest catchy tune travels through the town on the lips of errand-boys who could not read its score if they saw it, but the fugues of Bach and the symphonies of Beethoven must be recorded on paper or on sound-track if they are to endure. In the same way the elaboration of a great idea and its application to the circumstances of time and place, to say nothing of the logical arguments to justify its acceptance, must be written down, at least for those who have to propagate it, and perhaps also to enable its author to get his own mind clear. Moreover, men have found it well to set down even the simplest ideas and propositions in writing so as to provide a standard of reference, if perversion of them in the process of transmission is to be avoided.

In recent years, of course, the mechanical multiplication of copies has enabled books to play a further part. They have become not only the source from which the missionaries of the idea obtain their doctrine but, as it were, missionaries themselves among the many. As a rule, however, it is not the master work itself which serves this purpose, but popularizations on paper doing the work of popularizers on platforms. There has generally been some book at the fountain-head having a lonely pre-eminence.

For the fact is unescapable that a very high proportion of the ideas that have shaped or turned the course of history either were given to the world in the first instance in a book or became the fixed form of civilization or political system as a result of being embodied in a book. The number of unwritten systems of ideas decisive in the political history of the world is in the nature of the case difficult to estimate but can hardly be large, even if we include those that belong to periods and places in which writing was not in general use and which are commonly termed prehistoric.

One very remarkable exception of this type is the widespread megalithic culture, which almost certainly represents a compelling complex of ideas, both political and religious, carried right round the globe without a word being written down, unless in Egypt. Several millennia later, in the age of printing, Freemasonry has exercised an equally widespread and perhaps even more potent political influence by methods very different from those of the megalith builders in every respect except this one, that its system was not moulded by any writing known to the world. Of political systems that have operated publicly in a world of books, Fascism was virtually bookless in its formative stage, consistently with its early slogan "deeds not words".

These three political systems or movements may serve as examples of the rare exceptions to the general rule, and each of them is attributable to some special cause. The general truth remains, that the major movements and phases of political history have each been marked by a book. It was said earlier in this chapter that something like an outline of European history could be made to emerge from a course of lectures on Creasy's fifteen decisive battles. Even more certainly a series of studies of the books decisive for the political-history of the world could be made to cover in outline the greater part of that history.

It is, of course, necessary in this connection to interpret the term "book" somewhat widely if we are to include the documents that have shaped or fixed the political and social outlook of the earliest civilizations, when writing was a rarity and the multiplication of copies rarer still. A document engraved on stone and copied at long intervals on to clay tablets is a book for our present purpose if it fulfils our other requirements. Furthermore, we cannot confine the term "book" to the work of a single author publishing his original ideas to the world. A Code of laws, anonymous or otherwise, may be as effective as a pamphlet, if not in originating a political philosophy, at least in systematizing, consolidating and perpetuating one; several of the decisive books of political history are Codes. Again, two places at least in any complete list must each be occupied, not by one book by a master mind, but by a group of memoirs recording the Master's sayings. But none of these qualifications nullifies the essential meaning of the term "book".

I have drawn up a tentative list of books that played a

decisive part in world history; and the present book treats of the first eight of these, written before the coming of Christ. I try to show how each has been decisive—that is the effect it has had upon the world's political history, and, in so doing, to outline the mental history of the world's political systems.

The word "political" must be stressed. Books decisive in the realm of pure thought or literature but playing no part except perhaps in the remotest way in political history, are excluded. On the other hand, the book need not itself be on politics to be admitted to the list. In certain circumstances a work of literature may hold together a people with no political unity, as did the Epics of Homer.

In the same way the great books of religion are not included as such in the selection, nor excluded. Some, like the Pentateuch, played an obvious and direct part in the moulding and perpetuating of a nation. Others, such as the Hermetic Books of Hellenic Egypt, exercised a vast and hidden influence upon the mystical speculations of many centuries without ever contributing to political construction or, except remotely and occultly, to political disintegration. The Way of Buddhist monasticism has *withdrawn* its millions of monks from participation in any political or social activities.

The choice of books for the list, therefore, has been determined more by their effects than by their topics; and this sufficiently accounts for the nature of the part played in the choice by the quality of the book. The fact that a book is in the front rank of books does not necessarily make it a decisive book in the sense defined. On the other hand, one great quality a book must have if it is to be decisive in world history. Somehow or other it must contrive to be mind-compelling.

The ways of compulsion are various, as we have already indicated. One book may cast the mind of an entire community in an immutable mould by a body of precepts sufficiently intelligible to be grasped by those who have to administer them, sufficiently practicable and congenial to be accepted by those who have to obey them and sufficiently self-consistent and well-ordered to give an enduring stability to the institutions moulded by them. A book of an almost diametrically opposed type may operate by one of those clear logical demonstrations that can enthral a certain type of mind, once its premises, true or false, are consciously or unconsciously accepted; and may extend its grip through the crystallization of its logical formulas into a few striking phrases similarly capable of fastening themselves upon the minds of those who are satisfied to feel that they are thinking. Yet another book may express universal principles, drawn from the depths of human or Divine nature, stating them in terms of political and social problems and inviting the application of them to particular conditions.

Thus, one book will fix the social structure of a community for a period measured by millennia. A second will so fix the minds of individual men scattered over a continent that they become impervious to other thoughts and ruthless agents of the destruction of all that lies outside their narrow range and the equally ruthless agents of doctrinaire construction in which their own narrow range of thought is made the measure of the lives of others. A third book will fix principles from which minds that *can* work may work, a millennium or two (it may be) after it first propounded them. In all these cases the book will have succeeded, for good or evil, in capturing and forming minds.

VI

Here are the eight books of the Ancient World which seem to me most completely to meet the specifications I have set out for a "decisive book".

First, the Laws of Hammurabi, that gave legal form and sanction to the first bourgeois civilization. It was composed in Babylon, probably in the eighteenth century before Christ.

Second, the so-called Book of the Dead, formed by a slow accretion of "chapters", mainly during the first half of the second millennium B.C., and catering for that preoccupation with another world that was largely responsible for the static character of Egyptian civilization.

Third, the Books of Moses, dating in the main from about 1400 B.C., the charter of the Chosen People.

Fourth, the Epics of Homer (written in the ninth or eighth century B.C.) that preserved the unity of the disunited Hellenes and made a single Greek culture possible.

Fifth, the Institutes of Manu, which fixed the caste system that still characterizes Hindu India. The surviving version goes back to a lost original probably not much younger than Homer's Epics.

Sixth, the sayings of Confucius, who was teaching in the years round about 500 B.C. They formed the minds, for long periods throughout two millennia, of the bureaucracy of the Literati, which for centuries ruled China.

These six books may be regarded as forming a group roughly distinguishable from the two books that close the series as, in the main, embodying precepts rather than the principles of political thinking.

The seventh on the list is Plato's *Republic* (about 390 B.C.), the picture of the State whose pattern is laid up in heaven.

The eighth and last of the first series, is Aristotle's *Politics* (about 330 B.C.), which discusses the State natural to man.

[*Publishers' note: the author died while his book was in the press. Had he lived, he would have written a second and third series. Readers may be interested to know what were the remaining books on his list.*]

The second series comprises ten books, all of which belong to or relate to the period when revealed religion took an active part in one way or another in the directing of states.

First in this series and ninth on the complete list come the Gospels (first century), brief records of God made Man and of His teaching concerning the grafting of human nature upon the divine Nature.

Tenth on the list is St. Augustine's *City of God* (*De Civitate Dei*, about A.D. 425), which sets side by side the pictures of the earthly and of the heavenly States.

Eleventh, *The Rule of St. Benedict* (about A.D. 525), which was as the leaven in the lump in the new society that arose on the ruins of the Roman State in the West.

Twelfth, the *Institutes* of Justinian (about A.D. 530), which enshrined the legal absolutism of the Roman State still surviving in the East and preserved it in writing against the day when it entered Western Christendom as a revolutionary and transforming force.

Thirteenth on the list is the Koran (about A.D. 630), the sacred book of the militant theocracy of Islam.

Fourteenth, the so-called *Decretum* of Gratian (A.D. 1148), setting out the relations of Church and State in terms of Canon Law.

Fifteenth, the *Summa Theologica* of St. Thomas Aquinas (about A.D. 1270), which provided a framework of thought for a balanced scheme in which the natural rights of the state could once again receive full recognition and at the same time be brought into relation with supernatural ends.

Sixteenth, the *Defensor Pacis* (1324), of Marsiglio of Padua, the protagonist of the secular state and the absolutism of the people.

Seventeenth, Machiavelli's *The Prince* (*Il Principe*, A.D. 1513), that taught statesmanship without morals.

Eighteenth, Calvin's *Institutes* (*Christianae Religionis Institutio*, A.D. 1536), the first systematic Protestant theology, on which was based the theocracy of presbyters and the first anti-Catholic "International".

The third and last series represents the epoch of post-Christian political secularism—the era of Liberalism and of the revived totalitarianism that arose out of it.

The first of the series and the nineteenth on the list is John Locke's *Two Treatises of Government* (1689), the fountain-head of English Whiggism and Liberalism and of the doctrines of the American Revolution.

Twentieth comes Rousseau's *Contrat Social* (1762), the handbook of the absolutist democracy that took charge of France during the French Revolution.

Twenty-first is Adam Smith's *Wealth of Nations* (1776), that translated Liberalism into terms of economics.

Twenty-second, *The Principles of Morals and Legislation* (1789), by Jeremy Bentham, the father of Utilitarianism.

Twenty-third, Hegel's *Grundlinien der Philosophie des Rechts* (1821), which provided reviving absolutism with a philosophical foundation.

Twenty-fourth, Charles Darwin's *Origin of Species by Means of Natural Selection* (1859), which provided a biological pretext for the elimination of morals from politics.

Twenty-fifth and last, Karl Marx's *Das Kapital* (A.D. 1867), which, in the name of historical determinism, challenged the bourgeois State whose charter was provided some four thousand years earlier by the first book on the list.

I

THE LAWS OF HAMMURABI
AND THE FIRST BOURGEOIS STATE

I

THE LAWS OF HAMMURABI

AND THE FIRST BOURGEOIS STATE

I

OF the ancient stable civilizations of the river-basins, the earliest was probably that of Mesopotamia.[1] Be it noted that the word used here is "civilization" and not "state". It was not until long after its civilization was settled that Mesopotamia was stabilized as a single state, mainly (it may be said at once) by the action of the "book" we are to discuss in this chapter.

For, until nearly the end of the third millennium B.C., Mesopotamia was a land, not of one state, but of many. It was predominantly a land of city-states, that is to say, of little states each consisting of a single city dominating the territory immediately surrounding it, like those of ancient Greece or Renaissance Italy. The land had not even a single name but was known as Sumer and Akkad.

The use of the two names, moreover, reflects a duality of racial origins. The part known as Sumer, the fen-country in the south-east, at the head of the Persian Gulf, had, for its ruling race, the Sumerians, concerning whose origins there have been many speculations. They themselves believed that

---

[1] The claims of Egypt have eager partisans (less assured, however, in recent years than formerly) and the assertion in the text is a debatable one. But it would defeat the purpose of this book, which is to elucidate the history and achievements of ideas, if all the debatable questions of archaeological or historical fact that arose in the course of the exposition were argued out in its pages. Where, as in the present instance, the answer to the archaeological question is not bound up with the main argument, it should be enough to indicate by a "probably" or the like that an alternative view exists which the writer is aware of but cannot accept.

they entered Mesopotamia with their great inventions already made. Akkad was dominated by a people who were akin in language and habits to the so-called Northern Semites, the Martu or Amurru (or Amorite) peoples of northern Syria. This kinship is not necessarily inconsistent with their own belief that their ancestors were aboriginal on the Mesopotamian plain. Their own region of Akkad, named after the city of Akkad or Agadé, comprised the north-westerly part of the plain, where the two rivers, the Euphrates and the Tigris, are at their nearest to each other. (Their more or less parallel courses through the plain are what caused it to be known as Mesopotamia, Greek for "mid-river land".) The Semites, however, were not confined to this north-westerly region but were to be found also scattered over the whole country.

These Semites of Akkad were peasants and villagers; it was the Sumerians who took the lead in city life. They seem to have been the great inventors of the early world. It is apparently to their genius that mankind owes the wheel and the ox-drawn plough and the great political invention of the city-state. Certainly it was in Sumer that these states chiefly flourished in early Mesopotamia. Each of them, at this period, was ruled by an official called a *patesi* who was both a prince and a priest. As priest he represented the god of the city and it was as the god's representative that he was the prince of the city. In other words, the government of these Sumerian city-states was theocratic, for theocracy (of which we shall be hearing much more in the course of this book) is the system under which direct political authority is wielded by one who possesses religious authority and is wielded by him in virtue of his possession of religious authority.

These city-states of the Mesopotamian plain were ordinarily independent of one another and constantly at war. Naturally, also, there were spells when one city took the lead and exercised for a time a hegemony over the rest. But it was the Semites of Akkad, where inter-city rivalry was less acute, who manifested the strongest impulse towards unifying the country and the greatest capacity for it. The most notable of these early Semitic unifiers was Sargon, the founder of Agadé, who ruled the whole of Sumer and extended his conquests as far as the

Mediterranean Sea. Moreover, he founded a dynasty that lasted five generations. This date was perhaps about 2480 B.C.[1]

The overthrow of Sargon's dynasty by invaders from the north was followed by a period of confusion; then the ancient Sumerian city of Ur, in the south, took the lead, perhaps 2123 B.C. Under her suzerainty (for she did not rule despotically) the culture of the Sumerians reached its peak, but this was their last political rally. In 1894 B.C. (if the preceding dates are right) another Semitic ruler came to the front. One of the Amorites (that is to say, "Westerners") who dominated northern Syria, established himself at Babylon, a city hitherto unimportant but with an admirable strategic situation on the Euphrates, in the "waist" of the plain. Here he founded the First Dynasty of Babylon. Under its fourth king, who reigned for forty-two years, perhaps from 1792 to 1750 B.C., Mesopotamia was once again given political unity, this time so effectively that it remained politically united, not only when the First Dynasty was swept away by the great Hittite raid of 1595 B.C., but even under subsequent foreign conquests. The whole country, moreover, continued through the vicissitudes of nearly a millennium and a half to look to Babylon as its capital and became known to all the world as Babylonia.

It would, indeed, be difficult to find more striking testimony to the thoroughness of this work of unification than the fact that it was not undone during the centuries of Kassite rule (effective in Babylon from after the Hittite raid till 1169 B.C.). These Kassites were foreigners (probably Indo-Europeans) wholly alien in language, religion and customs to the Babylonians and possessing but little initiative or force, but at the end of the period the country still cohered around Babylon and was but little changed in character. It continued to be a political unity through the long alternation between native and foreign dynasties that followed the fall of the Kassites. Both the kingdom and the capital survived the savage assaults of the

---

[1] The range of dates assigned to Sargon by archaeologists of the highest standing is fully 500 years. The date given here has been supplied to me by Mr. Sidney Smith of the British Museum. The reasons for adopting this and other dates given in the early chapters of this book, and some account of the causes of the wide differences in chronology between authorities of standing, will be found in the Note on Chronology appended to this chapter.

Assyrian kings and annexation by Assyria; and when Senna-cherib had sacked Babylon and carried off the image of its god to Nineveh, his son Esarhaddon found it prudent to rebuild the city and restore its god.

By this time (the second half of the seventh century B.C.) Babylon was "a city as effete and rotten with intrigues as Baghdad in the days of the later Abbasids";[1] but the govern-mental scheme that had held Mesopotamia together was still strong enough to afford a framework for a final national revival. In 612 B.C. Babylonian armies took a fearful vengeance upon Nineveh and then Nebuchadnezzar, the captor of the Jews, almost wiped out the memory of Assyrian grandeur by the supreme magnificence of the New Babylonian Empire. Under him Babylon became at the same time by far the grandest and by far the oldest capital city in the world.

In 539 B.C. it fell to Cyrus the Persian, almost without a blow, and became no more than one of several capitals of another's empire. Sixty years later it was deprived by Xerxes even of this position. But it could still draw to itself Herodotus the Greek, to gather materials for his history, and Alexander the Macedonian, to plan in it a world empire under its head-ship. At the division of Alexander's conquests after his death in 323 B.C. it did actually become the capital of his general Seleucus, who dated the "Seleucid era" from his firm possession of it. Even when he had displaced it by his new foundation of Seleucia some forty miles away, Greeks thought it worth while to provide it with a Greek theatre and gymnasium. Presently the Greeks went; but amid crumbling mud-bricks a community struggled on there somehow until the last Babylonian tablet in the old Babylonian script was written and filed there two years before the Christ was born.

Now, the fourth King of the First Dynasty of Babylon who began all this was Hammurabi, and what made his work so enduring was not so much his armies as his Laws.

II

Even the greatest of law-givers can only succeed if his work concerns itself with the actual everyday life of the people; and

[1] Sidney Smith in the *Cambridge Ancient History*, vol. III, p. 70.

the everyday life of the inhabitants of Mesopotamia had seen a good many developments during the five or six hundred years that preceded Hammurabi. One of the reasons for outlining the pre-Babylonian phases of the political history of Mesopotamia was that some knowledge of them is required to make the economic and legal developments intelligible.

The basic mechanical problem to be solved if the economic life of the country was to rise above a very rudimentary level was that of irrigating the plain. Among the great river-basins that have nourished the great stable civilizations of antiquity, Mesopotamia and Egypt have a geographical feature in common that marks them out from all the others; they both lack regular and sufficient rainfall. It follows from this that, if any extensive area in either country is to be brought under regular and permanent cultivation, the river water must be artificially applied to that area in a controlled flow.

The technical problems thus set to Mesopotamia and Egypt respectively have affinities even in detail, together with some important differences. In Mesopotamia (which is all we are concerned with here) the region nearer the Persian Gulf suffered on the whole not so much from deficiency as from excess of water. It was a land of swamps and lagoons as a result of the constant blocking of the mouths of the two rivers by the silt they carried down.[1] In the upper reaches of the rivers the heavier gravel that was deposited there was always liable to create an obstruction that might suddenly divert the stream into a new course or cause it to flood the whole of the adjacent plain.

The main problem, therefore, was how to carry off the surplus river water during the flood season and cause it to flow harmlessly and, if possible, profitably, over the rainless flat-land. It is a difficult engineering problem for any age and the way in which the inhabitants of the country tackle it will to some extent be conditioned by their political evolution and

[1] In the early days of Mesopotamian civilization the Euphrates and the Tigris flowed separately into the Gulf. The single channel that now serves as an estuary for both rivers only came into existence as the heaped-up silt gradually extended down the Gulf, converting mile after mile at the head of it into more or less dry land, through which the rivers cut converging beds and merged their streams.

to some extent condition it and, with it, all their subsequent
economic and legal history. (If they do not tackle it at all, they
will have no history and mind will have succumbed to matter.)

It was solved in the end by the creation and maintenance
between the two rivers of an intricate network of canals raised
(like the cities themselves), by constantly renewed embankments,
above the level of the plain. Every period of political unity
brought the system further towards completeness and the
requirements of the unending task of construction and maintenance continuously weighed the scales in favour of political
unification over ever larger areas, for little could be achieved
on a large scale by rival cities quarrelling over water rights.
Considerable progress was made during the second half of the
third millennium B.C. and Hammurabi himself was a great
canal builder. Once created, the system kept Mesopotamia
fertile for some three thousand years under successive waves of
conquerors, until it broke down in the eleventh century of the
Christian era under the neglectful savagery of the Seljuk Turks
and the land reverted to the desert familiar to travellers to-day.

But the genius of the Sumerians for mastering and exploiting
nature did not stop at this achievement. They were pre-
eminently (as has already been said) the creators of a city-
civilization. Upon a firm foundation of the ceaseless cultivation
of the richest soil in the world, and an industrial craftsmanship
of a high order, they built a towering superstructure of
commerce. The very canals that irrigated the fields became
highways for the transport of goods; and the situation of the
country, in the geographical centre of the ancient world, was
utilized to make it the effective centre of the world's trade.
Seamen passing down the Gulf circumnavigated Arabia and
made contact with Egypt, or turned east to India. Up-stream,
traders and colonists reached mountain passes by which they
penetrated to the heart of Asia Minor, or else turned westward
to make the caravan routes that are still in use across Northern
Arabia to Syria. The foothills of the Zagros mountains that
wall in Mesopotamia on the north-east led to the highly cultivated and flourishing cities of Iran, and across Iran lay the
routes to the Punjab and to China.

To the exploitation of this commercial abundance, the inventive genius of the Sumerians contributed the basic elements of a commercial technique. They devised a sufficiently convenient system of writing, a numerical notation, an accurate method of book-keeping, a first approximation to a coinage in the shape of standardized weights of the precious metals, and a well-developed system of bankers' cheques. Thus arose the world's first money-economy and with it the world's first bourgeoisie, four thousand years before Marx deemed it due.

III

As early as the days of Sargon the merchants were beginning to be independent of the wealthy priesthoods, of whom they had originally been the agents. To the conquering dynasts they made themselves indispensable as dealers in the loot of conquest, in slaves and gold and silver. Amid semi-feudal land-tenures and semi-feudalized peasants they made land an object of purchase and labour of hire. When the Semitic dynasty of Agadé collapsed, they adjusted themselves to the renewal of inter-city strife by supplying the combatants with metal weapons and armour of constantly improving types. When Sumerian Ur restored unity and security, they obtained legal codes in their home-cities and founded their own colonies abroad. When the political leadership of the now much intermingled population finally reverted to its Semitic elements, they profited by the organizing ability of the First Dynasty of Babylon and, above all, of Hammurabi.

He was the first to centralize in some degree the administration of the entire country; and the civil service he created with this object reinforced the middle class with a large professional element possessed of assured money incomes. The same effect followed from the supersession of the *patesis* of the cities by royal officials for all except lesser local purposes. The increasing secularization of the civil government that this implied was a further factor in ensuring the predominance of the merchant's point of view; and the process was completed when the priesthood itself became professionally interested in money. Deprived of most of its governmental functions, it acquired a virtual monopoly of the most pervasive of economic activities by becoming the bankers of the community.

For the priestly corporations that in each city controlled the temple of the city's god, and had been behind the *patesi* when the *patesi* was the prince, had become great landowners, owning perhaps half the land of some city states, from which they drew corresponding revenues. They had accumulated, in addition, great stores of precious metals out of the temple offerings. They had consequently become the resort of all those who wanted agricultural or commercial loans and the situation only needed regularizing for the temple to become the leading bank of the city.

This necessarily gave its priests an interest in almost every great business-undertaking and a hold, direct or indirect, on the great majority of free citizens; for, wherever money circulates freely, its ultimate control tends to be concentrated in a few hands. In times of financial difficulty the small wage-earner incurs liability to the pawnbroker, the peasant to the landlord, the craftsman to the merchant, the shopkeeper to the wholesaler and all to the banks. With every change in the value of money (and there were many during this period) the large dealers in money can always gain in one way or another, so long as the law protects the monetary system itself. They are particularly well placed to do this when, like the Babylonian temple corporations, they can supply their own needs as consumers from landed estates large enough to be self-contained and therefore independent of money.[1]

The emergence of the priesthood in this financial role was of a piece with the general character of Sumerian religion, particularly after it had been modified by Semitic influence. The Sumerians had always been a most religious people and their Semitic rulers preserved practically without alteration the Sumerian myths and cults. But Sumerian religion had always been concerned primarily with the purposes of this world and Semitic influence had only accentuated its innate tendencies. By contrast with the contemporary religion of Egypt it was singularly vague about the next life and indifferent to it; by contrast with Buddhism it had a remarkably practical sense of the main chance in the present life.

[1] See, for this and several other points made in the present section (iii), Gordon Childe's *What Happened in History*.

Thus the idea of a heaven and a hell had but little place in the religious life of Babylon. "He has gone to his fate" is the standard phrase in the Laws of Hammurabi for "he has died" and it seems that in all the extensive religious literature of Babylonia there is only one isolated text that discriminates between the fates of the good and the bad. The common account given of the after life was of a shadowy existence in a gloomy underworld, "the Land from which there is no Return", where the shades fed on dust or mice. Only if the dead went unburied, or were buried without food or drink, did they return to plague the living; once satisfied, they disappeared from sight and soon from mind. As little money as possible was spent, at the time we are now speaking of—the age of Hammurabi—on the burial itself, which was often coffinless, or in a chest under the floor.

Consistently with this absence of interest in a future life, all votive offerings and prayers to the gods recorded in surviving documents are for health or wealth in this life. Literature presents a like phenomenon. The bulk of the written documents that have survived from Hammurabi's day are business documents.

IV

Here, then, we have all the ingredients of the complete bourgeois state; but more than the ingredients were needed to give it a pattern or permanence. A medley of races, some immigrant, some indigenous, had been included in the state created by the strong arm of Hammurabi. A long tradition of local self-government existed to strengthen resistance to uniformity and to maintain local laws; even tribal customs survived to add to the confusion. Family blood-feuds and private revenge still kept a footing in the administration of justice. Only the sword enforced unity and such uniformity as existed; and what force had brought together, force could dissipate, so that the overthrow of the dynasty might mean, as so often before, a reversion to chaos.

But, this time, he who wielded the sword wielded also the pen. The simplifying and organizing genius that gave a fixed mental form to the blindly cohering material seems to have been that of the conqueror himself, who at one stroke secured for his upstart capital both recognition as capital for nearly a millennium and a half and an ascendancy in the international universe of merchandise as great, relatively, as that of nineteenth century London and many times more enduring. In Babylonia he made it the headquarters both of her merchants and of her mental life. In the world at large it set the standards of business technique for the coming centuries. Its forms of contract were copied in the heart of Asia Minor and its language became the business language and, as a natural consequence, the diplomatic language of all the Middle East. Three and a half centuries later its kings were corresponding in it with the kings of Egypt concerning the safety of their caravans in Palestine and with the kings of Cappadocia concerning brigandage in northern Syria. Centuries later again the currency of its language was being renewed and extended by the merchants of Tyre and Sidon.

This master-stroke of Hammurabi was the promulgation of his Laws. "That he was not the inventor of these laws, numbering some 285," says a recent writer,[1] "is now well known, for Sumerian originals exist; but it was his genius which codified them and published them abroad in his Empire"; and the same writer asserts: "Great though his deeds [as a soldier and ruler] may have been, they pale before his wonderful creation, the Code of Laws, one of the most important documents in the history of the human race."

This is a sweeping judgment but not necessarily an extravagant one. It will not be thought to be so if the immensely long primacy of Babylon in its own country and the vast extension of its prestige in the international world of business can be shown to be derived to an important extent from the promulgation of the Laws and from the character of the Laws themselves.

We may note in the first place the effect of the promulgation upon the status of the monarchy in Mesopotamia. Many of the Laws were, it is true, copied from earlier collections—it would have been strange and unstatesmanlike not to have copied many; but the publication of the new collection in the existing circumstances was none the less an act of law-making on the part of the king. Henceforward the king, and no longer the

[1] R. Campbell Thompson, in the *Cambridge Ancient History*, I, ch. xiii, p. 492.

cities, nor their priestly rulers, nor custom, local or tribal,
appears as the source of justice; and what is true of the formulation of law is true also of its administration. Under the judicial
system set up by Hammurabi to administer his Laws, the judges
are supervised by the king and the right of appeal to the king
is carefully maintained. Hammurabi's dynasty and many others
passed away, but this new understanding of the situation remained and one of its consequences was undoubtedly the new
readiness to accept a permanent capital for the whole country.

Even more important was the fact that, for the first time, a
comprehensive body of law for the whole country was set down
in writing. Oral tradition was superseded and the administration
of the law could be checked at last everywhere by reference to a
definitive text. The effect was doubtless enhanced by the literary
merits of the text, for the opinion has been expressed that "a
consummate mastery of prose is exhibited by [its] wording".[1]
It was certainly both enhanced and perpetuated by the foundation, by Hammurabi or his successor, of schools of jurisprudence. The laws of the country became an object of study
and reflection and Hammurabi's continued to be studied practically throughout Babylonian history, "even down to the 7th
century B.C. . . . apparently under the name of 'The Judgments
of Righteousness which Hammurabi, the great King, set up'."[2]
Copies of them were found at Nineveh in the library of Assurbanipal, who died in 626 B.C. A century later Babylonian law
was adopted by Babylon's Persian conquerors and its influence
is alive today in the Books of Moses. Here we have a great part
of the explanation of the continuity of the administration of the
country through such violent vicissitudes and under such alien
conquerors.

In the third place, the promulgation of these laws was a
genuine attempt to create a Common Law, which is a sort of
generalization from many diverse local and tribal laws and
customs. The idea of a Common Law is so familiar today that
it is hard for most of us to realize how great a step this was;
but students of English medieval history will see in Hammurabi's

---

[1] Sidney Smith in the *Encyclopaedia Britannica*, vol. II, p. 848 (a), (14th
edition).
[2] R. Campbell Thompson, *loc. cit.*

work a parallel to that of Henry II, the first Plantagenet, and by that parallel be enabled to gauge its greatness. It constituted a return upward towards the simple conception of a universal justice—a return analogous in the sphere of morals to a return from the degradations of polytheism to the primitive worship of one God.

Indeed, there may well be more than merely political significance in the fact that among Hammurabi's many activities was the promotion of unity of religion within his empire. He had to contend with the traditional rivalries of the city gods and "endeavoured by poetry to teach his subjects that their gods, although different, were by no means enemies".[1] He carried this syncretism further towards monotheism by assimilating to the attributes of Enlil, god of the ancient city of Nippur, those of Marduk, the god of Babylon, who henceforward began to take Enlil's place as the supreme god of the Mesopotamian pantheon. In the event, the prestige of Babylon as a Holy City outlasted its commercial hegemony and even its status as a political capital.

V

Whether we regard the actual contents of the "Code" as the final testimony to its greatness will depend to some extent, no doubt, upon our political and economic standpoint. It can at least be said of the legal principles it enshrines that they were entirely without parallel in the eighteenth century before Christ and were accepted as axiomatic in the Anglo-Saxon world in the nineteenth century after Christ.

This assertion applies only to the principles of its provisions in the sphere of what we would now call civil law, the law of property and contract. The criminal law of the collection was hardly less crude than that of its predecessors. The *lex talionis*, the principle of "an eye for an eye and a tooth for a tooth", was worked out in often grotesque detail, and savage mutilation was a common penalty. For example, if a surgeon, operating on a gentleman, caused his death or the loss of an eye, his hands were to be cut off, and if he caused the death of a poor man's slave by operating, he had to render slave for slave.[2] Or if a

[1] C. F. Jean in *European Civilisation*, vol. I, p. 270.
[2] Laws 218, 219.

jerry-built house fell on the owner and killed him, the builder
was to be put to death but, if it killed the owner's son, the
builder's son was put to death.[1] But to judge the Code by these
and similar sections would be to miss its historical significance
as the intellectual framework of the first bourgeois state, in the
shaping of which the civil and not the criminal law was the
determining factor.

Even in this sphere we meet with elements of the slave-state,
of both the ancient and the modern type, such as chattel slavery
and conscription for public works; but chattel slavery in
Hammurabi's Babylon was on a very small scale—four slaves
was an exceptionally large number for one man to own; and
there was no state-compelled labour on a scale comparable
with that of Egypt under Cheops or Russia under Stalin. In
general, the collection recognized two of the leading principles
of Adam Smith and of nineteenth-century economics and
jurisprudence, namely, equality of status before the law and
freedom of contract. The latter was extended even to land, that
last stronghold of the family and of feudalism, for it might be
bought and sold or let on a variety of terms, at will. Property
rights were protected by elaborate penalties for damage. The
freedom to dispose of property by will was, it is true, severely
(and reasonably) restricted by the rights created by marriage,
divorce, judicial separation and the birth of children; nevertheless provision is made for the bequest of the bulk of a man's
property to a favourite son.[2] Contracts might be made for
services at wages, for commercial agency on a profit-sharing
basis and for loans at interest—a freedom and variety made
possible only by the widely extended use of equivalents of
money and by a strict rule that every contract, from marriage
to pawning, had to be set down in writing and written receipts
given at every stage. "Almost any possible business transaction
was reduced to the form of a contract," says an American
jurist,[3] "and was executed with the same formalities, i.e. with
witnesses, notary and signature."

All this had a tendency that constantly manifests itself in

[1] Laws 229, 230.
[2] Law 165.
[3] G. C. Lee, *Historical Jurisprudence*—New York, 1900, p. 38.

societies in which (in the classic phrase) contract is superseding status. An archaeologist has affirmed that " Babylonian law as codified by Hammurabi might be said to 'secure the creditor against the debtor and consecrate the exploitation of the small producer by the possessor of money' ". It legalized enslavement for debt by permitting the debtor not only to mortgage his land, but also to pledge his children, his wife, or himself. It regulated trading partnerships "in the interest of the capitalist, and fraud by the working partner was severely punished".[1]

Allowance, however, must be made for the apparently Marxist standpoint of the author of this account, and against it must be set the fact, admitted even in the same passage, a page further on, that "to the peasant and the small man the . . . king appeared as a saviour from the rapacity of usurers, the extortion of officials, oppression by the nobles and abuse by the soldiery". Hammurabi himself claimed to have published his laws "to make manifest justice in the land, to destroy the wicked and the evil-doer and prevent the strong oppressing the weak", nor is there any reason to doubt that the king was sincere in these intentions.

Nevertheless, to restrict is at the same time to permit and to regulate is to provide a pattern for an activity. That Hammurabi either foresaw or desired the ultimate consequences of a purely contractual society is inconceivable and what he saw of its abuses he minimized according to his lights. The fact remains that the same effort of genius that contemplated the jungle-growth of the new monetary economy and reduced it to some sort of order did, in pruning and fencing it, give it an enduring strength, in virtue of which its seat at Babylon came to symbolize Mammon for the ancient world. The personified Babylon of the Hebrew prophets is something worse than a tyrant. The all too seductive host of the Jewish exiles could do more harm to the Chosen People than Babylon's conquering armies. The Babylon of the Apocalypse has seduced the kings of the earth. Even now, if we wish for a name for a great city in which all the world forgathers to worship merchandise and money, we can think of none better than "a modern Babylon". It is our unconscious tribute to the decisiveness of Hammurabi's Laws.

[1] Gordon Childe, *What Happened in History*, p. 141.

NOTE ON CHRONOLOGY

I

Questions of chronology present a peculiar difficulty in writing a book of this kind. On the one hand, the subject of the book is, in the main, the history of ideas, and this has two consequences. First, it is only rarely that great precision in dating is important, particularly in connection with early times, when the diffusion of ideas was slow and irregular. Secondly, the writer of a book on such a subject will not be expected to have made an independent investigation of every disputed date that falls within his narrative, involving (as that would do) research in a large number of specialized archaeological and historical fields ranging over four millennia. On the other hand, the history of ideas becomes a mere blur if strict attention is not paid to chronological sequences and (almost as important) the approximate length of the intervals between the various phases.

Moreover, the particular method by which the history of ideas is treated in this book involves again and again a consideration of the interaction between ideas and states or institutions, so that a clear picture of the political history that formed the setting for the operations of an idea, and was (in its turn) influenced by it, is absolutely necessary for the reader if he is to obtain a clear picture of the growth and influence of the idea. But a clear picture of political history is unobtainable without a clear framework of dates.

Possibly all this so far has seemed to some readers much ado about nothing. "Very well, then," they may be mentally saying to the writer, "look up the dates in the proper histories and put them into your book." For it is extraordinarily difficult for most of us, living in an historically self-conscious age, when almost every important event is immediately put on record with a date attached, to realize how impracticable such a demand is. Only those who have had occasion to compile chronological tables for themselves from "standard authorities" can fully realize how numerous are the discrepancies in dating between even quite authoritative histories, even for comparatively recent times; and only those who have read for themselves a certain number of the original authorities on which the modern standard histories are based will be able fully to sympathize with the historians of our own day in their inability to agree with one another.

For the historians and biographers of earlier ages were, more often than not, maddeningly vague about dates, and even the sequence of events. And sometimes the modern historian has not even these vague writings to guide him but is reduced to reconstructing the chronology of a period from such "sources" as broken inscriptions, dateless coins, conflicting king-lists or pottery patterns. The scope for disagreement, therefore, in reconstructing a series of historical events and assigning years to them is often large and sometimes practically limitless and, of course, generally (though not always) increases as we go back towards strictly pre-historic times.

Consequently the writer of a book like the present, though his subject is not primarily the history of political events and though he is conscious that, even when he is concerned with them, it would be folly on his part even to attempt an independent investigation of disputed dates in a long series of specialized fields, nevertheless cannot escape from the necessity of making some decisions for himself on disputed chronological questions. He must at least decide for himself which of the differing modern authorities to follow and, in some cases, the range of dates offered is a very wide one. In others, though the range of choice is not wide, yet our estimate of the political influence of the book under consideration will be considerably affected by the choice and there is no "standard authority" whose verdict in the matter commands general acceptance. A case in point is the question of priority as between the Rule of St. Benedict and the *Corpus Juris Civilis* of Justinian, as will appear in due course.

As for differences in dating, between standard authorities, amounting to really long periods of time, we have only to turn to the first five chapters of this volume to find quite startling illustrations. For early Mesopotamian history, even if we include only works published in the last thirty years, the differences amount to several centuries. For early Egyptian history they are for the most part on the same scale but, if we are to include all schools of thought, we must reckon almost in millennia. For the early history of the Hebrews, of the Greeks and of the Hindus the discrepancies are, again, often enormous, for various reasons.

The variety of reasons must be stressed. The reader who has never looked behind the scenes at any of these chronological reconstructions is in danger of regarding the different sizes of the discrepancies as representing simply different degrees of vagueness, perhaps in the evidence, possibly in the historians. But this is far from being the case. When, for example, we find a date back in the third or fourth millennium B.C. given by one authority, not in round figures, but to a particular year, and, by another authority, also to a particular year but to a year perhaps three or four hundred years away from the first authority's, it is evident that some cause of uncertainty has come into play other than mere lack of precision in the data or in the instruments of measurements such as accounts for the ± sign so often affixed to the calculations of the physical sciences.

II

These other causes do in fact exist and in considerable variety. To mention only those conspicuously affecting the dating of events important to this book, we may note, first, the different ways of interpreting the figures obtained from the king-lists of some of the ancient Mesopotamian city-states. The figures are precise enough but it is going to make an enormous difference to our computations whether we regard, say, two dynasties claiming to rule some particular territory as following one upon the other, or as partly overlapping; and they might well overlap if, for example, they were rival claimants established at different capitals. In particular, the dating of Hammurabi's reign turns largely (though not, of course, entirely) on the question of how much overlapping there was between the First Dynasty of Babylon (in its later phases) and the Kassite dynasty.

Now, the choice between these two interpretations is often a very open one, into which considerations of various kinds may enter. There will probably be evidence or indications from sources other than the king-lists, that bear on the reigns in question. There will be the general effect of the longer or the shorter system on the reconstruction of the country's history as a whole or on synchronisms with events in other countries, and so on. Sometimes considerations enter that are essentially subjective, such as personal prepossessions in favour of early or late dates or the fashion of the moment in archaeological scholarship, for there are such fashions.

Thus, volume I of the *Cambridge Ancient History*, published in 1922, which might seem to be an obvious "standard authority" from which an unspecialized work like the present might safely take its dates, represents an already "dated" phase of archaeological opinion upon chronological questions. This is not to say that it was not a fully considered view—a whole chapter is devoted to a discussion, by four of its leading contributors, of the principles on which its chronological schemes should be based. Nevertheless it has proved transitory. Even at the time of publication the dates given for the periods before 1500 B.C. only represented the opinion of those who accepted the longest chronology possible. Since 1930 many new sources have become available, and no one now doubts that the enumeration of dynasties *seriatim* is an error; there were large overlaps, as some scholars had long maintained.

Mr. Sidney Smith, of the British Museum, himself an extensive con-tributor to the *Cambridge Ancient History* on later Babylonian and Assyrian history, has very kindly supplied me with two chronological schemes that are in the field to-day. Of these, the one with the largest number of adherents at present would appear to go to the extreme in the opposite direction. This is the scheme first propounded by Professor W. F. Albright of Johns Hopkins University, Baltimore and adopted by (amongst others) R. T. O'Callaghan, S.J. in *Aram-Naharaim*, published by the Pontifical Biblical Institute at Rome (*Analecta Orientalia*, 26). For the events for which dates are given in the preceding chapter, Albright's dates are as follows:—

Sargon of Agadé, accession ..	.. about 2360
Third Dynasty of Ur	.. about 2070-1960
First Dynasty of Babylon begins	.. about 1830
Reign of Hammurabi	.. 1728-1686
Hittite raid on Babylon	.. about 1550
Kassite Dynasty begins	.. about 1600

Sargon's date in this scheme is about 500 years later than that given in the *Cambridge Ancient History* and Hammurabi's 395 years later.

I have preferred, however, to use Mr. Smith's own dates. These, though fully allowing for overlaps, are not quite as low as Professor Albright's—there are, of course, many issues, besides that of the overlapping of dynasties, dividing archaeologists in this field and forming an immensely intricate web of indications and inferences, of which the reader can get a glimpse who cares to consult the chronological chapter to which I have referred and then the chronological note prefixed to the second edition (1923) of the same volume.

It will be seen that Mr. Smith's date for Sargon is 120 years earlier than Albright's and, for Hammurabi, 64 years. But the actual periods allotted respectively to the various dynasties by Mr. Smith are approximately the same, not only as those in Albright's scheme, but also as those in the *Cambridge Ancient History*.

III

When we turn to the early history of Egypt, of which we shall have to say something in the next chapter, we find that different views on this question of the overlapping of dynasties again account for many of the differences in dating to be found in various authorities. Indeed, the peculiarity in the geography of the country that caused it frequently to fall apart into two rival kingdoms of Upper and Lower Egypt gives this factor special importance there, and the differences due to it are even greater than in Mesopotamian chronology.

Another disturbing factor has an astronomical basis. It turns on the fact that the first day of the Egyptian year coincided with what is known as the heliacal rising of Sirius, the dog-star, every 1460 years. (This period constitutes the so-called "Sothic cycle", the years of the coincidence being called by some Egyptologists "Sothic years".)

The first consequence of this is that Egyptologists have differed by as much as 1460 years as to the date of the 7th year of Senusret III, a king of the 12th Dynasty (comparatively late in Egyptian history), which would appear, from a certain astronomical statement, to have been the 905th year of the Sothic cycle. The lower of these two dates is 1876 (1872) B.C., but this dating requires us to suppose an immense amount of overlapping in the king-lists for the confused period of the Hyksos invasion between the end of the 12th Dynasty and the beginning of the 18th Dynasty in 1580 B.C. Flinders Petrie, therefore, put Senusret III a whole Sothic cycle earlier (it speaks volumes for the deep uncertainties of Egyptian history that it should be possible even to contemplate adjustments on so generous a scale).

Hardly any Egyptologists would now be found to follow Petrie in this extreme course, but many (including H. R. Hall in the *Cambridge Ancient History*) have attempted compromises based on the supposition that

Egyptian astronomical calculations were to a greater or less extent in error, and modern astronomers have added their quota of uncertainties.

But since the *Cambridge Ancient History* was published, the situation has been revolutionized by Scharff, who has attacked the problem from the other end, namely from the dating of the year of the introduction of the calendar, which must have been a Sothic year. Hitherto most Egyptologists have held this year to be 4241 (or 4237) B.C., though a few have favoured 5701 (or 5697) B.C. Now, Scharff has shown strong reasons for thinking that the calendar was introduced under the rule of King Zoser of the 3rd Dynasty, and his great minister Imhotep, the probable designer of the famous Step Pyramid of Sakkara, which inaugurated the era of pyramid building. (It certainly seems clear that the calendar was known to the pyramid builders of the 4th Dynasty and there are unmistakable references to it in the inscriptions of the 5th and 6th Dynasties, so that at least it cannot be *later* than these dynasties.)

But if the inauguration of the calendar is to be placed thus well within the dynastic period, then the year of its inauguration must be 1460 later than has hitherto been generally supposed, for the dynasties cannot go back to 4500 B.C. In that case all Egyptian dates will come down with it and the 7th year of Senusret III cannot possibly be earlier than 1876 (or 1872) B.C.

The dates thus reached harmonize very well with the lower Babylonian datings. The approximate dates given in chapter II of this book are based on Scharff's hypothesis and have received a general endorsement from Mr. Smith.

IV

When we pass to the early histories of the Hebrews, the Greeks and the Hindus, wholly different causes for the disagreements over dates come into view. We can only mention with the utmost brevity one or two in each case that conspicuously affect the dates required for this book.

In the case of Hebrew chronology, the great dividing line is between those who accept the historical books of the Hebrews themselves more or less as they stand and those who regard them as late and largely mythical compilations. The former have a scheme that can be worked out with considerable precision for the most part (though, even for them, discrepancies between the versions, including the Septuagint, amount to substantial totals, one of the items being a solid block of 230 years). They can claim, moreover, a certain amount of corroborative archaeological evidence from such sources as the Tel-el-Amarna correspondence, the excavations at Jericho and, more recently, the Ras Shamra discoveries.

The rejection of the books, on the other hand, strikes not only at a scheme of dates but at the whole story that the books tell and at the very existence of some of its leading characters and events. Chronological questions in the ordinary sense of the word become subordinate to literary analysis and this, again, to theological prepossessions. Differences in opinion on archaeological grounds, amounting to perhaps 10 or 20 years, concerning the dates of some of the universally accepted events of the latter part of the narrative are trivial by comparison with the enormous uncertainties created by the Higher Critics.

The chronology of early Greek history or pre-history, particularly in relation to the Homeric epics, has, until recently, been in somewhat the same case as Hebrew chronology. Here, again, the national traditions gave a fairly precise chronological framework and, here again, an era of intense scepticism brought about a disintegration (in the minds of scholars) of the traditional account of early history and also of the literary compositions with which it was traditionally bound up—in this case the Iliad and the Odyssey.

At this point, however, the parallel becomes less close, for, in the case of Homer and the Greeks, the support given by the anti-traditional criticism to the anti-Christian movement was only indirect, so that the hold of this criticism on the typical scholar of the period was less strong than in the case of the Old Testament, and it was possible for scholarship to recover its balance more quickly. Consequently something not unlike the traditional view of Homer and his narrative finds a place in a number of recent works of high standing, including even the *Cambridge Ancient History*. And wherever it prevails, the chief chronological uncertainty left is as regards the date of the Epics themselves and this is a genuine difficulty of literary history, of a very common type, arising simply from a deficiency of both internal and external evidence for the date of the compositions in question.

In this feature we have a link with the chronological problems of early India. We are not concerned in this book with the pre-Aryan civilization of the now famous prehistoric cities of the Punjab—Mohenjodaro and the rest, whose affinities are with early Mesopotamia and whose chronology has to be approached by strictly archaeological methods. We are concerned mainly with the first millennium of the Aryan age; and for practically the whole of this long period there are literally no precise data, either literary or archaeological, for a chronological scheme. There are a number of writings, from the early hymns of the invading Aryan warriors (the Rig-Veda) down to the early Buddhist texts; but few of them concern themselves with historical events, and those that do (like some of the Vedic books) treat of them without even an attempt at chronological arrangement. And the writings themselves are considerably less datable even than those of Homer by either internal or external evidence. As for archaeological evidence, there was no building in stone or brick in India during this period, so that there are practically no material remains.

In these circumstances, historians can do little more than distinguish the various cultural and social phases reflected in these various writings, place them in an historically probable order and check this by their topographical allusions, which mark the penetration of the Aryans eastward and southward from their point of entry into India in the north-west. They thus arrive at a scheme of relative dates both for the writings and for the historical phases and then make more or less probable guesses at the intervals of time that must have elapsed between the successive phases. (The guesses at the date of the Aryan invasion itself differ by hundreds of years; there is practically nothing to go by beyond vague synchronisms with vaguely dated Aryan movements elsewhere and, more recently, with the quite dateless ending of the Mohenjodaro civilization.) Not until the Greek period, that is to say to the period of inscriptions and written records inaugurated by the invasion of the Punjab by Alexander the Great, do we get any chronology much more definite than this.

The case of China is wholly different again. Chinese records are full of dates and these are by no means necessarily unreliable until they recede backward beyond, say, 2000 B.C. into an obviously fabulous past. But that remote period does not concern us in this book; and from the time of Confucius onwards the chronology of the Chinese historians is more than sufficiently full and precise for all our purposes.

Returning to the West, and coming down to the fourth century B.C., we shall find that the dating of those works of Plato and Aristotle with which we shall be dealing is, like that of Homer (though in a very much less degree), vague from deficiency of either internal or external evidence; but the political setting of these books is under the full light of history and, except in rare cases, the chronological uncertainties amount at the most to a very few years. This continues to be true for the remaining books of the series and it takes a very extraordinary combination of circumstances to make an uncertainty of only half a dozen years of any consequence from the angle from which this book is written, until we come down to periods when even that degree of uncertainty ceases to exist.

II

THE BOOK OF THE DEAD

II

THE BOOK OF THE DEAD

I

THE so-called Book of the Dead of the ancient Egyptians has been described as an illustrated guide to the other world, provided for a man's soul after death and buried with him. It reached this form under the Eighteenth Dynasty of united Egypt (from 1580 to about 1360 B.C.), the period of Egypt's "New Empire".

But our modern term for it is misleading. A recent writer,[1] perhaps erring to some extent in the opposite direction, has said of the Eighteenth Dynasty compilation:—

"The Egyptians themselves knew of no 'book' . . . There were current among them large numbers of spells or recitations, selections from which were combined on rolls of papyrus and placed in the tombs. No two rolls contain the same selection, and while some of those found in the tombs of rich men are over fifty feet long and contain as many as 130 spells, those found in the less magnificent tombs are often but a few feet in length and include only a few of the more vital sections."

They differ also in their selection and treatment of the vignettes, or coloured illustrations. The so-called Theban Recension (or edition) of the Book of the Dead is a collection of 190 chapters drawn from the funerary papyri of the New Empire, whose capital was at Thebes in Upper, that is to say southern, Egypt.

The suggestion that these chapters consist in the main of

[1] T. E. Peet, in the *Cambridge Ancient History*, vol. I, ch. ix.

magical formulas is one that can be challenged, as we shall see, and in other respects also the description just quoted seems unduly to minimize these writings and their unity. Budge[1] claims for the collections a very ancient nucleus, a work called *Per-t em hru*, that is to say, "Coming Forth by [or "into"] the Day." The Egyptians believed this to have been written by the god Thoth, the scribe of the gods, and to have been discovered by a high official in the foundation of a shrine during the reign of King Semti, the fourth king of the First Dynasty. Three thousand years later "the papyri and coffins of the Roman period afford evidence that the native Egyptians still accepted all the essential beliefs and doctrines contained in it. . . . Many additions had been made to it but nothing of importance seems to have been taken away from it".[2]

All authorities, however, agree that our modern title is apt to create an illusion. There was no book in our modern sense but only a combining and recombining of infinitely varying selections from a large and growing body of short documents relating to the after-life and found only in tombs. For the book, such as it was, circulated only among the dead.

It is this last feature of it that must strike us as the strangest of all. But it seemed entirely natural to the Egyptians; and there lies the very heart of the matter that we are to discuss. For they, beyond all other historical peoples of antiquity, had a belief both firm and vivid in a life after death. The pre-historic Celts of Britain seem to have had as vigorous a faith in it, inherited perhaps from the mysterious builders of the megalithic tombs, but they have left no monuments in writing. The ancient peoples that have histories—the Babylonians and the Hebrews, the Greeks and the Romans and the remote Chinese—were alike in this, that they pictured the dead as mere unsubstantial shades in an underworld of gloom and yearning, not an altogether inadequate representation of the actual state of the disembodied soul in Limbo before the coming of Christ. Some of the secret cults that circulated in the Hellenic underworld in the last centuries before Christ did indeed assure their initiates of

---

[1] E. Wallis Budge, *The Book of the Dead* (British Museum), p. 4. This is not the complete translation (to which reference will be made presently) but a useful handbook, now out of print.

[2] *Op. cit.*, pp. 13, 14.

something better; but in this matter they were the offspring of the Egyptian religious tradition.

For the Egyptians, though their original picture of the life after death had been gloomy enough, were early converted to a religion that taught them to think vividly and hopefully of the next world, chiefly in terms of their bodily life in this one. In startling contrast to the Hindu sages, who viewed with horror the prospect of an endless cycle of bodily lives and taught that the highest to which man can aspire must be sought through the cessation of activity, the Egyptians desired above all things to reproduce their bodily life after death in every pleasant detail and came to believe it possible to do so. They believed almost too easily in a resurrection of the dead, for they hardly troubled to distinguish it from coming back to life. In the mind of the average Egyptian (there were exceptions to the rule) his resurrection would not be to a new life, but to renew the old one. Many a Christian has given away all his worldly wealth in the expectation of heavenly treasure, but it took an ancient Egyptian to make a loan in hard cash in this life in return for an undertaking to pay him in hard cash in the next.

So overpowering an expectation naturally absorbed an immense proportion of the surplus energy of the people. We have seen that the bulk of the documents that have survived from Hammurabi's Babylonia were business documents. Nearly all those surviving from ancient Egypt deal directly or indirectly with religion; and the life of the other world is by far the most prominent among their religious topics. In science the chief achievement of ancient Egypt was the embalming of corpses. "Artists of all kinds", says a recent authority,[1] "found ample scope for their talents in the decoration of the tomb and its appurtenances", and they included some who have never been surpassed in their departments.

The tombs themselves absorbed, in most periods a large proportion, in some periods an enormous proportion of the labour of the population; and comprise some of the largest and most accurately executed constructional works achieved by the human race. The Great Pyramid of Cheops (Khufu), which was

[1] *Cambridge Ancient History*, vol. I, p. 320.

simply a tomb, was originally nearly 480 feet in height; its square base had a side of nearly 760 feet, laid out (without any modern instruments of precision) to within three or four inches of perfect accuracy—some have said to within an inch. It was built of 2,300,000 blocks of limestone fitted so accurately "that often one cannot insert a pen-knife between the joints of the stone".[1]

The building of it was almost the sole act of King Khufu's reign of twenty-three years, and his obsession. This was perhaps about 2700 B.C.[2] Twelve hundred years later, under the Eighteenth Dynasty and its two successors, corridor tombs up to 650 feet in length, were being cut into the limestone cliffs of the narrowing Nile valley of Upper Egypt. And it all meant something. The great pyramids of Gizeh are "the external symbol of the Old Empire and express its inmost character. The whole state is concentrated in the person of the 'great god' (the Pharaoh); its supreme task can be summed up as follows: to assure to the sovereign after his death the continuation of his power for eternity".[3]

II

Belloc has somewhere a passage to the effect that nothing contributes more towards giving a man moral vigour than a firm belief in personal immortality. The assertion is profoundly true but it requires clarification. It will have its full truth only if it relates to a belief rooted in a realization of eternity, which is something quite different from a mere prolongation of time and altogether transcends it. A belief thus rooted in eternity can so link the present life to eternity as to impel a man to live every moment of it as if it had eternal value, and to make sure that it does have it. An earthbound Valhalla may enable a man to face death like a hero, but does not enable him to face life because it does not enable him to transcend life. It provides an alternative to life, not a transformation of it. Similarly, belief in a heaven that is no more than "a better world" will provide an escape from life, not a conquest of it. It is this that gives plausibility to the Marxist slogan that the belief in another life is escapism and religion the opium of the people. Another life

[1] *Loc. cit.*, p. 281.
[2] See the Note on Chronology appended to Chapter I.
[3] Quoted by C. F. Jean in *European Civilisation*, vol. I, pp. 281, 282.

that is merely a future life can never be part of the present life; only when it is life in eternity can it be begun now.

It is possible, therefore, to have a belief in another life that does not enhance moral vigour and may even diminish it; and such a belief may, furthermore, quite literally subtract from this life by taking some of it away. If we wish to prepare now for the next life, in whatever way we conceive it, we must live now with an eye on it. Now, to live this life with an eye on eternity is not to diminish this life but to enhance it, by giving it an eternal meaning. But those who think of the next life as simply the present life lived in pleasanter surroundings elsewhere may think it necessary to make for it the kind of preparation they would give to another spell of this life. Consequently they will give to it a large portion of their time and energies in this life, not eternalizing them by consecrating them to eternal ends but diverting them to what are in effect other temporal ends.

The worst effect of all is when this diversion of a proportion of time and energies to merely external and physical preparations for a future life is regarded as the *only* necessary preparation for it. In that case the ordinary activities of this life will not be brought into any sort of relationship with the next, since a man's fate in the next world will not depend in any way on his outlook and conduct in the affairs of this world but solely on the time and energy, or time and money, he has diverted from its normal activities into external and material preparations for the next world.

Moreover, what is true of each individual applies with at least equal force to the community as a whole and to its communal and political activities. To plan the corporate activities of a state to serve eternal ends while serving, and in the very process of serving, temporal ends is to enhance their vigour and their stability and to give more meaning to the civic life of the citizens. To plan the state's activities with the thought that ruler and subjects alike will carry them on better after death, will make many indifferent to the fate of the state before their death. To divert a great proportion of them to physical preparations for their continuation in the next world will lower the standards of the physical life of the citizens here. To consider that this diversion exhausts the obligations of the state to the future life is to lower also the moral standards of the citizens.

If, then, the Egyptians individually and the Egyptian state, for all their high conviction that death was not the end, should succumb at one time or another to all these perversions of their belief, they would inevitably suffer sooner or later from all these evils. And their conviction had no supernatural shaping or sanction from revelation such as might have enabled them not to succumb. Though they may well have derived it in the first instance from the primitive tradition of mankind, they came to hold it in a form that has every mark of having been moulded in part by the accidents of their setting and their temperament.

There may well be something in the suggestion that the natural preservation of corpses in the dry soil of Egypt predisposed the Egyptians to attach importance to the preservation of the corpse. There is almost certainly some truth in the notion that the physical vitality of the Egyptians and their naturally merry dispositions gave them a horror of physical death and inclined them to give credence to any suggestion that it could be overcome. Again, the exceptionally restricted and rigid form imposed upon their everyday economic life by the geography of the Nile valley seems to have made them intensely conservative, and fanatically eager to perpetuate the familiar and the customary.

But the shaping of a cultus and its attendant beliefs by external conditions must necessarily diminish the truth and the authority that originally belonged to them. Furthermore, it will cause them to appeal to men's weaknesses rather than to their strength, since the modifications that they suffer will be the product of wishful thinking. They will then be easily distorted still further and may even sink to that level at which the rational and moral bases for beliefs and actions alike have disappeared. And this also happened, in part, to the cultus of the dead in ancient Egypt.

III

Two rival systems of belief, theologies if we like, competed in providing the ancient Egyptians with a picture of the after-life. One was dominated by the worship of the sun-god, Re (pronounced like the English "ray" though the words have no connection). The other centred round the god Osiris. Their developments and interactions and respective contributions to the Book of the Dead must be briefly reviewed but they are so closely bound up with the political history of Egypt that at least the bare outline of the latter must first be given in order to make the review intelligible.

The beginnings of Egypt as a united kingdom date from what is known as the First Dynasty, whose founder, perhaps about 3100 B.C.,[1] united what had previously been the separate kingdoms of Upper and Lower Egypt. (Lower Egypt is the Nile Delta, in the north; Upper Egypt is the 600-mile long stretch of narrow river valley between the apex of the Delta and the First Cataract, near the modern Assouan.) Under this dynasty occur those striking resemblances between the royal maces and the royal tombs and burial customs of Egypt and Sumer that give substance to the suggestion that the Sumerians had a hand in the building of both civilizations.

The dynasties from the third (or, as some would have it, from the fourth) to the sixth constitute what is generally called the Old Kingdom. It was the great period of the monarchy, when the kings (or Pharaohs, to give them the title by which all kings of Egypt were eventually known) were worshipped as the sons of Re, and the nobles were grouped around them as little more than courtiers. It was also the period of the great pyramid tombs of the kings. The first pyramid belongs to the Third Dynasty and the greatest pyramids of all, those at Gizeh, to the Fourth. Like most of the pyramids they were built near the capital of the Old Kingdom, namely Memphis, near the modern Cairo, just south of the apex of the Delta. Near Memphis also was the city that the Greeks called Heliopolis ("Suncity"), the great city of the priests of Re.

Towards the end of this period a sort of feudal nobility grew in power and independence, and the power of the monarchy waned. It collapsed entirely under the Sixth Dynasty, which (on the chronological scheme adopted here) was estab-

[1] For this date and those in the next two paragraphs see the Note on Chronology appended to Chapter I, and particularly section iii of the Note.

3

lished towards 2400 B.C., not long after Sargon of Akkad began to reign in Mesopotamia. Feudal anarchy and foreign invasion followed and the confusion did not end until the beginning of the second millennium B.C., when Amenemhet I, with popular support, put an end to anarchy and founded the Twelfth Dynasty and what is known as the Middle Kingdom. Once more there was a strong monarchy, but one that in a large measure over-rode class distinctions, gave opportunities to all, and made itself the champion of the common people. The last kings of this dynasty were contemporary with beginnings of the First Dynasty of Babylon.

With the Thirteenth Dynasty civil war returned, opening the way to an invasion from Asia by a people called the Hyksos, who ruled the country (adopting its manners and religions) until, about 1600 B.C., the princes of Thebes, in southern Egypt, began a war of independence which ended in the expulsion of the Hyksos and the foundation of the Eighteenth Dynasty (and the New Empire) with Thebes as its capital, in 1580 B.C. Inspired by the military spirit thus aroused, Egypt became for a period an imperial power, the greatest of the conquerors being Thotmes (or Tuthmosis) III. In the fourteenth century one of his successors, taking the name of Akhenaten, tried to force on the country some sort of approximation to monotheism, learnt perhaps from the Hebrews, who had recently been sojourning in the Delta. In the reaction against this reform, the Eighteenth Dynasty and its Asiatic empire collapsed together.

There followed a long period of slow decline broken by occasional partial revivals of Egypt's power in Palestine and Syria on a scale significantly small in proportion to her vast resources. By 1090 B.C. the monarchy had become so completely discredited that the High Priest of Ammon (or Amen), god of Thebes but identified with Re as Amen-Re, thrust the reigning Pharaoh aside and took his place, founding the Twenty-first Dynasty. While David and Homer sang and Zoroaster spoke, feebleness and civil strife became the ordinary portion of Egypt until, in 668 B.C., Assurbanipal sailed up her Nile and made her part of the last Assyrian empire.

The political revival of Babylon, which first shook and then put an end to the Assyrian power, allowed Egypt a final spell of independence under the Twenty-sixth Dynasty (663-525 B.C.). "The Egyptians . . . believed that they had once again become a great nation, and proudly went back to the Old Kingdom for their models in the art";[1] and priests, artists and the cultus of the dead played as great a part as ever in Egyptian life. But the power was gone out of it. The country is said to have been invaded by Nebuchadnezzar, the king of Babylon, in 568 B.C. and was certainly annexed in 525 B.C. to the Persian Empire, which had recently swallowed up the last Babylonian Empire, liberated the Jews made captive by Nebuchadnezzar, conquered half the Punjab and the Greek cities of Asia Minor and was soon to invade Europe. Egypt remained under Persian rule until she welcomed a new master in Alexander of Macedon and then we are in the period when the Pharaohs were Greek and the Hebrew Scriptures were translated into Greek by Hebrew scholars resident in Egypt. And then came the Romans.

IV

To return to the rival religions of early Egypt, it is the worship of Re that has pre-eminence in the funerary inscriptions in the earliest inscribed tombs, those of the Old Kingdom. It was essentially the royal cult ; and every prayer and every formula depicted on the walls of rooms or corridors within the pyramids was intended to aid the dead king to preserve his life and power as a tutelary deity of his country. The nobles had to be buried round the king as if at court. The common people had no part in the rites of Re.

Re's realm is the eastern sky and the king, his son, must go to him, ferried or flying across a lake, and join him as his companion in his daily voyage across the sky, from which their joint power pours down upon the land. The priests of Heliopolis knew more than this. They strove to return from the many to the one and under the Fifth Dynasty left records of their speculations on the unity of the divine power manifested by the sun's creative rays. Under the next dynasty these thoughts became known outside the priesthood but the days of feudal

[1] T. E. Peet, in *European Civilisation*, vol. I, p. 495.

anarchy had come, when every noble exalted his local deity, and polytheism closed over them again.[1]

The other theology told of Osiris and his son Horus. It was no new thing in Egypt. It had been prominent in the Delta, and may even have been the official religion there, in pre-dynastic times. When it hid itself before the magnificence of the Memphite monarchy and the Sons of Re, it was cherished by the common people, who aspired to be like Osiris after death.

Osiris, according to a common version of the story, had been slain, when a king on earth, by his wicked brother Set. He had then been nailed up in a coffin and thrown into the sea. He had been cast up on the shore at Byblos, on the Syrian coast, where he was found by Isis, his sister and wife, who took the body back to Egypt. There Set tore it to pieces and scattered its limbs but Isis found them, brought them together and embalmed them. Then Osiris began to live again, now incorruptible, and to reign in the underworld, becoming judge of it and promising resurrection and immortality to every follower of his who had led a life of truth and sincerity on earth.

Thus the funerary cultus of Osiris had two distinguishing accompaniments. One was embalming (Osiris was always represented as a mummy); the other was a strong ethical element. Neither is found in the royal burial rites of the great days of the Old Kingdom. It is only with the weakening of the monarchy under the Fifth and Sixth Dynasties that they find their way into the great tombs, when the nobles no longer consent to be buried around the king but claim tombs and cemeteries and ritual of their own and access to heaven in their own right. But, when that time comes, it is not only the tombs of the nobles that reflect the new trends. Ritual and writings in the tombs of the kings themselves are affected by the rising tide of Osiris-worship. Embalming begins to come to the fore (it is found in a primitive form under the First and Second Dynasties), though it remains pre-eminently a rite of the people until the Middle Kingdom. Similarly, ethical elements in an Osirian setting intrude themselves into what are known as the Pyramid Texts.

[1] See C. F. Jean's chapters in *European Civilisation*, vol. I. I am very considerably indebted to them for the interpretation of Egyptian religions and political history in their mutual relations offered in this section.

These texts are the writings found cut on the walls of chambers and corridors in a series of five pyramids in the royal cemetery at Sakkara, not far south of Memphis, one of which belongs to the last king of the Fifth Dynasty and the rest to kings of the Sixth. In these writings the priests have interpolated, among chapters of the older type, thoughts about justice and a judgement to be undergone before Osiris. The king is sometimes referred to as "righteous" and there is a fragment of the so-called "negative confession" which, as we shall see, figures prominently in the Osirian texts of a later date. No attempt is made to harmonize these texts with the older elements; indeed, the rooted conservatism of the Egyptians forbade them to reject altogether anything they had once adopted. They simply let the two strata of ideas and formulas stand side by side.

It was with the Middle Kingdom that the great change came. Then any man, whatever his original rank, could enter the ranks of the governing class; and in like manner the Osirian texts and the Osirian rite of embalming entered every tomb. Long new chapters concerning the judgement of Osiris were added to selections from the Pyramid Texts and were written, as a rule, on the inner surfaces of the lids or sides of the coffins or sarcophagi, where they would be visible to the corpse. A modernized form of the traditional hieroglyphics, akin to the running script of everyday use, began to be used for this purpose. Occasionally, owing to their increasing length, these writings were done on rolls of papyri placed inside the coffins.

The climax of all this came under the Eighteenth Dynasty. By that time the funerary religion of the whole population was founded on the story and the justice of Osiris, "who makes mortals to live a second time". The kings themselves desired nothing better than to be identified with Osiris after death; and the ordinary way of referring politely to any dead man was as "the Osiris so-and-so"—a kind of deification for all. Everyone who could afford it was embalmed as Osiris had been embalmed and the art of embalming reached its peak. Nor was any coffin complete without its papyrus roll, long or short according to what the dead man's family cared to spend, containing chapters describing the ordeals through which he must pass or giving the words of the prayers and spells and hymns he must recite to get to heaven. The very nicest service you could render to your dead friend was to place a good-sized roll of these chapters in his coffin before it was fastened down.

V

It was during this period that there came into existence the compilation commonly known as the Book of the Dead. For the convenience, no doubt, of those who wished to make selections of chapters (for themselves or for their dead friends) to suit their sentiments and their purse, standard collections of chapters were made. They were drawn from contemporary funeral papyri but (since these papyri were themselves composed of chapters preserved by the priests from earlier periods) many of the chapters in the Theban editions contain, in a modernized form, chapters of immense antiquity. Mention has already been made of the Egyptian tradition of the finding of *Per-t em hru* under the First Dynasty. Another, and longer, version is said to have been found, cut on the plinth of a royal statue, under the Fourth Dynasty, in the reign of the king who built the third pyramid of Gizeh. The earliest portions of the Theban compilations found by modern archaeologists actually inscribed in tombs are certain chapters of the Pyramid texts. The later compositions are almost wholly Osirian in character.

Since the subject of this chapter is the formative effect of this so-called Book of the Dead on the Egyptian mind and, through it, on the growth, character and fortunes of the Egyptian state, some account, however brief, must be given of the contents of the collection; but something ought first to be said of certain terms used to describe it by archaeologists of our own day, and particularly the term "magical". This term has been freely applied to certain chapters of the Book, particularly to distinguish those dating from the Old Kingdom from the more ethical chapters from the later tombs, which are said to represent a higher phase of religious belief, attained (apparently) through some law of religious progress. But the archaeologists and ethnologists of the last two generations have as a rule been without experience of religious reality and strongly biased against acknowledging its existence, so that they are not the best judges of the relation between religion and magic.

For example, they like to lump together as magical all set formulas used in religious worship. But it is one thing to pronounce a formula with the idea that the mere uttering of certain words is an act of preternatural potency (which is simply magic) and an altogether different thing to pronounce a formula valued only because it gives a set form to an invocation or blessing (or the like) uttered with faith in an omnipotent God who hears it, and will respond to it as He sees fit. To confuse the two kinds of utterance is an act of either malice or gross ignorance.

Moreover, even those ethnologists who admit that there may be a distinction between the two kinds of utterances in the minds of the utterers almost invariably assume that in the course of history the act of magic comes earlier and the act of religion later. In point of fact, however, it is psychologically impossible, humanly speaking, for the pronouncing of a formula as an act of magic to become elevated to an act of religious faith; but it is neither impossible nor particularly uncommon for the words of a prayer or a blessing to sink to the level of a magical charm when religious faith has been lost and the original meaning of the words forgotten. Nor is the presence or absence of ethical phrases an adequate criterion of a genuinely religious element. Ethical phrases may be embedded in a formula that has become a mere mascot or may become themselves the shibboleths of the wholly unreligious mind, while prayer or praise from the heart may dispense with the language of ethics.

These considerations, then, must be borne in mind when we are confronted with the facile relegation of every set formula in the Book of the Dead to the plane of magic or have to interpret the historical sequence of the Book's component parts, ethical or otherwise. In regard to the earliest texts, for example, it is likely enough that some of them had become almost as unintelligible to the Egyptians of the Eighteenth Dynasty as to the archaeologist of the twentieth century, so that their recitation might well have become an act little above the plane of magic; but it is possible, and indeed probable, that they originally had a perfectly intelligible, even if symbolical and esoteric meaning, known at least to the priests who carved them.

As to the supposed rise of Egyptian funerary religion from the magical to the ethical level, the appearance of a plainly ethical element for the first time in the Pyramid Texts and to an increasing extent under the Middle Kingdom is fully accounted for, if the foregoing reconstructing of Egyptian religious history be accepted, by the invasion of the domain of public and priestly funerary ritual, hitherto a royal preserve, by the nobles and the lower classes, who brought with them a cultus that had been ethical from its beginnings.

VI

With all this in mind, let us make a very brief examination of the Book of the Dead in its Theban Recension. For the sake of both brevity and clearness the chapters have in most cases been arranged in groups, according to their topic or their religious character. It must be remembered, however, that any systematic grouping of the chapters must, in one respect, give a false impression of a document whose sequences are mostly haphazard, whose inconsistencies are many and violent and whose contents range over the greater part of two millennia and two religions.

All the great papyri of the Book of the Dead, says Budge, open with one or more hymns to Re, to be sung by the dead man. In these we find the theology of Heliopolis at its best. Here are some phrases culled from three variants found in different papyri :—

". . . Thou perfect one, thou who art eternal. . . . O divine youth, who art self-created, I cannot comprehend thee. Thou art the Lord of heaven and earth and didst create beings celestial and beings terrestial. Thou art the God One, who camest into being with the beginning of time . . . self-begotten and self-born . . . thou art unknowable . . . thou existest alone" (pages 9, 12, 13, 14).

Chapters 15 and 17 have a similar religious outlook. They comprise another hymn to Re, with illustrations, and a descrip-

---

[1] I have used, as material for the following analysis, Budge's *The Book of the Dead. An English Translation of* . . . *the Theban Recension, with Introduction, Notes, etc.*, second edition, 1909. For quotations, however, I have used (where there is no indication to the contrary) the renderings included in the British Museum handbook already referred to. Page numbers in brackets after a quotation show where the corresponding phrases are to be found in the complete translation.

tion of Re put into the god's mouth: "I am the only one . . . I am Re, who rose in primaeval time, ruler of what he had made" (p. 93).

The introductory hymn to Re is usually followed by one to Osiris, and Chapters 180 to 185 contain other hymns to him. The following phrases are from Chapter 183: "Let me follow this majesty as when I was on earth . . . I have come to the city of God, the region that is eternally old, with my soul (*ba*), my double (*ka*) and my spirit-soul (*dakhu*), to be a dweller in this land. Its god [Osiris] is the Lord of Truth" (p. 628).

The story and attributes and mysticism of Osiris occupy a number of chapters scattered through the collection. Thus, Chapters 111 to 113 tell parts of the legend of his son Horus, and Chapter 138 relates to the ceremony commemorating the reconstituting of the dismembered Osiris. Chapter 14 is a prayer to him to be spoken by the deceased on his arrival in the other world: " . . . Wash away my sins, Lord of Truth . . . may this god be at peace with me" (pages 62, 63), and so on. In Chapter 43 the deceased assumes the character of Osiris; in Chapter 154 he claims the effects of this: "I shall not decay, nor rot, nor putrefy, nor become worms nor see corruption. I shall have my being, I shall live, I shall rise up in peace" (p. 520). And the highest elements in the Osirian portions of the Book of the Dead are epitomized in the oldest section of all, to which reference was made almost at the beginning of this chapter and of which the longer and shorter versions between them constitute Chapter 64 of the Theban Recension. Amid a confused medley of petitions and aspirations, it seems to feel after a mystical absorption into the god—"Thou art in me and I am in thee; and thy attributes are my attributes."[1]

Thoth, the scribe of Osiris, is another god with whom the deceased seeks to be identified, but it is identification on a lower level, with a distinct suggestion of magic. In Chapter 18 the deceased has entreated Thoth to ensure that he is declared innocent at the judgement. In Chapter 94 he is enabled by means of certain formulas to take the books of Thoth and assume his

[1] From the complete translation, p. 220. The sentence is taken from the shorter and earlier version of *Per-t em hru*, belonging, according to Budge, to the First Dynasty (*op. cit.*, Introduction, pp. xxxiii–xxxvii).

3*

character and so obtain his immunity. He is identified with Thoth again in Chapter 123, with Ptah in Chapter 82, with Horus and other deities in Chapter 66, and so on. The purpose in all these cases is to obtain the powers or the privileges of the god.

Besides these great gods with whom identification is desired, there are many other gods and spirits who are approached in one way or another in the dead man's journeyings. Among them are the seven spirits who punish sinners (Chapter 71), and the spirits of East and West, that is to say, of the beginning and ending of the passage across the sky (Chapters 107 to 109). Some of the deities require altars and offerings (140 to 142); others, including Isis, give protection when the appropriate formulas are written on, or recited over, amulets (156 to 160).

Here we are certainly moving on a plane very different from that on which we started. We are still on it when we come to the numerous spells for enabling the deceased to satisfy both bodily and spiritual needs on his way through the other world and to protect him against evil powers that lie in wait for him there. Thus, Chapter 5 provides for the performance of the agricultural labours assigned to the deceased and Chapter 6 consists of spells to be inscribed on the so-called *ushabti* (or *shauabti*) figures (the word means "answerers")—figures of servants buried with the deceased to perform manual tasks for him beyond the grave.

Again, Chapters 91 and 92 are spells to preserve the dead man from having his soul imprisoned in the underworld or in his tomb; Chapter 89 brings him to his body in the underworld; Chapters 21 to 23 and 25 to 29 are meant to restore to him, or preserve, his bodily powers, Chapter 44 to prevent him dying a second time and 90 to preserve him from mutilation. Chapters 46 to 63 are to promote in various ways his bodily welfare; they come in an odd conjunction with number 45 which is to prevent the decay of his mummy. (We shall have something to say presently of this puzzling anomaly—the provision for the welfare of the body in the tomb and, simultaneously, for that of the body in the underworld.) Chapters 65 to 70 give the dead man various freedoms in the other world; Chapters 77 to 88 enable him to assume a variety of forms; number 132 enables him to return to earth and revisit his home there and number 152

provides him with a new house there. All these should be reinforced by the very ancient formulas of Chapter 137, which
should be recited daily by the survivors to enable the dead man
to become a living soul for ever.

Other spells provide for his actual travelling in the other
world. There are several[1] to provide him with the various boats
necessary (the Re cultus is prominent here) together with a
knowledge of their parts and of the use of these. Chapters 76
and 104 obtain for the traveller the services of the insect known
as the praying mantis as a guide through the bush and to the
great gods. (The Chapter numbers are worth recording if only
to bring home the extraordinary confusion of the order in the
original.) Chapters 144 to 147 provide him with the names of the
porters of the various halls and gateways through which he
must pass; by using them he may compel the porters to admit
him; the three following chapters supply other names necessary
to know.

All this really leads up (if that is the right term in dealing
with such a medley) to the most famous of all the Chapters,
number 125. This is the judgement scene, in which the heart is
weighed in the Judgement Hall of Osiris after the deceased has
made, to forty-two assessors respectively, forty-two denials of
the forty-two sins enumerated in the Code of Osiris. The list is
inserted to enable the deceased to be word-perfect.[2] This scene
in its turn leads (though not in the order of chapters in the
collection) to the description and illustrations of the land of
the blessed contained in Chapter 110 and its vignettes.

This "Elysium" (the Greek and not the Egyptian name for it)
is an idealized Egyptian farm, a flat country intersected by
canals of running water without fish or water-snakes. In the
midst of the canals is an island, the Island of Truth, where
Osiris lives with his saints. The ferryman will only take across
those who, at the judgement, have been declared "true of word"
in the presence of "the great god who destroyeth sin". The

---

[1] E.g. Chapters 98–102, 130, 131, 135, 136.
[2] A brief description of the scene will be found in Budge's book on *Egypt*
in the Home University Library, pp. 159, 160. Another easily accessible account,
also short, but containing the whole of the forty-two items of the Negative
Confession, is to be found in *Studies in Comparative Religion*, No. 9, "The Religion
of Ancient Egypt", by A. Mallon, S.J. (C.T.S.).

dead man's ancestors meet him on the Island. The beatified are seven cubits tall and have the use of boats that carry them where they will, without fatigue—doubtless a constant dream of the Nile-dwelling boatman—and grow celestial wheat or barley, three cubits high.

Here is part of the prayer concerning his life in this Elysium put into the mouth of the deceased in this Chapter:[1] "May I eat therein, may I drink therein, may I plough therein, may I reap therein, may I fight therein, may I make love therein, may my words be mighty therein, may I never be in a state of servitude therein, but may I be in authority therein." It is, in fact, a programme "Of doing everything even as a man doeth upon earth", to quote the last words of the Chapter's title. There is little left of the mysticism and the high theology of the earlier speculation. But since the gods themselves, as ordinarily pictured, lived on much the same plane, "ate the same food, drank the same drink and wore the same apparel"[2] as the beatified, and lived as they lived, and since this life was everlasting and exempt from earthly troubles, it could be regarded as blessed and in a sense divine.

VII

There can be little doubt, if these renderings are not misleading, that there was much of great nobility and high religious meaning in the Book of the Dead. It is equally clear that the amount of sheer magic in the funerary cultus under the Eighteenth Dynasty must have been very considerable, especially in its later phases. Quite apart from the questions raised by the use of set formulas with apparently no ethical meaning, we have the indubitable fact that even plainly ethical texts were used in ways that, if not originally magical, must soon have become so.

Thus, it was possible at this period to buy rolls in which the judgement scene included a verdict of acquittal with a blank space left to be filled in with the purchaser's name. The Negative Confession is invariably written with satisfactory answers to the questions asked, and may well have sunk, in an age without revealed religion, to the level of a charm endowed with a magic

---

[1] Here I am using the rendering in the complete translation, p. 327. Budge's British Museum handbook gives a most misleading account of this Chapter.
[2] Budge, op.cit., Introduction, p. lxxii.

force compulsive even on the gods.[1] Moreover, charms could be bought, to be placed on the corpse's breast, to silence the guilty conscience of the dead man, who might feel impelled to blurt out the truth when confronted with the assessors. On these charms would be inscribed some such phrase as "Oh, my heart, rise not up against me as witness".

The commercialization of the cultus no doubt played a considerable part in these developments. It was the priests who put together the texts, sold the rolls, composed the formulas for the charms, and so forth, and derived a large part of their income from doing so; and the great corporations of a married and more or less hereditary priesthood, lacking the supernatural aid of the sacraments, are not likely to have contained at that late stage of Egyptian history any great proportion of sincere and zealous men capable of resisting the temptation to turn popular superstition into cash.

The whole question of the magical element in the cultus is complicated by the puzzling problem, that happily need not be decided here, of the relation between all this provision for the welfare of both soul and body in the other world and the provision made for the welfare of the mummified body in the tomb. The complication is not lessened by the fact that Egyptologists are not agreed on the precise meaning given by the Egyptians to their various terms for soul and spirit and on the precise relation of any of them to the corpse; nor are they agreed as to whether it was the *ka* or the *ba* or the body itself that was supposed to feed upon the food-offerings and make use of the other provisions for bodily needs which were placed in or near the tombs (and included even lavatories, in some Second Dynasty tomb-chapels). Nor is it certain for what length of time the corpse needed (to the Egyptian way of thinking) to be preserved. It is not even clear that the preservation of the body was regarded as the primary intention of the embalming. Originally it was almost certainly not the main intention of the rite, which was primarily part of the process by which the dead man was identified with Osiris in the god's resurrection. The more materialistic view, however, may well have prevailed in later times.

[1] See T. E. Peet in the *Cambridge Ancient History*, vol. I, pp. 354, 355.

Only two things are certain amidst a welter of confusion in this regard. One is that the ancient Egyptians remained to the last capable of entertaining simultaneously any number of logically or historically incompatible notions. The other is that very few of them were capable of conceiving the life after death except in terms of the bodily life of this world. Only in a few hymns does "the contemplation of the gods in all their splendour" take its place among the attractions of the other world beside the physical and even sensual pleasures of the Elysium where Osiris reigned.

Consequently the broad effect of the cultus of the dead in ancient Egypt was to paralyse or divert energies rather than enhance them. The conservatism of the Nile valley had bred for centuries a political pessimism born of the feeling that nothing would ever again be as good as it had been in the past. Faith in an infinite and eternal God who calls us to eternal life with Him would have made it possible to transcend this pessimism and give to a transitory and unsatisfying life an eternal value by living it for the love of God and as a prelude to this eternity with Him; and to those thus seeking the Kingdom of God first, other things would have been added. Alternatively, the loss of their vivid belief in an after-life worth living might, for a time, have turned the energies of the Egyptians to trying to make this life pleasanter here and now. As it was, their capacity for facing this life constructively, as if it were worth improving, was reinforced in neither way. The nature of their beliefs was such that their minds and creative faculties were preoccupied, and their surplus energies largely taken up, with what were in effect preparations for living this life more pleasantly elsewhere. The effect was inevitably to confirm them in the tendency to regard political activity as not worth while.

VIII

There must have been times when their cultus of the dead meant something more. It is possible that it meant something more, when it was at its height as the monopoly of kings, to the toilers on the great pyramids; for it is hard to think that the royal power to coerce, in an age of puny weapons, could have exacted labour so prolonged from so many labourers together if it had not been reinforced by their desire that the royal power to bless should be prolonged. Nor is it likely to be without significance that the reconsolidation of the kingdom under the Twelfth Dynasty with the co-operation of all classes, after a period of confusion and despair, coincided with an uprush of the cultus of Osiris at its best and most mystical and the breaking of the barriers that had kept out the low-born from the priestly rites. It is likely, again, to be more than an accident that the sudden emergence of the Egyptians as a conquering people coincided with an enormous multiplication of the facilities for securing admission to a life beyond the battlefield.

Nevertheless, the broad and long-term effect of bad theology remained. Political despair came very easily to the Egyptians and it was never for long at a time that they displayed political vigour as a people. To perpetuate the ancient ways of life through periods measured by millennia and spells of almost inconceivable political confusion was their characteristic and supreme achievement as a community. Their conception of the next life as a replica of this one confirmed them in this capacity but never allowed them to transcend it for long. Then, when the best that their cultus of the tomb had to offer had been standardized and stereotyped once and for all in the Book of the Dead, they entered upon a period of very slow but very sure decline.

Naturally, over so long a period—far longer, even if we reckon only down to Roman times, than the history of England since the Norman Conquest—there were interruptions and even temporary reversals of the process of decline, alike on the religious and on the political side. The latter we have already noted ; the former are intertwined with them. Under the rule of the priest-kings of Amen-Re, much was done by the dynasty to bring Re back to his ancient pre-eminence in the funerary texts; and during this period were written the largest and most finely illustrated papyri of chapters from the Book of the Dead. One of them, known as the Greenfield Papyrus, measures 123 feet by eighteen and a half inches. A more interesting fact about it is that (as the choice and wording of the chapters shows) the princess for whom it was written had, in spite of the official cult, a great devotion to Osiris and was able to regard Osiris and Re as two aspects of the same god.

The subsequent submergence of Egypt, first under civil war and then under Nubian rule, put an end to this phase; and the next national revival, under the Twenty-sixth Dynasty, was associated with a revival of the religion that lay nearest the nation's heart. The worship of Osiris was once more completely triumphant and the Book of the Dead enjoyed as great a vogue as it had ever done. Moreover, more popular versions of it appeared, largely replacing *Per-t em hru*. They were shorter documents, written on smaller sheets or strips, instead of on the large rolls, and consisted of hymns and litanies dealing with the sufferings, death and resurrection of Osiris.

All this must have been the product of much genuine religious belief and feeling, embodying something of those yearnings for a truly divine Redeemer that were stirring all the world over, during those centuries. But the weakening of what may be called the more solidly theological element, associated with the cultus of Re as his priests had maintained it, was also making itself felt. As the deities commonly worshipped lost their greatness and dignity in men's eyes, the dignity of man also diminished and irrational creatures filled the void. For ages gods had been represented to the imagination by beasts; now the beasts that had represented them became the gods and Egypt began to swarm with myriads of sacred animals. But since these were obviously mortal, their entry into heaven had to be ensured by the only means known to the Egyptians, and beasts were admitted to the rites that had been reserved to men and embalmed with the ceremonies of Osiris. When Greek globe-trotters reported that the Egyptians worshipped the bull Serapis, they were recording the fact (though they knew it not) that the bull (Api) had been canonized as Osiris-Api after embalmment.

But for the most part it was the smaller and more companionable beasts that were thus mummified, for religion in Egypt was fast sinking to the worship of pets, and of cats in particular, which were first domesticated there. Under this same Twenty-sixth Dynasty, the last before the Persian conquest, they were mummified in hundreds of thousands, for the Book of the Dead still determined the outlines of every cult. It still determined also the outlook of the Egyptians on the political world. Few of them had been stirred by the humiliations that the land had suffered under the Assyrians. Even fewer gave heed to what they were likely to suffer at the hands of Darius. They transferred their emotions to the cemeteries of innumerable cats and Egypt slept on under her successive conquerors.

III

THE TORAH OR THE BOOKS OF MOSES

III

THE TORAH OR THE BOOKS OF MOSES

I

THE books on our list have been chosen for their formative influence upon states and nations and political thinking; and none of them has had a simpler and more direct influence of this kind than the book we have now reached. Some of them have given fixed form to some particular state or civilization already well developed; others have supplied the creative inspiration for many states. But the Pentateuch, or Five Books of Moses, gave a single community, the Hebrew nation, its own unique form, and preserved it in that form through vicissitudes in which every other formative mould or bond or unity was lost. It may be added that the nation so formed has been one of the longest lived of the nations and, in some respects, the most influential of them all.

Nor should we be deterred from recognizing the importance of this book by the plea of the twentieth-century "Liberal Jew" that Judaism is the product of natural reason and religious evolution—"the highest form of natural religion", as he likes to call it, so that its sacred books, which tell quite another story, need not have much importance attached to them. Even if these books could be made to yield a picture of "religious progress" (and a favourite method of doing this is to label all the loftier passages as late on *a priori* grounds and then assert that Higher Criticism proves that the earlier documents know nothing of higher religion), even then the historical fact would remain that what has formed the Hebrew nation, at least since its exile in Babylon, has not been the Judaism of the twentieth-century Liberal synagogue or the composite "Hexateuch" as it emerges from Higher Critical analysis, but "the Books of Moses" taken as they stand and read in their natural meaning.

It is equally indisputable that, read thus, they have nothing to say of progress or the advance of reason and much to say of revelation and of perverted reason stubbornly resisting it. They provide for the nation a background of divine selection, divinely inspired leadership, miraculous deliverance, special revelation and a divine sanction for the Law that they contain. It was that picture, whether true or false, derived from the words of the Book and no offspring of nineteenth-century progressive thought, that actually formed the minds of Jewry; and it was the Code so sanctioned that formed their way of life.

We shall be on safe ground, therefore, as students of history if, in analysing the political influence of these books throughout the period when Jewry most influenced the world, we take them as they stand. As for those occasions on which the truth or falsity of the picture they present might be held to affect our estimate of its political and historical influence, it may be said at once that I accept the picture in substance as it was accepted, from Exilic times at least, by the nation, which was, after all, in the best position to compare it with its own national memories.

II

What, then, are the contents and characteristics of the Mosaic writings that gave them their formative power?

First, they contain a narrative of stupendous events amid which the nation came to birth and they present this narrative in the grandest of historical settings. For they begin with the creation of the world and proceed to narrow down world-history, stage by stage, by shedding, step by step as we come down the millennia, all that is extraneous to the origin of the Hebrews. By the time we reach Abraham, Isaac and Jacob (who was given Israel for his other name), all collateral branches of the human race have disappeared from view except in so far as they reappear at intervals in the narrative as peoples with whom the "children of Israel" come into contact. Thus, the call of Abraham, the promised birth of Isaac, the training of

Jacob, the descent into Egypt and the segregation of the people there, and finally the Exodus and the birth of the nation, are presented as the culmination of a long process that began with the creating and populating of the world and was continued in the gradual sifting and winnowing of the peoples until attention is focused on one people only, the Chosen People. And in the last phase of the narrative, Moses, the God-appointed leader of the nation, steps onto his own stage.

In the second place, the Books of Moses are the documents of a covenant or compact, made between this Chosen People and the God who chose it. It is the compact which Jehovah (or Yahveh) made with Abraham, Isaac and Jacob and afterwards, through Moses, with the whole nation descended from them. Its terms were that He should be their God and they should be His people and that He would bless them for all time provided that they worshipped only Him.

Thirdly, the Pentateuch contains the essentials of a revelation of monotheism. Here is something unique and distinguishing among the formative books of antiquity. It is something, further-more, that transforms the character of the covenant. That each tribe or city or nation should have its special god is a notion familiar enough to polytheism. That this god should be regarded as refusing to tolerate the worship of any other god within the nation or even within the territories that his nation ruled was also not unknown among the ancient empires. It is the con-ception that students of religion have termed "henotheism", the exclusive worship of "one" god as distinct from the worship of "the only" God. But the God of the Pentateuch and of the Covenant is the only God, ruling all nations and knowing no other god. Abraham speaks of "the God of heaven and earth" who "judges all the earth";[1] and Moses of a God who is one, the only God, besides whom there is no God, whose name is "I who am".[2]

Thus the God who has chosen the Hebrew people to be His own people turns out to be self-existent Being, the omnipotent Creator, God of all. Without diminishing His special relation-ship to the people of His choice, He makes Himself known as

---

[1] Gen. xxiv, 3 ; xviii, 25.
[2] Deut. vi, 4 ; xxxii, 39 ; Exod. iii, 14.

the master and sustainer of every nation and of every man. He manifests Himself, that is to say, in two roles, and this duality imposes upon His Chosen People a special mission.

They were given every opportunity of being aware of this mission. From the very first of the revelations to Abraham[1] it was made plain that through him and his descendants all the peoples of the world were to receive a blessing; and, in an immense variety of forms, this divine intention continued to be repeated. God, who cares for all, would ensure that no nation would for all time be excluded from His special favour; and it was through the privileged people that the privilege was to be spread. It was their special tragedy that, from their possession of the universal God as their own God, they chose to learn, not the universalism of love that would have shared Him, but the exclusiveness of pride, that made "heathen" a term of contempt instead of pity. It was the direct result of this that, when at last their own God came humbly among them and began to manifest Himself to the unprivileged, all but a few of the most generous-hearted closed their minds against Him, destroying thereby the very reason for their existence as a separate people.

The fourth distinguishing mark of the Pentateuch as a formative book is that it contains a code of laws. The God and Judge of all the world, the ultimate source and arbiter of right and wrong in the breast of every human being, gave through Moses special laws to His own People.

From our modern standpoint it was a highly composite body of law. First, there was the moral law, summarized in the Ten Commandments and applied in a number of special prohibitions directed against idolatry and other sins. Here and there we find analogies with moral precepts enunciated amongst other peoples; indeed, it could hardly be otherwise, seeing that none of this legislation, though drawn on this occasion from a special revelation, went beyond the natural moral law known, or capable of being known, through the common conscience of mankind.

Then there was a quantity of ceremonial law, a complete religious ritual. Here again we can find analogies elsewhere, as

[1] Gen. xii, 1–3.

in contemporary Egyptian customs and, more plentifully, in the contemporary tablets from Ras Shamra in Syria. The latter at least prove what sceptics have denied, that Semitic peoples could appreciate elaborate ceremonies in the Mosaic period and also put them into writing.

Third and fourth, in this analysis of the Mosaic legislation, come the essentials of a criminal law and of a civil Code. Both exhibit some striking resemblances in detail to the Laws of Hammurabi, though their moral background is very different. It would have been strange indeed if a law-giver "learned in all the wisdom of the Egyptians" had never resorted to devices with which every educated Egyptian would have been familiar. Finally, there are administrative and political regulations, for the appointment of judges (for example), of which there will be more to be said in a moment.

These distinctions between the different kinds of law contained in the Mosaic Code are, however, anachronisms. The Mosaic Code is one, covering indifferently what we now separate as religious and secular matters, moral and positive law, public and private law, or civil and criminal law. Indeed, it makes no attempt to sort out its items under what we would now regard as their proper headings. In the Hebrew nation there was to be no distinction between Church and state, so that it was entirely appropriate that civil, criminal, administrative and canon law should be incorporated in a single code. No alternative course could, in fact, have occurred to the Hebrew mind at that time.

The fifth and last of the characteristics of the Pentateuch that give it a place among the great formative books of political history is that it provides the blue-prints of a complete theocratic state. They are implied in the narrative of the leading of the nation by Moses, the mouthpiece of God, and by the comprehensive character of his legislation, as just described. They are explicit in the administrative provisions contained in the Code. This is political formation at its most direct.

Yet, strangely enough, through the greater part of the history of the Hebrews, and for an overwhelming proportion of the period after the Torah (to give the Law its Hebrew name) came fully into operation, the nation was not a theocracy, at one time because it chose not to be, at others because the opportunity was denied to it by political forces beyond its control. The Law of Moses continued to be operative and to be the bond of union of the nation but it was the Law itself that ruled rather than the political constitution that it prescribed. For this reason the word "nomocracy" has been suggested as more appropriate than "theocracy" to this phase of Hebrew history.[1] We must anticipate what must be enlarged on later and add that in no other way during those periods could the nation have been held together at all.

III

For the first centuries after the first promulgation of the Law and the settlement of Israel in the land promised to them, theocratic rule prevailed after a fashion but more by a living and personal tradition than under the guidance of any writings. On the death of Moses, Joshua, his chief general, stepped into his place as leader, though he made no claim to succeed him as lawgiver or prophet. The so-called "Judges" who ruled from Joshua's time until the effective rule passed to the Prophet Samuel were in a similar sense the successors of Moses. Whatever of the Torah was then in writing must have been preserved by the priests and Levites who accompanied and ministered in the Tabernacle (or tent) that was the shrine of God where the Mosaic ritual of worship was kept up. Without something to direct the priests and guide the procedure and judgements of the Judges, there could have been little continuity in the national life. But in an age of warfare and settlement and (in defiance of the strictest prohibitions of Moses) inter-marriage with the heathen inhabitants of the land and partial adoption of their ways, the writings must have been known only to a few. Many have yielded to the temptation to infer, quite illogically, that none existed.

This period lasted from about 1400 to something like 1025 B.C. Then the leaders of the people deliberately and in set terms rejected the theocracy and with it their political distinctiveness from other nations. (In fact, it was in order to be like the others

[1] By J. Bonsirven, S.J., in *Studies in Comparative Religion*, "Modern Judaism", p. 5.

that they demanded a monarchy.[1]) It is true that the kings were consecrated; they were "Jehovah's anointed", but they were no theocrats. Prophets in the succession of Moses and Samuel continued to be the ordinary vehicle of God's pronouncements. In that capacity they frequently advised or rebuked the kings but they did not take over their functions. The priesthood continued to be attached to the Tabernacle and, presumably, to preserve the writings of the Law.

The Torah, in fact, continued to provide a thread of continuity in the nation's life. King David, who began to reign a little before 1000 B.C., brought the Tabernacle and its attendant priests and Levites to his newly captured capital of Jerusalem and it is not likely to be a mere coincidence that some of the hymns attributed to him are full of allusions to the Torah and his delight in it. So, too, the description of the Temple built by his son Solomon to replace the Tabernacle shows it to have been designed in close conformity with the ritual requirements of the Torah. Moreover, though it would certainly not be true to say that the Torah shaped the nation's polity at this time, nevertheless state and religion remained so closely interwoven that when, about 930 B.C., the state broke in two, the secession of the North took the character of a religious schism.

Then followed a long period during which religious and political decay went on together. The northern kingdom lapsed into semi-paganism and in 722 B.C. was completely destroyed by Assyria. The Kingdom of Judah alone remained, and henceforward we may speak of "Jews". Even amongst them the observance of the Law grew more and more lax and intermittent, until the mass of the people, and even the royal family at Jerusalem, were once more in a state of ignorance of even its most fundamental ceremonial and moral requirements. The prophet Hosea (or Osee) writing in the eighth century laments that the Torah has become to the people "an alien thing".[2]

At last, in 622 B.C., under King Josiah, came the rediscovery of "the Book of the Law",[3] the restoration of the proper worship in the Temple and the extirpation of idolatry. This is the

---

[1] I Kings (= I Samuel) viii ; see especially verse 20.
[2] Hosea viii, 12.
[3] IV (= II) Kings xxii, 8 sqq.

event which the anti-Christian movement of the last quarter of the nineteenth century seized upon to be the pivot of a reconstruction of Hebrew history that became Gospel-truth for all non-Christian and many Christian scholars. The event was represented, not as a rediscovery of the Law, but as the publication under royal patronage of the newly or recently written Book of Deuteronomy, or part of it. We are expected to believe, for example, that someone who wished to impress upon the people the moral teachings of the contemporary prophets composed, with this object, a series of speeches purporting to have been delivered by Moses to the Hebrews just before they began their invasion of Canaan and, in an unhistorical age, gave his invention verisimilitude by filling these speeches largely with instructions as to how to meet situations that must have occurred at least as long a time before the forger wrote as Magna Carta is before our own day.

Thus the speeches[1] include warnings against entering into friendly relations with the inhabitants of Canaan (long since disappeared), regulations for the sanitary arrangements of the camp of the invaders, instructions to Joshua on taking over from Moses, and a plan for cities of refuge which had certainly not, in the time of Josiah, existed for hundreds of years. And all this strain is put on our credulity by the critics because an early date for writings containing the lofty moral and theological teaching of Deuteronomy did not suit the nineteenth-century rationalist's idea of religious progress. It is but a small thing after this, that the ritual regulations of the Torah are assigned to an even lower date as obviously an exceptionally late development, though in fact it is just these that find the closest parallels in the fifteenth-century B.C. Ras Shamra tablets.

However, we shall soon be reaching that lower date and then all schools of thought can concur in tracing the formative effects of the Torah as it has been known indisputably for two and a half millennia. Meanwhile we may note that the immediate effect of Josiah's discovery was small, for the religious revival came too late to save the monarchy. In point of fact it was not even sustained by the next king; and the monarchy fell before the onslaught of the last dynasty of Babylon. The final blow was

[1] Deut. i–xxx.

struck in 586 B.C., almost exactly at the midpoint of the last native dynasty of Egypt. The Jewish state was extinguished and, except for the labourers on the land, almost the whole body of citizens, including the priests and Levites and the royal family, were carried off by Nebuchadnezzar to Babylonia.

IV

At this point, against all human expectation, the Books of Moses began to manifest as never before their unique formative power. They were by now supplemented by chronicles recording the confused period of the Judges and the reigns and events of the monarchy, by genealogies (the compilation and preservation of which became almost a national cultus), by prophetic writings belonging to the last two hundred years and by the preaching of the prophet Ezekiel then living in Babylonia. But it was the Torah that held the place of honour among the writings salvaged from the general ruin and played by far the greatest part in ensuring for the nation a future.

The community had been torn up by the roots and planted in the vast heathen and commercial city of Babylon, which made all too great an appeal to the national weaknesses. It would have been the easiest thing in the world for it to have become assimilated to Babylonian life and religion and, eventually, completely lost in it; indeed, many members of it were thus lost. It was the Torah that was the principal instrument in bringing it about that a substantial number of the exiles preserved their separateness and national identity and their racial and religious self-consciousness. For, as we have seen, it comprised an account of the miraculous birth of the nation, unequivocal testimony to the uniqueness of its God, and precepts providing for a complete way of national life. By making the public reading of the Torah an integral part of their religious worship and by practising at least a substantial portion of such ritual and moral precepts as were applicable to a nation that had lost both its temple and its land, these exiles could and did preserve the essential minimum of a national life and self-consciousness. It was the first Jewish experiment in existing as a stateless nation and owed a great part of its success to a book.

Suddenly Cyrus the Persian captured Babylon and in the following year, 538 B.C., let the Jews go. Not all of them availed themselves of the offer but some forty thousand formed caravans for the long trek and found their way to the deserted sites. Under many difficulties they made some sort of start under a Persian governor and succeeded in building a pitiful imitation of the wonderful temple of Solomon. But the community did not really find itself, nor achieve the essential purpose of its return, until it found leaders in Ezra, the priest-scribe, and Nehemiah (or, as many are beginning to think is their true order, Nehemiah and Ezra, or Esdras). It was under them, probably in the second half of the fifth century and the early years of the fourth century B.C., that the Torah was once more promulgated to the people and, this time, became definitely the pattern of an actual state.

Their work could hardly be better summarized than in the following sentences:[1]

"Nehemias is especially memorable for his rebuilding of the walls of Jerusalem, his insistence on the moral renovation of priests and people, who were lacking in the very elements of their religious duties, and his renewal of the covenant with Yahweh . . . (Under Esdras) Jews who had contracted marriages with non-Israelites were ordered to put away their partners, and Judaism was effectively founded. Idolatry was at an end; Yahweh alone reigned over his people."

V

The young theocracy, however, went through many phases, in the course of which its political character, never very closely defined, fluctuated wildly in conformity both to external forces and to the spiritual state of the nation.

The first determining external fact was that, for very nearly the whole period from the return from Babylon to the destruction of Jerusalem and the Jewish state in A.D. 70, the nation was subject in one way or another to the overlordship of a foreign power. It was part of the Persian Empire for two centuries.

---

[1] By J. M. T. Barton, D.D., in *Studies in Comparative Religion*, "Post-Exilic Judaism", p. 6.

Then Alexander the Great, the Macedonian conqueror, defeated and took the place of the last Darius in 332 B.C. and was overlord of Jerusalem for nine years. When he died his empire was divided between his generals, and Palestine became disputed territory between the Greek dynasty of the Ptolemies in Egypt and the Greek dynasty of the Seleucids, who held, among other regions, northern Syria. Finally it fell to the Seleucids in 198 B.C. Then, after many vicissitudes of which we shall say something presently, Jewry became completely independent in 129 B.C. under John Hyrcanus. But in 63 B.C. the Kingdom (as it had by now become) was annexed by the Romans and remained either under their direct rule or under puppet kings installed by them until the end.

Now, this foreign overlordship, though sometimes little more than nominal and very seldom oppressive, had two distinct effects upon the nation. First, it tended to make the Jewish rulers of the nation subservient to the foreign power upon whom their position ultimately depended and, consequently, often venal and corrupt. Secondly, it kept alive in the rest of the nation a spirit of nationalism. This did not at first aim at political independence in the legal sense, for that ambition was for a long time beyond the horizon of a nation returned in feebleness from exile. Still less, during the first centuries after the Return, did the people pay much attention to those who interpreted politically the foreshadowing in the Law and the Prophets of a Messiah ("God's Anointed") destined to establish a universal rule of truth and justice, and who understood them to refer to a king who was to emancipate the Jewish state and lead it to conquest. The nationalist movement at this time was animated primarily by a zealous concern for the integrity of the national religion, the real seal of the nation's unity and uniqueness.

But, vague and ill-defined as were these two attitudes or interests provoked by foreign overlordship, they were persistent, and were crystallized, in the course of time, in classes and parties. For the first three hundred and fifty years after the Return, the headship of the Jewish state was normally attached to the line of high priests; and it was they and the group of families in whom the priesthood was hereditary that felt, and generally succumbed to, the temptation to subservience to the paramount power and to bribery and corruption in pursuit of office. This opportunism, and a growing scepticism and materialism in religious belief, came to characterize the hereditary priestly aristocracy, the Zadokites or descendants of Zadok (for this is generally held to be the origin of what, in a later phase, was known as "the sect of the Sadducees"). Similarly, concern for the purity of the national religion was naturally conspicuous among those charged with the care and the interpretation of the Books of the Law, by now the final and unchallenged authority in religion. These duties in the course of time became the monopoly of a professional class of laymen, familiar to us under the name of Scribes or (sometimes) Lawyers.

These functionaries not only copied and commented on the Torah but applied it in judgements in the courts, which dealt without distinction with what we should now term secular and ecclesiastical cases. The immense prestige which they derived from their association with the Torah eventually gained them a place in the supreme Council and Court of the nation, the Sanhedrin, where they sat alongside of the Elders and the representatives of the priests. They became also the repositories of a vast quantity of oral tradition claiming to be based on the Torah.

These two developments were clearly marked by the beginning of the second century B.C. They represent the two main reactions of the theocracy to the fact of foreign overlordship.

A second external factor of the first importance to the evolution of the little Jewish state was the rising tide of Hellenism, the late Greek culture spread over the Middle East by Alexander's conquests. This, with its heritage of some of the most brilliant poetry, drama, sculpture and painting, history, philosophy and scientific speculation that the world has ever known, was by far the highest culture in the world at that time and was presented in the most flexible of languages and with an unerring eye for physical beauty. To a people whose background had hitherto been the oldest Empires of the ancient world, Hellenism had also the compelling lure of modernity. It was saturated, unhappily, with religious and moral associations utterly repugnant to Judaism but was nevertheless very hard to resist. The priestly families, with their vested interest in humouring Greek overlords, grew less and less inclined to resist it and eventually went so far as to provide facilities in Jerusalem itself, in the shape of nudist gymnasia, for the younger generation to enjoy themselves openly, not to say shamelessly, in the Greek manner. This, and the seductive form in which the pagan outlook was presented to the eye and the mind of the intellectually curious—and to a people, be it remembered, to whom even the representation of the human form in art was forbidden—all helped to weaken the national powers of resistance to a direct challenge to the Torah when it came. On the other hand, it brought about the formation of a society known as the Chasidim, who, in a period when the Scribes were becoming too much an official caste, took up the cause of religious nationalism, with the strict observance of the Torah as the first item on their programme.

VI

The direct challenge to the Torah, when it came, was the work of both these external forces, foreign overlordship and Hellenic culture, linked in a most dangerous combination.

An integral element in Hellenism at the period we have now reached, the first quarter of the second century B.C., was the new ruler-cult, the rendering of divine honours to the head of the state. It had, of course, existed in Egypt since time immemorial; it had made sporadic appearances in the cities of Mesopotamia and elsewhere in the Middle East, and towards the end of the fourth century B.C. had begun to filter through to the Greek cities, including even the University city of Athens. Alexander the Great, who had come across it when he conquered Egypt, had been impressed by its political possibilities and exploited it there and elsewhere for his own purposes. The dynasties founded by the generals who had divided his Empire followed his example—first the Ptolemies, then the Seleucids. Rather more than sixty years after Alexander's death, Antiochus II, the Seleucid King of Syria, made the cult an integral part of the machinery of his state. In the circumstances of the time and place it served a number of political purposes, which it would serve no useful purpose to detail here—one of them was to provide a bond of unity in a very heterogeneous empire rather as loyalty to the crown has done in the British Empire under the Statute of Westminster. But neither Alexander, nor the Ptolemies nor the Seleucids had pressed the cult upon the Jews.

Then, in 175 B.C., there came to the Seleucid throne at Antioch a man seemingly devil-possessed, who apparently believed in some way in his own divinity. This was Antiochus IV, surnamed Epiphanes, or "God-made-manifest". Not content with his already considerable successes in his drive for the Hellenization of Palestine, he set about forcing upon the Jews the worship of himself. He outraged every sentiment both of piety and of national pride by setting up a statue of himself as a god in the Holy of Holies in the Temple at Jerusalem and then sent portable altars all round the countryside before which incense had to be offered to his divinity.

So gravely had the partial acceptance of Hellenic culture weakened the moral fibre of the nation that the great majority of Jews were ready at first to acquiesce even in this gross and open violation of the central tenet of their religion. There were some, however, particularly among the Chasidim, whom this drove to desperate measures. Led by five brothers, known as the Maccabees, of a family of priests, they broke out into armed rebellion, gathered a number of recruits and, after heroic exploits, fearful defeats and almost miraculous recoveries, succeeded in re-establishing the worship of the true God in Jerusalem after an interval of three years. Then, after the death of the persecutor, they went on to consolidate their position and even to vindicate the rights of Jews in the surrounding territories. Making dexterous use of rivalries for the throne within the Seleucid family and of the readiness of the expanding power of Rome to favour rebellion against potential enemies beyond her frontiers, they succeeded in their objects both at home and abroad. Jonathan, the second of the brothers to take the lead, accepted nomination to the High-priesthood by a pretender to the Seleucid throne, adding the office to that of generalissimo (as a member of a priestly family he was technically qualified for it). His brother Simon continued this combination of posts. It was Simon's son John Hyrcanus who made the state completely independent and his grandson Aristobulus who, in 105 or 104 B.C., adopted the title of king, without ceasing to be High Priest.

Such events could not take place without profoundly altering the spiritual atmosphere of the state and the relations of the parties within it. The descendants of Maccabees became absorbed in their dynastic ambitions (their dynasty is known as the Hasmonean, after their family name). The Sadducees (the name appears about this time) followed their usual course of making up to the powers that be and, since these were for the moment not foreigners, supported for the moment a native dynasty and the cause of national independence. They numbered, now, some twenty thousand. The Chasidim, now known as the Pharisees and about six thousand strong, had decided, after much wavering, that the combination of High-priesthood and kingship in one person was against the interests of Judaism, at any rate when the person was as secular-minded as the later Hasmoneans had become. They went so far as to call in a descendant of Epiphanes, the persecutor, against the native king Alexander Jannaeus and then Pompey the Roman against the last Hasmonean king, Aristobulus II. They claimed to be following this policy as champions of the national religion, and fanned popular zeal for the ancient ways and racial segregation. To impress the masses they punctiliously observed the external details of the Law and promised an avenging Messiah.

This unstable situation brought about its own end. Pompey took Jerusalem in 63 B.C. and, when he returned to Rome, left in virtual control an Idumean timeserver named Antipater, who had a son named Herod, who took after him. This son, while still only an adventurer, obtained from the Roman Senate the designation of King of the Jews and then proceeded to justify it by taking Jerusalem with the aid of Roman legions and ousting the last Hasmonean High Priest. This was in 37 B.C. By cruelty and cunning he maintained his position for more than thirty years, humiliating the Sanhedrin and all the parties alike and almost doubling the size of his kingdom. His last exploit of note was to order a massacre of babies, designed to eliminate a possible rival, a King of the Jews recently born with a better title than his own.

His kingdom was divided among his sons but, ten years after his death, the son who held Judaea was deprived of it by the Romans, who henceforward governed it direct by Procurators, under whom the Sanhedrin fulfilled restricted functions on sufferance. The Jewish parties were re-aligned to meet the new situation. Direct government by the heathen gave Messianic expectations a final twist towards a political form, except in the minds of a very few. A Pharisee of the left wing became one of the founders of a new society, the Zealots, that dreamt of direct action in the original tradition of the Maccabees. The bulk of the Pharisees made themselves more exclusive than ever by their observance of the minutiae of the Torah and of the body of commentary and oral tradition for which they virtually claimed the authority of the Torah. In the circumstances of the time, an exclusiveness on this basis was regarded by them with some reason as a passport to popular applause.

So it came about that when, under Pontius Pilate's procuratorship, a young religious leader appeared outside their ranks who seemed to be supplanting them in popular favour, they dogged his footsteps to collect instances when the Torah could be alleged to have been violated. To the Sadducees his popularity was equally obnoxious, but for other reasons. Dependent once more upon foreign rulers, they had a horror of agitators whose power over the populace made them dangerous in the eyes of the Romans and might give the Emperor a pretext for taking away from the High Priest and his Council their last remaining privileges.

Moved thus by diverse hatreds against the same Person, the rivals joined hands for long enough to hand over to the heathen oppressor one who was coming to be regarded as at the same time the religious and the political hope of the nation. And when the Roman saw through their motives and pronounced for an acquittal, fanatics and sceptics joined hands once more to invoke the Torah itself against its Author. "We, too, have laws," they told the Procurator, "and according to our Law he ought to die, because he claims to be the Son of God."

By that act they flouted, and at the same time fulfilled, the
Law. The Torah-made state had brought its doom upon itself.
It had condemned by the Torah and by the Torah it was con-
demned, and in forty years it was dead.

VII

The political influence of the Torah now entered upon its
longest, most widespread, strongest and most potent phase.
The people whom the Torah had formed for the supreme purpose of history had missed their hour and now existed and
persisted without a state, without an historical purpose, and
with only one common purpose in their own hearts, to strike,
openly or secretly as opportunity allowed, at the Church
founded by the Messiah whom they had crucified. Nevertheless,
their persistence as a stateless and a scattered nation was also
the work of the Torah.

Something of the sort had already been accomplished by the
Torah for the Jews of the Dispersion. These were the Jews
scattered over the known world. There were many Jewish
colonies in Mesopotamia, some being the relics of the deporta-
tions, others the result of commercial enterprise. Within the
Roman Empire, which now included Egypt, there were probably
between three and four million Jews, perhaps a fifteenth of its
population.[1] In some countries their larger colonies had a considerable measure of independence. At Alexandria, where the
Jews numbered some hundreds of thousands, they had their
own quarter in the city and formed "a state within a state".
Almost everywhere their peculiar ways were tolerated, and they
constituted closely knit *collegia*, as the term was. In varying
degrees they accepted Hellenization but in every case there was
some observance of the Mosaic Law, particularly in the matter
of kosher (or ritually clean) food and the annual observance of
the Paschal Festival; and the Torah was read every Sabbath
Day in the Synagogue, the place of worship that had come into
existence in every Jewish centre out of reach of Jerusalem.

Until A.D. 70 the Temple at Jerusalem, the only place in the
Jewish world where the divinely prescribed sacrifices could be

---

[1] J. B. Bury, in his *History of the Later Roman Empire*, vol. I, p. 62, accepts
the figure of 54 millions for the population of the Empire at the death of Augustus,
A.D. 14.

offered, had served as a centre of unity. Regular visits were paid to it, by multitudes of Jews, for the great Festivals, particularly Pentecost. In A.D. 70 the Temple and its sacrifices came to an end together (that which they had foreshadowed was now a reality) and the Sadducaic priesthood lost its functions and its power. The Zealots, who had taken the sword, perished with the sword. The Pharisees and the Teachers of the Law (who were mostly Pharisees) were left to direct the future of a broken people.

They established themselves at Jamnia, south of Jaffa, where they set up a Patriarchate. There the Canon of their Scriptures was settled, and there and in the Rabbinical schools of Babylonia was compiled the Mishnah, a complete code of an elaborated Mosaic Law, and the Gemarah, a learned, closely argued and highly legalistic commentary upon it. Together, these works form what is known as the Talmud.

Thus expanded and expounded the Torah displayed a fresh and altogether unexpected vitality. The commonest criticism of the Mosaic religion has always been that it is too legalistic; but the legalism of the Torah as it stands in the Old Testament is as nothing compared to the labyrinthine legalism of this new recension of it; and yet it was just this aspect of the renovated Judaism that seems to have been its strength. It had no political power behind it and not even an effective central religious authority to enforce it, for the Patriarchate at Jamnia was extinguished by the Empire in the fifth century and its successor in Mesopotamia was increasingly cut off from the West. But this exaggerated legalism gave it an immense toughness, partly mental, partly moral. It reduced religion to two things, first, obedience to a mass of minute regulations affecting some of the commonest activities of life; secondly, as its only mental activity, the study of the most closely knit reasonings on the most arid and technical points of ritual law. The first toughened the will to support an almost but not quite intolerable burden of religious practice; the second toughened the mind to a temper that may partly account for the fact that at the present day the Jews produce more than their share of the leading physicians, physicists, economists and chess-players of the world.

Thus amplified, the Torah more than ever went on moulding

Jews, dispersed over the world, in the ways of life and thought that made them Jews, and preserved them as a nation. It did more than that. Surprisingly enough it made Judaism for several centuries what it has never been on that scale before or since, a missionary religion. Deprived of the supports, and at the same time freed from the limitations, of a visible community, the new Judaism made a strong appeal to all who felt the attraction of discipline, either of the mind or of the will. It converted whole communities, as in North Africa and southern Russia, had its synagogues in China, and was regarded as an active rival by the Catholic Church. Not until all Europe, North Africa and the Middle East had been decisively partitioned between Christianity and Islam, was it tacitly recognized on both sides that Jewry must live, and might be allowed to live, as a once more "hereditary sect, on the fringe of Christendom".[1]

Thenceforward it lived on in numberless segregated communities, within Christendom but not of it, favoured at times by secular rulers because it could deal in money in ways forbidden to Christians; liable for that very reason (amongst others) to outbursts of violence on the part of the populace; consistently protected by the Popes on grounds of Christian morality; making, for its own part, certain concessions in its way of life to its Christian environment; but still held in the mould of the Talmud, through which the Torah now operated with a morbid intensity upon sufferers from enforced inbreeding, physical and mental.

VIII

Meanwhile the same Torah had been exercising its formative power over another community, and doing so more in accordance with its original purpose, though the community in this case was not a Hebrew one. For the other community that it was helping to form was the community that the Hebrew nation had been intended to become, the Christian Church, the congregation of the *Christos*, the Messiah. In this community its

---

[1] This quotation is taken from an article by G. Schmerling in *The Tablet* of 27.5.50, to which the foregoing description is indebted in more ways than one.

operation was balanced, and indeed outweighed, by the Gospels, but never superseded. St. Paul, Hebrew of the Hebrews but Apostle to the Gentiles, had conceived of the Torah as the *paidagogos*, the attendant who escorted the boy to the school of Christ. He was speaking then of its historical function down to Christ's appearance, but the conception remained to a large extent valid if applied to the part played by the Old Testament in forming the minds of Christians in the Christian era. With its ritual prescriptions dropped, because reality had replaced the allegory and the new wine had been put into new wine-skins, it was still a religious document of immense value.

Its moral standpoint, though naturally not on the plane of Christian perfection, was far higher than that of the despairing pagan world. It could warn the convert against the dangers of reversion to idolatry, a very real danger in the first generations of the faith; and could provide for both earlier and later generations a necessary foundation and, as it were, a lower story, for the edifice of grace. It supplied a discipline and training for the lower nature, and for lower natures.

Furthermore, the world-picture contained in the Books of Moses could do for the Catholic Church very much what it had done for the Hebrew nation; it could provide a setting in world-history for revelation and thereby throw a flood of light on the inter-relation between the two. It had a special interest here for intelligent Gentiles, for it cast them for the role of residuary legatees of the unique place in God's world-dispensation that the Jews had rejected; and in this way the sense of being a Chosen People was carried on from Jewry into Christendom. Finally, the Old Testament, as a whole, provided an historical story-book and a body of moral tales for the simple, a psalmody for the worshipper, proverbial wisdom for the preacher, and a luxuriance of prophetic symbolism for the expositor and the mystic, throughout the Catholic centuries.

Thus the Books of Moses, become part of a Christian whole that supplemented their limitations and transformed their spirit, played a subsidiary but important part in the building and shaping of medieval Christendom.

The coming of Protestantism brought with it, in Luther and Calvin, an unbalanced emphasis on the omnipotence and absolutism of God—unbalanced, that is, by any strong sense of God's membership of the human race whereby His redemption of it was effected from within, with man's co-operation. This was in effect a partial reversion to Judaism, where this sense is in the nature of the case entirely absent since it depends upon a belief in the Incarnation. Certainly Protestantism in its early forms was associated with a strong emphasis on the Old Testament, and the Torah became for many purposes divorced from the Gospels again. Old Testament studies became the special mark of minds formed by the new theologies, with the result that the Torah became the chief formative influence upon many of the most active Protestant bodies, particularly upon the off-shoots of Calvinism, such as Presbyterianism in Scotland and Puritanism in England. It played a special part in fostering the theocratic tendencies of Calvinism in all its forms (a whole chapter will be devoted later in this book to the political implications of Calvinism).

All this time the Jews within the area of Christendom (comprising the great majority of the nation) had remained in a sense outlaws, expelled from some countries altogether and, in the rest, confined to, though protected by, the ghettoes. Outside Christendom they had in many cases floated into power in the worlds of learning and administration on the Moslem wave, but it was within Christendom that they best preserved their separate national identity. This was because confinement in the ghettoes of the great business centres, combined with the linking of ghetto to ghetto in a network of international commerce and money-lending, operated as a second Exodus in welding the Jews into a close and exclusive unity again, with the Torah for a code of law for all their ghetto purposes and a perpetual reminder of their first formation.

One more profound change in the formative work of the Torah came with Emancipation. Protestant Holland and Cromwellian England led the way in inviting the Jews to employ their financial talents in the open. With the French Revolution and Napoleon came a general emancipation of the Jews from the restrictions of the ghetto, which exposed the nation afresh to Gentilizing and secularizing influences just when rationalism was the leading intellectual force on the Continent. The result

4*

of this exposure, after one hundred and fifty years, is the contemporary atheist Jew, disowning the God of the Torah but with the stamp of the Torah upon him and upon his policies still. Jewry still retains, with the peculiar twist given to it by the ghetto, the national character formed during millennia by the Book. Jews have not, as a body, lost the consciousness of their uniquely long astonishing historical past, known to them chiefly through the Book. They have not lost the Book itself, nor their reverence for it as a national possession, even when they have ceased to reverence it as the Word of God. They still consider its religion, "which they do not practise, an inalienable inheritance, and if any one of their members passes over to Christianity they accuse him of deserting the nation".[1]

And if they have not lost the sense of their historical past, neither has their "unassimilated" core lost the sense of a political destiny. The Messianic hopes of the last century of their statehood are reproduced, without a Messiah or a God, in the fierce nationalism of the Zionist state—Zionist because Palestine was the land to which the Hebrews were led by Moses.

Nor have they lost the sense, created by the Book, of themselves as the Chosen People. In a new form it has survived even the loss of their belief that they are the repository of a divine revelation and the instrument of a divine purpose. In spite of centuries of suffering, it survives in unassimilated Jewry as a sense of themselves as the unique and superior nation, able and destined to master and remould the world-order and, in doing so, to obliterate all traces of the Christian era. This is the Messianism of the atheist from the Torah's mould. It is not particular as to its choice of methods. It has lately found a use for the ideology whose prophet is the Jewish atheist, Karl Marx.

[1] J. Bonsirven, S.J., *op. cit.*, p. 4.

IV

THE EPICS OF HOMER

IV

THE EPICS OF HOMER

I

THE Greeks of antiquity, Hellenes (οἱ Ἕλληνες) as they called themselves in their great period, resembled the Jews of the Christian era in being a nation, and one of the greatest political forces among the nations, without being a nation-state. Until their greatest days were over they were not united in a single state of any kind and when, towards the end of the fourth century B.C., most of them did for a short time come under a single rule, their ruler was a Macedonian and their various cities were all separately included in an Empire far bigger than any nation and predominantly Asiatic. Even in their great days, in the fifth century B.C., many of their cities were under non-Greek rule, notably those in Asia Minor, which included what had been some of the most brilliant. And those which governed themselves did so as separate states, often at war with one another and always fiercely insistent on their political separateness.

This was true even within the limits of the land we now call Greece; and the Greek states, so far from occupying a single country, were scattered along the shores of the inland seas from Marseilles to the Crimea. The very word Hellas, which we commonly translate "Greece", was frequently used by their great historians, Herodotus and Thucydides, to denote collectively all the scattered territories that the Hellenes then inhabited.

Yet the Hellenes were undoubtedly a single nation and thought of themselves as such. Throughout their great period, and for long before and long after it, they were conscious both of their own unity as a people and of their separateness from other peoples. For non-Hellenes they had a special term, just as the Hebrews had (and still have) for non-Hebrews. It was *barbaroi*, but it did not mean "barbarians" in our modern sense. It could be applied to cultivated peoples with an older or more luxurious civilization than the Greek, such as the Egyptians or the Persians. Probably it was intended originally to mock at the sounds made by those who speak an unintelligible language, but it came to mean much more than that—so much more, indeed, that Aristotle, the greatest intellect produced by the Greeks, actually tried to justify the owning of slaves by the Greeks on the plea that the *barbaroi* were slaves by nature.[1] Admittedly he was uneasy in doing so, but that he should make the suggestion at all testifies to the strength of his conviction of the difference between Greek and non-Greek in respect of the capacity for the use of liberty (for that, as we shall see better when we come to discuss the book in which the passage occurs, was at the back of his mind when he made it).

What, then, were the bonds of union that made these scattered and disunited Greeks one nation and at the same time distinguished them, in their own eyes and in actual fact, from other peoples?

First, there was their belief in their descent from a common ancestor whom they called Hellen and held to be the son of Deucalion who, in their world picture, played the part of Noah. But this, as their own Herodotus pointed out, though necessary to their unity, was not sufficient.

A common language was an important factor, as it nearly always is in creating nations. The Greek language, though apparently of mixed origin and further diversified by dialects, was essentially one; and it had the advantage of being capable of being developed for the purposes of literature into one of the most flexible and beautiful instruments of expression that mankind has used.

Thirdly (and this is a factor that in the case of the Greeks must be ranked high) they had common standards of beauty, based on a singular objectivity of vision. They saw nature simply and unselfconsciously, so that they needed neither to exaggera ˄ nor to minimize, being happy just to see.

[1] *Politics*, I, ii, 2-4.

They had, fourth, a common religion, using the term in a somewhat loose sense and including under it the holding of the great pan-Hellenic festivals and the originally religious intra-Hellenic games. Fifth, they had common moral standards, for what they were worth, of which more presently.

Sixth, they had a common passion for political liberty, only faintly suggested by the now obsolete claim to be a free-born Englishman. A closer analogy may be found in the political rhetoric of the U.S.A.

Seventh, though they had no common territory and no common government, they had a common patriotism, capable of being aroused when a number of Greek cities were together threatened with foreign conquest, and directed particularly against the Asiatic. (The geographical boundary between Europe and Asia, so far as the Greeks knew anything of either, was drawn by them where it is drawn today.)

Finally, there were the Epics of Homer, in which most of these bonds of union found expression and without which some of them would not have been preserved or even have existed at all.

II

Our exploration of a remarkable situation may well start from a fact scarcely less remarkable, the fact that this supremely intelligent people at the height of their intellectual and literary activity, had only the sketchiest knowledge of their own past. Their two greatest historians both confined their main narratives to events within their own lifetimes. Thucydides confines his account of the more distant past to a slight preliminary sketch and Herodotus to scattered and incidental notices, and these as a rule consist of little more than statements about the migrations and settlements of the different Greek-speaking peoples within the Greek world, about the foundation of cities and about the genealogies of royal houses—often mere lists of names and places. The only systematic written presentation of these genealogies and the rest is in the *Theogony* of the poet Hesiod, who reduced to some order the confused stories of the gods and their descendants, writing in the eighth or ninth century B.C.

If we went further and asked why there was no more Greek historical writing concerning this past—at any rate, none that has survived—part of the answer would no doubt be that for various reasons, to be touched on later, the Greeks had nothing that we should call historical records to draw on. Another part of the answer would certainly be that any Greek of the great age setting out to write history would know that any possible reader of his book would already have read, or listened to the reading of, Homer and would be satisfied with that.

And yet Homer was not an historian. He did not even write historical epics. This does not mean that he professed to be telling history in poetical form in his epics but was in fact grossly inaccurate and misleading. What is meant is the simple truth that neither in the Iliad nor in the Odyssey did the author set out to present the history of the Greek people in poetical or any other form. The very plan of his poems proves that. The narrative contained in the twenty-four books of the Iliad does not, as do so many early sagas, cover a series of generations of the childhood of the race. It does not even cover the ten years of the Trojan War. It covers about six weeks of the war and deals with a single episode of it. As for the Odyssey, it recounts the adventures of one man, and only of the last six months of that man's ten years of travel.

It is true that, by the marvellous artistry of the poems, the few weeks or the few months are made to mirror the whole Greek world in which the heroes lived. But the mirroring of an age in a single episode is the achievement of a poet, not of a chronicler, of a Shakespeare, not of a Holinshed—Homer gives no chronicle of his times. (In passing, we may note that the consummate epic architecture of the poems which makes this achievement possible is one of the facts that make the dissolving of Homer into a score, or ten score, of wandering minstrels spread out down the centuries rather ridiculous. Occasional interpolations apart, there can at most be room for two composers of the Homeric epics; and, if for not more than two, then probably for not more than one.[1])

[1] "If we admit the single authorship of each of the epics, it is difficult not to ascribe both to Homer. If there had been two poets equally great, the names of both would surely have been remembered." J. B. Bury in the *Cambridge Ancient History*, vol. II, p. 507, footnote.

How, then, did the Greeks come to accept the epics as a sufficient picture of their past? Partly, no doubt, from the very fact that, in the poet's way, so much is mirrored in them; partly, and quite illogically, from the sheer glamour of the poetry. But two reasons may be given on the more strictly historical plane. First, the great poetic episodes not only appealed to their national pride as glorious pictures of their own heroic age; they felt them to be true pictures of it. The heroes who moved and spoke in them were what they could imagine their ancestors to have been; their gods, their virtues, their emotions, their dress and their weapons were none of them very far removed from their own; they differed chiefly in being presented on the heroic scale and with the simplifications felt to be appropriate to the race's childhood.

In the second place, the poet had managed to fit the episodes with great precision into the chronological and topographical setting provided by the oral historical traditions. These genealogies and foundation-stories, going back to the gods, meagre though they were, did provide a scaffolding of pegs and dates; and the names and cities of the Homeric warriors all fitted exactly into this framework at the point that the supposed period of the episodes required. They fit, in fact, into that mysterious early world that archaeologists know as the Mycenean age, the last phase of the "Minoan" culture, which the Greeks knew as the age of demi-gods and the beginning of their civilization. No more than this combining of a saga of idealized Greek heroes with the accepted origins of Greek culture was needed to convince the Greek mind of the truth of Homer. The epics were unquestioningly accepted as historical pictures of the ancient Greek world, the only pictures that existed, and all else that they contained was accepted with them as the compendium of how all modern Greeks should feel and think.

III

Here, perhaps, we might leave this aspect of our subject, for, if the Greeks really thought like that about the epics, it might seem to matter little for our present purpose whether their thoughts were well-founded or erroneous. Up to a point this is of course true, as we saw it to be, up to a point, in the case of the Torah; but, as in that case also, a point does come when the objective truth or falsity of the nation's belief about itself must affect our interpretation of its history. It must certainly affect our estimate of the formative power of the Homeric epics and of poetry in general; for on one view of the matter the Greek people was cut off from its real past and its normal course of historical development by a piece of sheer historical romanticism; but in actual fact (as I believe) the unifying power of the epics, and therefore their importance in political history, depended on their combining an enormous psychological anachronism with an almost pedantic historical precision.

No adequate account of their political influence can be given, therefore, without taking a definite line as to the historical truth or the unhistorical origins of the various elements in Homer's picture, so that the present section must consist of an attempt to reconstruct the process by which it was put together. Since the reconstruction is in several respects a novel one, some reasoned justification of it can reasonably be asked, but since this is necessarily somewhat lengthy and technical it has been relegated to a Note appended to this chapter, which has been so planned that it could conveniently be read at this point. The result of this procedure is inevitably to give what follows here an air of dogmatism that ill befits an unproved hypothesis and is very far from representing the writer's state of mind. The reader is assured, therefore, once and for all, that the " ifs and ans " that would be too tiresome here, positively swarm in the Note in question.

The Trojan War, then, was fought and won about 1200 B.C. by the Greek-speaking peoples whom Homer, naming (in poetic fashion) the whole from the part, called the Achaeans. These Achaeans inhabited the cities of the Greek mainland in the last or Mycenean phase of the so-called Minoan culture of the Aegean, the great prehistoric culture whose headquarters were in Crete, where it first blossomed under stimulus from Egypt.

It seems, however, that in this population we must distinguish a governing class, the Achaeans in the more limited sense of the word, who were comparatively recent comers to this Minoan world. The evidence of Greek genealogies suggests that they entered it about 200 years before the Trojan War was fought, time enough for them to have been assimilated fairly completely into the culture they had entered—far higher and older than theirs. (We may compare the conversion in an even shorter time of the Vikings who settled in what was to be Normandy, under Rollo, into the Christian and Gallo-Romanized Normans who conquered England under Duke William.) They had had time also to impose their own Greek language upon their subjects, a very common phenomenon when a highly organized language meets one of a lower type. It was they who provided all the leaders of the Greek forces in the Trojan expedition.

A hundred or a hundred and fifty years after the Trojan War the Dorians overran the Mycenean world, from a centre in northern Greece. They belonged to the same stock, and spoke virtually the same language, as the Achaeans but when the Achaeans moved into the Minoan culture-world they had remained on its fringe, much as the bulk of the Teutonic tribes did when many of their kinsmen in the third and fourth centuries of our era infiltrated across the Rhine-Danube frontier into the Roman Empire and were Romanized. Consequently they had preserved their original tribal culture and religion, which was very much the same as that of the closely related Aryans, who, at much the same period, were invading Persia and the Punjab. To the now civilized Achaeans they appeared as destroyers, though their kinship in language was recognized. And, in fact, their incursion was almost entirely destructive. They practically obliterated the Mycenean culture and brought upon Greece a "Dark Age" comparable with that brought by the Vikings upon parts of Western Europe.

During the next few centuries these Dorians acquired some of the habits of civilized life. But they had destroyed so much that there was little positive culture left for them to assimilate; and they long retained, in sharp contrast with their neighbours, the survivors of the decadent Myceneans, that simplicity of outlook and manners and that love of the martial virtues always so much admired, at a distance, by an over-civilized generation. (We may recall how the supposed virtues of the German tribes across the Rhine were held up by the historian Tacitus to the admiration of the decadent Romans.)

Meanwhile the Dorian invasion had set up other movements of the population. In particular, great numbers of the peoples displaced or threatened by the Dorians went overseas and settled in the western and south-western coastal regions of Asia Minor, where earlier Greek colonists had already settled and which now became for several centuries more Greek than Greece and was destined to remain Greek under a long series of non-Greek rulers until 1922.

These movements were going on from about 1000 B.C. onwards. Chief among the emigrants were the so-called Ionian Greeks. These are distinguished from the Achaeans in the stories of the migrations (in which the term Achaean seems to be used in the narrower sense), and seem to represent the most civilized element of the basic population of Greece of the Mycenean age. Though other Greek-speaking peoples, including Dorians, had their settlements in Asia Minor, these emigrant Ionians, together with the Ionians of Attica, the most considerable region of Greece proper not to be Dorianized, formed a world very much on its own among the Greeks, a world with longer memories than the rest and a greater capacity for responding both to intellectual and to aesthetic stimulus when the time came for them to become fruitful again after long centuries of lying fallow.

In this world, in the ninth century B.C. or not long after, two events took place, both almost certainly in Asia Minor or its islands. First, through intercourse with Phoenician traders, the Ionian Greeks had become acquainted with the Semitic consonantal alphabet and one of them had the brilliant idea of supplementing it by adding signs for vowel sounds. Secondly, there was born among them, just at the right time, a genius capable of taking full advantage of the new invention and putting into writing the lays that had been chanted by the court minstrels in the Ionian world ever since the days of the Trojan War.

But this genius, who is more likely to have been Homer than a series of editors, did much more than put into writing the traditional lays. He had the architectonic mind that could incorporate many separate poems in a single lengthy whole and plan the whole with a purpose. Furthermore, he could view physical and human nature alike with a detached eye; and with a robust piety he combined a strong sense of humour. He was sensitive to beauty both of the eye and of the ear, he commanded an unfailing flow of imagery, and had the great poet's power of conveying through the particular image a universal thought. And he built up and adapted to the written word a metre that still stands unrivalled as a medium for epic verse.

Thus equipped, he took first the old minstrel-theme of the Trojan War and used it to convey a picture of what he doubtless regarded as the glorious childhood of his race. To give verisimilitude to his picture he had to satisfy two major requirements. First, he must conform with precision to the genealogical and civic traditions of a people who clung to them all the more tenaciously because they had been dispossessed of their ancient cities. Secondly, he must depict the ancestors of the race, not as the sophisticated and commercial people that the Ionians in Asia Minor were rapidly becoming, but as cast in a simple and heroic mould, ruled by princes who were, credibly, only a generation or two from the gods themselves.

The first of these requirements could be met quite easily (in so far as the traditional lays did not fulfil it) by the accurate use of genealogies and the like. The second was met by Homer with surprising daring. Since his fellow Ionians could not supply him with models, he drew the simpler, still half-barbarian Dorians, now living side by side with the Ionians as fellow-members of the Greek-speaking world. By a stroke of irony that he may or may not have appreciated, he moulded his Achaean heroes in the likeness of their later conquerors.

However, he had too scientific a mind and at any rate too much of the archaeologist's scruples to be wholly satisfied to leave matters at that. Unlike the compilers of the Arthurian romances with whom there is good reason to compare him,[1] he took some trouble according to his lights to adjust his picture in matters of detail to the actual trappings of the period. But it is significant that he left the Dorian dress severely alone, though he must almost certainly have known, from the Mycenean works of art he describes, that the warriors and

[1] See the Note at the end of this chapter.

princes of the period did not wear Dorian dress.[1] He was
following the same instinct that made the sculptors of the
eighteenth century depict in Roman togas statesmen who in
real life wore tail-coats and knee-breeches. And in the larger
matters of religion and character, whether as an archaeologist
he knew better or not, as a poet he knew better than to archaize
at all.

IV

Thus Homer, combining precise chronology with a gigantic
anachronism tempered by an element of deliberate but intermittent archaism, created a composite picture, highly artificial
in the main, but given life and unity by the magic of his poetry
and capable of giving unity to a people as composite as itself.
Indeed, it was by its very compositeness, as much as by the
magic of its art, that it succeeded in unifying the Greek nation.
By fathering upon the Achaeans of the Mycenean age, to whom
the oldest portion of the nation traced their pedigrees, an
idealized portrait of the Dorians, who were the ancestors of
most of the Greeks of the historic period, he established that
portrait as the model for all sections of the Greek-speaking
world and in the end triumphed over a disunity that was cultural, geographical, political and (taking into account the large
pre-Achaean element) racial also.

Indeed, so profound was this disunity at first that it is only
in the light of later events and by using terms derived from
later Greek nationhood that one can give any intelligible
account of the evolution of the Greek-speaking world during the
centuries immediately following the composition of the Iliad
and the Odyssey. It was an age (so far as the Greeks were
concerned) without historical records and, except for the
Ionian cities, of only the very crudest culture—so complete had
been the obliteration of the older world by the Dorians. Even
in the Ionian cities, it was several generations before cultural
activity became at all general. Then in such cities as Miletus,
Ephesus and Colophon, whose commercial contacts with the

[1] He actually distinguishes the " Ionians" (by which he seems to mean the
Athenians) as wearing the long trailing dresses that were general among the
real Myceneans (Iliad, xiii, 685).

wealthy East had made possible for them the "free, leisured and luxurious life",[1] a period of intensely brilliant activity began. Passionate lyric poetry was written, and metres were invented for it that were in use for a thousand years. Philosophers, Thales and the rest, put forward man's first speculations on the nature of the physical world. There were political experiments, in aristocracy and plutocracy, from which, towards 600 B.C., sprang despotisms, as in the late medieval Italian cities; and the despots, as in Italy again, became in their turn the patrons of the arts.

It was from the flame lighted among the Greeks in Asia that European culture was carried to Europe. Further expansion eastward had been increasingly blocked since about 750 B.C., by the Assyrian Empire, and the conquests of Sennacherib about 700 B.C. made it altogether impossible. So the migrations of the Greeks turned westward, first back to the Greek mainland, and then beyond, to Sicily and southern Italy, which became "Greater Greece".

It was about this date that in Greece proper we get the first glimpses of an emergence from its long "Dark Ages". The political sequences of Ionia were repeated there and, in every department of culture, progress became continuous until, in the great fifth century, Athens took the lead, earning her place not only by the pre-eminence of her Ionian intellect and senses but by the valiant part she played at the battles of Marathon and Salamis, in the years 490 and 480, in throwing back the Asiatic. For the recently created Persian Empire had by that time swallowed up the Greek cities on the Asiatic coast and was threatening to swallow up those of Europe. And since it is the peculiar characteristic of European culture that it can only flourish characteristically among Europeans whom Europeans rule, European culture was by this time confined to Europe and only just escaped complete destruction.

But even this danger did not drive the Greek city-states to unity. A fierce exclusiveness, based originally on clannishness and sanctioned by religion, possessed them all. Greeks travelled freely from one city to another, frequently settled and practised their arts in other cities, even received privileges in other cities

[1] The phrase is Dr. Hogarth's (*Cambridge Ancient History*, II, 550).

but always as aliens. "No Greek city had a law of naturaliza-
tion." Nor could two neighbouring cities of importance easily
have been found that had not at some time been at war with
each other.

Such visible bonds of unity as existed were for the most part
religious. Among them were, as was said earlier, the intra-
Hellenic, inter-city athletic contests; and the Greeks with some
reason reckoned their dates from the year of the first of the
four-yearly celebrations of the oldest of them, the Olympic
games—the year we call 776 B.C. There were also festivals at
which the god or goddess of one particular city was venerated
by the whole Greek world and when a truce was observed in
any inter-city war that might be going on at the moment.
Special Leagues used to come into existence for a time to
encourage a common cultus of this kind among a group of
cities. Then there were permanent shrines to which the whole
Greek world resorted, where priests or priestesses gave divine
responses. Pre-eminent among these was the Oracle of Apollo
at Delphi, almost in the centre of Greece, just north of the Gulf
of Corinth.

But without a unifying mental and emotional background
none of these things would have sufficed to give to a multitude
of separatist states such mental and emotional unity as nationhood demands, and the required background was supplied by
the Homeric epics. How the cultus of them arose and why it
arose just when it did are fascinating questions that have never
been satisfactorily answered and the materials for a satisfactory
answer do not appear to exist. But there are traditions of public
recitations of the epics at civic festivals at the end of the seventh
century B.C.; and by the middle of the sixth century they had
come to be regularly recited at the pan-Hellenic annual festival
in honour of (significantly enough) Athene, the goddess from
whom the Ionian city of Athens took its name. Nearly two
hundred years later the philosopher Plato, no friendly witness
as we shall see, could write of a crowd of 20,000 gathered at
one of these festivals and moved alternately to tears and laughter
by these recitations. A whole professional class supported itself
by thus reciting the epics in public.

The epics became also an inseparable part of the ordinary

school education, and by far the largest part. As a recent authority has said: "Reading, writing, dictation, above all, memory lessons were largely confined to Homer.... It was not uncommon for a Greek boy to know both the Iliad and the Odyssey by heart" together with the correct actions to accompany his recitation.[1]

The same writer goes on: "But more than this. Homer was taught in school as the one great authority on all that regarded Greek religion, history and patriotism, not to say as the chief source of knowledge on most other subjects." And when school days were over: "Homeric poetry . . . was . . . the training-ground of every literary artist, every man of taste and education, throughout the Greek world."[2]

V

But if Homer provided the background, what kind of background did he provide?

In the first place, he provided the Greek world with its only civic religions. The Mycenean age, as the archaeologists have reconstructed it, had shrines, but they were rooms, not temples. It had images, but they were little figures for the wall-bracket, not statues for the pedestal and public view. It had a cultus of the dead, drawn ultimately from Egypt, but that was for the family—perhaps for the royal family, but not for the state. It had nature deities and rites, and these survived to Homer's time and later, but they were holy trees and shapeless fetishes and farmers' festivals. "Mystery" cults—secret rites, that is, based on secret beliefs, also came down to the historic Greeks from the Mycenean age, but they were private cults, open only to the initiates, nor were they confined to citizens or even to Greeks; slaves or barbarians might be initiated; there was nothing civic or national about them. Finally, though individual shrines might be tended by a priest or priestess, there were not even the rudiments of a national priesthood; there was no professional body corporately capable of systematically bringing together the gods worshipped by the prehistoric Greeks and organizing a national worship.

[1] H. Browne, S.J., in *A Handbook of Homeric Study*, p. 30.
[2] C. Norwood, *op. cit.*, p. 36

But two laymen (to use our modern and wholly un-Greek distinction), both poets, stepped into the breach. With Homer leading the way and Hesiod following and systematizing, they provided the Greek world with a pantheon, a collegium of Greek gods and goddesses who lived above men in the open on a mountain-top and invited public worship. However diverse the origins of their cults and names—and Homer certainly achieved an astonishing *tour-de-force* when he brought the mystery-loving Mycenean deities into the comradeship and open rivalries of an unmistakably Aryan pantheon under the presidency of the Aryan sky-god—henceforward they were grouped, Aryan and Mediterranean deities alike, as the dwellers on Mount Olympus and public figures for all the Hellenic world.

It is true that not even the creation of a national pantheon called a national priesthood into existence. That was never the Greek way; and to the Dorians (as to their compeers of the Rig-Veda) it was as alien as to the Mycenean Greeks, though their substitutes for it were different. But the systematization and popularization of the pantheon did much to promote the public and official worship of each individual deity by the appropriate city-state and, furthermore, made all the deities collectively known and reverenced by all the Greeks.

In the second place, the poets gave the gods intelligible relations and individual functions. It was a Greek of the great century, Herodotus the historian, who said of them that they "made the genealogies of the gods for the Greeks, gave them their names, distinguished their offices and crafts and portrayed their shapes".[1] By this they made it possible for every Greek to feel that he could enter into personal relations with the deities, not only as a pantheon, but individually, and that in more than one way.

For, by giving clear-cut Aryan personalities to the formless local deities of the Mycenean world, Homer at one stroke created a religion capable of being propagated by the poetic art and used that art to depict an age when heroes had constant and bodily intercourse with these humanized deities and were themselves only a generation or two removed from them. He and Hesiod added an appeal to civic and ancestral pride by

[1] *History*, ii, 3.

identifying these god-like and god-descended men with the figures that stood at the head of the genealogies of the Greek-speaking world. Thus they captivated simultaneously the poetic and the patriotic sensibilities of Ionia and gave Homer's hybrid deities with their Aryan features an enduring place both in its imagination and in its family trees. As for the Dorians, it mattered little that they were less sensitive to the poetic appeal, for they would have had no difficulty in recognizing both the gods and the heroes as their spiritual kindred, even when their names were strange; and, if physical kinship needed to be proved, every Greek city had some equivalent of the College of Heralds!

It was, indeed, in the sphere of religion that the Homeric synthesis achieved its most astonishing triumph of unification; and it is safe to say that history affords no parallel feat of poetry. The religious traditions embodied in the Scandinavian sagas are, like those of the Vedas, almost exclusively those of a single race and spirit. Dante only gave imaginative form to one aspect of an already systematized world-religion; Milton did the same for an insular version of that religion. Homer by blending two religions in one poem made one nation out of two peoples. But it is probably also safe to say that only the Greek nation could have found its unity in a religion composed by a poet.

And it is a method for which a price, and a heavy one, must be paid. Polytheism necessarily degrades its gods (only believers in an Eternal Three in One can apprehend God made man without ceasing to be God and infinite). All polytheism, therefore, in making its gods, is reduced ultimately to a choice between the man and the mascot. Now, Homer, whatever his ancestral traditions may have been, had little use, as a poet, for the impersonal—either for the fetish or the divine plant, or for the dark and formless potencies behind them or the vaguely monotheistic memories of the mystery religions. He could have no conception of a truly supernatural power that transcends both human and material nature and he could not evoke beauty from the shapeless nor a scene of tender emotion from the use of a magical formula. All his deities have human faces. They are changeable though immortal men and women.

Moreover, as a poet he elaborated and played upon their human traits to an extent unknown elsewhere in polytheism before or since. They all have human stories of their own; they have human idiosyncracies and human frailties and lusts.

But they are not entirely on the human level. "Homer's gods", it has been said, "with all their shortcomings are the aristocracy of the universe."[1] Therefore, while they can keep their own affairs from the eyes of men, men cannot hide theirs from the gods, nor escape their interference if they choose to interfere. And in point of fact they are immensely interested in the affairs of men and like nothing better than to intervene nor, in these interventions, can they be coerced by men. They are still gods, who must be approached by prayer and sacrifice.

Moreover, however low their standards of personal conduct, the greater gods, at least, remain in the last resort, the guardians and vindicators of the divine law. This is particularly true of Zeus, the supreme judge. He is often capricious and changes his mind, he can be deceived and can even be made to look ridiculous by his wife, he has his lusts and passions, he frankly boasts that he rules by physical strength;[2] nevertheless it has been well said of him[3] that it is not difficult to distinguish between his behaviour in his private relations with other deities and his behaviour as the god who judges all mankind.

Nor should we overlook the fact that, if Homer was often betrayed by his poetry and his sense of humour into making great play with the frailties of the gods and goddesses, his standing as a theologian, if we may so express it, was saved by the very fact that his epics, even at the height of their cultus, were read as poems, not as sacred books. They were never thought of as revealed writings or as literally true. (That is one reason why the frequently used description of them as "the Bible of the Greeks" is a most misleading one.)

Consequently it was possible for the reader to enjoy and to laugh over the tales of the lusts and quarrels and treacheries of the gods, rather as a devout Catholic can laugh over absurd stories of St. Peter at the gates of heaven, and nevertheless

---

[1] W. R. Halliday in the *Cambridge Ancient History*, vol. II, p. 606.
[2] E.g. Iliad. viii, 18–27.
[3] By E. E. G. in *The Makers of Hellas*.

believe that in the end there was justice to be had in heaven and that there were powers who punished murders, laid low the proud, hated lies and lay in wait for perjurers.[1]

Certainly Homer himself seems to have believed in these things, though he can hardly have believed, except as a poet, in the reality of the characters in his own story. It is at least undeniable that he succeeded in making a religion that included these beliefs a reality for several centuries among an educated people imbued with a strongly rationalistic strain and a sardonic sense of humour, possibly because, true Ionian that he was, he had all those qualities himself.

VI

The moral ideals conveyed by Homer have been summed up by the anonymous writer already quoted.[2] Justice ($\dot{\eta}$ $\delta\acute{\iota}\kappa\eta$) is put first. "Irresistible justice working out three great ideas—the doom of Troy, the avenging of Achilles and the recognition of Hector—forms the inner motive-power which has held together the framework of the Iliad for nearly three thousand years." And since, in the Iliad, this sense of justice is so often swept aside by the might of passion, it may with even more truth be called the leading motive of the Odyssey, in which all leads up to the long-delayed but divinely planned home-coming and reinstatement of Odysseus.

Manliness ($\dot{\eta}$ $\dot{a}\rho\epsilon\tau\acute{\eta}$) comes next in this writer's list. This virtue, of which Hector is the pattern, is (in its Homeric context) essentially courage, but we must include both physical and moral courage. But in actual fact Homer gives far more prominence to the sense of honour, self-respect ($\dot{\eta}$ $a\dot{\iota}\delta\acute{\omega}s$), which should include a respect for the dignity and self-respect of others; it is almost the greatest offence of Achilles that he fails in this in his relations with Hector. All these virtues became and remained ideals of the Greeks. Sin was conceived as blindness of the heart ($\dot{\eta}$ $\check{a}\tau\eta$); and unbridled insolence ($\dot{\eta}$ $\check{v}\beta\rho\iota s$) was the manifestation of it most surely punished by the gods.

With all this went an immense zest for life—for this life,

---

[1] See some excellent paragraphs on this two-fold aspect of Homer's humanizing of the gods, by A. W. Gomme in *European Civilisation*, vol. I, pp. 575, 576.
[2] E. E. G., *The Makers of Hellas*, p. 283.

that is to say—and very little hope or thought for the next, in which only a dim shade survived, emptied of all the warmth of life and personality. The Greeks had to turn from Homer to the mystery-cults if they hoped to escape from their loathing of the grave.

Finally, the Greeks were perhaps the only people—the Japanese at one period may possibly have been another—who were held together to any important extent by a common sense of beauty; and, here also, Homer supplied the standard. He did this all the more effectively because he never talked about aesthetics or even praised things for their beauty but, having observed natural objects photographically and having delighted in their loveliness unselfconsciously, he described them by just the right epithets or made use of them in just the right similes. Sometimes he enables us to feel their loveliness by showing how men felt about them but he never falls into the "pathetic fallacy", so as to make them feel like men.

The extent to which he fixed the standards of art for all Hellenism is shown by the persistence of his standards when other forms of art arose, and other tempers of mind. The first great dramatic poetry, that of Aeschylus (who lived from 524 to 456 B.C.) sprang almost directly from the epics.

"Homer's technique," says a well-known authority,[1] "the shape and structure of his paragraphs, his balancing of themes and episodes, like figures on a vase or pediment, even the distribution of his images . . . all this was studied and adapted to dramatic purposes by Aeschylus. Whether he said it or not, his plays were slices from the Master's feast."

In the generations that followed, the technique of the new art moved away from the methods of the epics; Homeric subjects were avoided (for the significant reason that they were too familiar from public recitation [2]), wholly different mentalities came to the front—the "savage, sneering scepticism"[3] of Euripides, for example, the destructive ingenuity of the Sophists (professional dialecticians, of whom there will be more to be said in the chapter on Plato), and the diverse speculations of

[1] Sir J. T. Sheppard in the *Cambridge Ancient History*, vol. V, p. 114.
[2] See Gilbert Murray, *The Rise of the Greek Epic*, ch. xii, p. 297.
[3] The phrase is Father Martindale's, S.J.

physicists and metaphysicians; nevertheless Homeric standards of beauty, directness and restraint remained the norm, even in writers quite unlike Homer. Take, for example, the historian Thucydides—a writer as different as possible from Homer both in matter and in style. The essence of his art is, by general agreement, his objectivity of vision, and a writer we have already quoted defines this as "a clear, calm intuition of his subject; a vivid imagination which, while it hurries him along, never disturbs him in its course; a stately dignity, which prevents his ever saying a word too much". Having put the facts before the reader, he leaves him to draw his own conclusions; and the same writer adds: "We call this 'Greek reserve'—it is a true indication of strength. Strength nobly wielded—this is the real root of Thucydides; and what is this but to say that he, if any Greek, is Homeric?"[1]

Doubtless it was in the Greek nature to do these things, but it was nature given fixed form by Homer's art.

VII

It would be misleading if the impression were given that Homer went without criticism or that no protests were made against his virtual monopoly as a vehicle of education. In the second half of the sixth century B.C. a violent attack was made on Homer's polytheism and anthropomorphism by an Ionian of Colophon and in the second half of the fifth century complaints were numerous, on religious, moral and aesthetic grounds alike. Sceptics, of course (of whom the Ionian cities produced many), attacked his deities, their interventions and their vices. Thucydides tried to rationalize away the over-marvellous episodes of the historical passages. The sophists specialized in "debunking". One of the charges brought against Socrates that led to his execution by the democracy of Athens was that he used deliberately to quote the most embarrassing passages of Homer and Hesiod in such a way as to bring the poets and the deities they described into ridicule and contempt. His disciple Plato made more than one attack on Homer in

[1] H. Brown, S.J., in *A Handbook of Homeric Study*, p. 318.

his books. Writing early in the fourth century B.C.,[1] he criticized him for his anthropomorphism and for making God the author of evil when he portrays the gods as prompting men to violate oaths. He objects also that the Homeric gods bribe men to do good by promising rewards in this life and can themselves be bribed by sacrifices. And the great Achilles, says Plato (with substantial truth), behaves like an hysterical child.[2] He admits that he himself, like other Greeks, was brought up on Homer, to love and reverence him, but asks: "Who has ever been really educated or improved by him? Who ought to regulate his life by him?" Homer may be granted the title of the greatest poet but not that of the educator of Hellas.

The fact remains that Homer *was* the educator of Hellas but not in the schoolmaster's way; and this outburst of Plato's reads rather as if he were attacking Homer for writing a bad school text-book. No doubt some schoolmasters did present Homer in the manner Plato disliked, but Plato should have known better than to judge Homer by their presentation of him. He had a strong vein of poetry in himself that comes out again and again in his own philosophical writings and he should have been able to recognize in a fellow genius the dramatist's detachment from his own characters, whether human or divine. Only the many generations of school-room teaching of Homer that went before him can excuse him (or, for that matter, the pundits of our own dying classical tradition) for failing to see that Homer was getting a laugh out of his gods for their bad behaviour long before his too literal-minded critics were getting a laugh out of him for his bad theology.

And even those scholastic generations can hardly excuse him for not noticing that Homer, though he cannot displace Achilles from his traditional position as the great champion of the Achaeans, loses no opportunity for putting into the mouths of both Achaeans and Trojans the strongest criticisms of him, both for his savagery and for just that hysterical behaviour of which Plato complains; and, in one case (the killing of the Trojan prisoners to burn on the pyre of Patroclus), he so far departs from his usual practice as to speak outright in his own

[1] In *Republic* ; see ii, 377 to end; iii, 389, 390.
[2] *Republic*, iii, 388.

person of Achilles' "evil deeds".[1] But Plato is not the only critic who has missed Homer's capacity for detaching himself on occasion from his gods and from his heroes alike.

The truth of the matter is that Plato, when he wrote these criticisms, was passing through a phase of "hard-headed realism" of the kind that likes to call itself "practical" and has no use for poetry. In the same book in which they occur he banished poets from his ideal commonwealth, in which he makes the philosopher-rulers commit graver crimes against women and family life than could find sanction in the Iliad and the Odyssey combined. And, in spite of his lip-service to Homer as the greatest poet, he goes on to criticize him even as a poet, on the extraordinary but significant ground that he is too intensely dramatic.[2] But later in life he admitted that the greatest of pleasures for an old man like himself was to listen to a professional reciter reciting well the Iliad or the Odyssey.[3]

In any case, if we are estimating the political influence of Homer, we should remind ourselves that these criticisms, whether sound or unsound, did not become numerous or important until Homer had held unchallenged sway for many generations. Nothing can alter the fact that, with all his faults, he was the educator and unifier of Hellas during the whole period in which Hellas was rising to her greatest heights, upon which she achieved, in many modes of art and thought, works that have remained unmatched in all the world for the rest of time.

VIII

Even beyond this, in historical importance, is the fact that he caused Hellas permanently to exist. Whether Hellas would have come into existence at all as a psychological unit, after its dark ages, without Homer, is very doubtful but it is a question that can be debated because we know too little of the relative dates of the beginning of the Homeric cultus and of other forces making for unity to be able to dogmatize. But there can be no disputing the assertion that, without the mental and spiritual

[1] Iliad, Book xxiii, 176.
[2] Republic, iii, 392–394. See also chapter VII of this book, section ix.
[3] Laws, ii, 658.

5

unification of Hellas by Homer's epics, its existence would have been uneasy and ephemeral.

If the Hellenes, in their days of dispersion and diversity and amidst the political particularism that followed their dark ages, had not all seen themselves mirrored in a single picture of the past in which every branch of them could recognize something that it knew for its own, they could only with the utmost difficulty have struggled into self-conscious existence as a separate people. If the image had not been kept continuously before their eyes, they could not in the face of everyday realities have retained that consciousness—above all when those realities included Asia. Most assuredly, indeed, the epics made history at the beginning of the great fifth century when the Greeks faced the Persians.

Inter-state rivalries were making it the likeliest thing in the world that the hopelessly outnumbered Hellenes of the Greek mainland would succumb to the Persians as their kindred across the Aegean had done. But Homer had called the Hellenes into existence out of an historical void in the act of warring as a people against Asia, and it was the inspiration of this picture that turned the scale when the Hellenes were called upon to stand up against Asia once more.

With Ionian Athens in the van, they stood up to Asia just sufficiently to throw Asia back and make a future possible for the European mind. Then the story was told in the great history of Herodotus in pages that renewed the Homeric theme;[1] and presently the epics were heard with a new awe as a voice from olden times prophesying for Hellas a world-role. A few generations passed and the prophecies were fulfilled when the tide ran eastward and the Hellenes overran Asia, under a leader who constantly slept with the Iliad under his pillow.[2]

In the wake of Alexander the Great, hundreds of Greek cities were founded between the Nile and the Oxus. But so thinly scattered were they that they might easily have lost their Hellenic identity and culture. This may seem improbable to, say, modern Englishmen, who are more English than ever abroad; but twentieth-century Englishmen have ten centuries

[1] See especially *History*, i, 3, 2.
[2] Plutarch, *Lives*, Life of Alexander the Great, section 8.

of common political institutions behind them and a strong colour-prejudice and the Greeks had neither. They had only a consciousness of a community of culture, a consciousness fixed once and for all by Homer.

But that was enough. Strong in that consciousness they retained their Hellenism, and their Hellenism Hellenized the Middle East. Greek became its *lingua franca*. Conservative Egyptians wrote in Greek; Hebrew and Christian Scriptures alike circulated in it. The great Greek writers were read and studied in it and a new Greek science was built up with it, this time in Asia and in Africa.

Presently the Romans conquered Greece and the lands the Greeks had conquered; but, instead of Romanizing them, they Hellenized themselves. Then the Catholic Church came out from Jewry and conquered the whole Roman world, with the result that it is with the European mind, and not with the Semitic, that she has done her thinking and her ruling ever since. Islam came out of Arabia and overran the Christian East and, under its banner, Jews studied Aristotle's philosophy in Syrian cities and transplanted it to Spain. Gaul heard of it and the Italian Aquinas teaching in Paris made it the framework of the official philosophy of the Catholic Church, the vastest synthesis that the European mind has achieved. And where would the European mind have been but for the Greek nation, and where would the Greek nation have been but for Homer?

NOTE ON HOMER'S ACHAEANS

I

The difficulty in accepting the Greek view of the poems would not be acute if, like the Greeks, we had only the poems to consider. There is fairly general agreement that, in seeing in them portraits of their ancestors, the Greeks were in one sense broadly speaking right; the warrior tribes whom Homer represents as inhabiting the mainland and islands of Greece and combining against Troy, and for whom his generic name is Achaeans, are possible ancestors for the Greeks in the sense that their ways and their weapons, their thoughts and their gods, and the rest, as Homer depicts them, are sufficiently akin to those of the Greeks of history for the latter to have been derived from them. It is, of course, arguable that the very fact that the Greeks accepted the Homeric poems as embodying the Greek ideal would have caused the Greeks to become like the Achaeans, so that their actual resemblance does not prove historical descent. But though this might well be true, up to a certain point, of their religious, moral and aesthetic outlook, it could hardly be true of resemblances in material things such as dress and armour. It is difficult to conceive of the Greeks or any other people making a national change in the traditional pattern of these articles by way of modelling themselves upon the heroes of a poem.

A chronological note at this point may help matters. The siege of Troy by the Greeks, if it is to be taken as an historical event and fitted into the traditional chronological framework of the early age of Greece, probably lasted from 1193 or 1192 to 1184 or 1183 B.C. The Greeks of the historical age had begun the public cultus of the Homeric poems before 600 B.C., but in view of the lack of evidence it is impossible to say, definitely, how long before. The actual composition of the Iliad (the poem of the siege) in its present form is dated, by a fairly general consensus of recent opinion, in the ninth century B.C., or perhaps the eighth, and is to be placed in one of the settlements of the so-called Ionian Greeks in Asia Minor, or just possibly at Athens, the earliest Ionian centre. The epics come, that is to say, a good deal nearer to the beginning of the cultus of them in the historical period than to the historical events which they profess to recount. It is, chronologically speaking, as if an epic relating to Alfred the Great and the Vikings had been written some time during the century preceding Chaucer and a public cult of it had begun during the Wars of the Roses and continued into the eighteenth century.

It may be granted, then, that the customs and weapons of Homer's Achaeans, though not precisely those of Homer's own day and still less like those of the historic period, have, nevertheless, a definite kinship with both, so as to be reasonably accepted as the forerunners of the latter. The difficulty of accepting the Greek view of the matter does not lie there. It arises when we try to relate Homer's picture of the Achaeans to the weapons, clothing and customs revealed by archaeology in the ruins of the cities in which his heroes lived and in the strata corresponding to the times in which they lived. The equipment and customs of Homer's Achaeans should be traceable in the remains of the Mycenean culture of the Greek mainland but, with a few exceptions, they are not. The types of weapons and armour, the dress, the arts, the burial customs and the gods of the Mycenean age, as known to archaeologists, all show notable differences from those of the epics. The Homeric heroes are fitted into the Mycenean age and sites with great precision so far as their dates and movements go, but their appurtenances are, in the main, not to be found there.

Such at least is the prevailing archaeological opinion today after nearly two generations of violent controversy. It seems that the contrary opinion can only be maintained by labelling as late interpolations all those numerous passages, particularly those referring to the Homeric warrior's equipment, that stubbornly refuse to be squared with the archaeological discoveries;[1] and a theory that depends on rejecting the evidence, when there is no other reason for rejecting it than that it contradicts the theory, stands self-condemned.

On the other hand, the disagreement between the setting that Homer provides for his story and the setting provided by the archaeologists is by no means complete. The settings are in agreement as to the ordinary materials of the weapons, namely bronze (it was iron in Homer's own day); as to the absence of trumpets, of four-horsed chariots and of cavalry;[2] and, rather more vaguely, as to the plan of the palaces. A few other resemblances in points of detail have been adduced.

We arrive, then, at the rather curious result that Homer's heroes are fully at home neither in his own age nor in the Mycenean. "Nor has any place in Greece been found", says a recent authority,[3] "where the archaeological evidence corresponds to the Homeric-Achaean culture or could even suggest its origin."

In face of this certainly very remarkable fact, some have denied all historical value to the Homeric epics; but scholarship has in general reacted in recent years against this facile type of solution, once so popular. Others have tried in one way or another to minimize the discrepancies between the archaeological and the literary evidence. Others, again, have maintained the essential truth of the Homeric picture of the Achaeans but dissociated the Achaeans from the Mycenean culture, either by representing them as very recent occupiers of the sites, using the conquered natives (who, on this view, were non-Greek speaking "Pelasgians") as mere serfs or retainers or, alternatively, by dating them much later than the Mycenean age. But there is no trace of any such duality of languages

[1] A good short summary of this tangled controversy will be found in the *Encyclopaedia Britannica*, 11th edition, vol. II, article on Arms and Armour, 3 and 4.

[2] See Bury in the *Cambridge Ancient History*, vol. II, p. 513.

[3] A. W. Gomme in *European Civilisation*, vol. I, p. 536.

and classes in Homer; and, in general, the dissociation of the Achaeans from the Mycenean ruling class is contradicted by the fact that Greek tradition independent of Homer traces its genealogies and civic histories to the Mycenean royal houses of the period in question with no kind of interruption or anything to suggest that there was a change either of rulers or of languages. There are, indeed, unmistakable signs that a catastrophe brought the Mycenean age to an abrupt end, but that was about 1100 B.C., when, according to Greek tradition, the "Dorian" invasion occurred. But the Dorian invaders, though generally believed to be speakers of a Greek dialect, were not Achaeans but their enemies and moreover are unknown (as an important and conquering people) to the epics.

It may be suggested, however, that the problem appears insoluble because it is tacitly assumed in these discussions that the external trappings and manners with which Homer invests his Achaeans were necessarily those which characterized them in real life and consequently afford a satisfactory basis for arguing about their historical identity. There is nothing incredible, or even improbable, in the supposition that he is using a perfectly true tradition of the presence and activities of the Achaeans at the times and places in question but has given his heroes the externals and the outlook that in their broad effect are those of a people with whom he was better acquainted than he could have been with the actual occupants of the Mycenean sites three hundred years before his time.

After all, it would be no more than the compilers of the medieval Arthurian cycle did for the Arthur and his warriors who upheld the Romano-British cause against the Anglo-Saxon invaders, when they dressed them in medieval armour and attributed to them medieval ideas of chivalry. It would be a less violent anachronism than Tennyson perpetrated, with less excuse, when, in retelling the Arthurian saga, he invested the war-lord, the *dux bellorum* of the chroniclers, with something of the manners and the sentiments of the Victorian gentleman.

II

This solution of the problem of Homer's Achaeans, that the poet was substantially right in his history and at the same time guilty of enormous anachronisms in his psychology and *mise-en-scène*, would account for a number of anomalies. It would account for the fact that his picture of the Achaeans, though in a general way conforming to the ideals and accoutrements of the Greeks of the historical period, strictly speaking corresponds to nothing at all. It is necessarily a medley, inconsistent with itself, because epic tradition, the observation and portrayal of contemporaries, an idealistic romanticism and an uninstructed archaism all played a part in its composition.[1]

[1] C. M. Bowra, *Tradition and Design in the Iliad*, ch. 7, has argued that Homer's language has something of this artificial and composite character.

The part played by archaism—by what Bury goes so far as to call "conscious and persistent archaism"[1]—is particularly to be noted in this connection. It explains both the existence of resemblances between Homer's picture and that of the archaeologists and also the sporadic and curiously selective character of the resemblances. For Homer, in so far as he did deliberately archaize, had not the equipment nor the historical training of the modern archaeologist. He had to pick up notions from the traditional lays out of which he wove his epics and from such impressions as he could gather from visits to the scenes of his narrative—for there can be little doubt that he did pay such visits.

For example, the topography of the Troad (the district of Troy) is on the whole very accurate,[2] though no one supposes that Homer was born or lived there. He has, too, a general notion of the lay-out of the Mycenean palaces such as might be gathered from a visit to their ruins. Some of the more conspicuous items of the equipment of the Mycenean warriors, such as the two-horsed chariot, he could have seen represented in Mycenean decorative art; and the general idea that weapons were of bronze he would have gained both from surviving specimens and from the universal tradition of an age of bronze preceding the age of iron. And many of these things, together with various details of court life, would have come down in the verses of the court minstrels in whose succession he himself stood.

But he is not completely consistent in any of these points—in the similes he is conspicuously non-Mycenean[3]—and, inadvertencies apart, there are in the narrative itself many very large matters in which he does not make even a beginning in archaizing. The Achaeans of his hexameters wear the Greek *chiton* or tunic and the loose mantle, and cremate their dead, which the Achaeans of the Mycenean age never did; and when he comes to the gods and their characters, their images and the rites with which they were worshipped or, again, to the ethos and spirit of the heroes themselves, he is either utterly unaware of the wholly different Mycenean beliefs and usages or else firmly resolved that in these matters at any rate he will not archaize but will adhere to the picture of the "heroic age" suggested by the manners and spirit of the contemporary people he has taken as his model for this purpose. The analogy with the medieval Arthurian cycle is in this respect very close. No wonder archaeology has unearthed nothing corresponding with any completeness to this bastard and highly literary "Homeric civilization".

Nevertheless Homer must have had some actual contemporary people in some actual phase of culture as the basis of his picture, as did the medieval composers of the Arthurian cycle, and we are brought up against the question of who they were. Here we may find a clue in the now very old-fashioned presentation of Homer's Achaeans as the western

---

[1] *Cambridge Ancient History*, vol. II, p. 513.
[2] So the *Cambridge Ancient History*, but C. M. Bowra, *op. cit.*, disputes this (pp. 159–161).
[3] See C. M. Bowra, *op. cit.*, p. 121.

counterpart of the Aryan tribes who, in the East, invaded Iran and India and are depicted in the collection of Sanskrit hymns known as the Rig-Veda. This presentation has been discredited only because archaeology has made it impossible to apply it to the kings of the Mycenean world. If we may apply it, not to the actual heroes of the Trojan War as revealed by archaeology, but to the non-Mycenean people who served as a model for Homer's painting of those heroes, there can be no objection to resuscitating it, for the parallel has always been a striking one, particularly in the matter of religion and of the characteristic temper and virtues of the warriors.

As regards religion, it is true that the names of the gods in Homer are for the most part not those of the Rig-Veda; only Zeus certainly has an Indo-European name and the goddesses Athene, Artemis and Aphrodite almost certainly have not. But a change of names of their deities may quite possibly have already been made by the people who were serving as his model; it is common enough that a migrating people settling in the midst of a well-established civilisation should identify their gods with those of the local shrines and accept the local names. In any case it was one of the changes that Homer himself was bound to make if he was aiming at even a minimum of verisimilitude, for these divine names of the Mycenean age were still very much alive in his own day and in his own "Ionian" world (of which more presently) and had many links, familiar to his audiences, with the Mycenean cities from which his heroes came.

Moreover, and this is the most significant thing, though he has changed their names, he has not changed their essential character. Under their Mycenean names they are, as a body, in their general character and in their grouping as a pantheon around Zeus, the Sky-father, recognizably the deities of the Rig-Veda and, as we shall see later, markedly out of harmony with what we know of the Mycenean religion. As with the heroes, so with their gods, the names and the places may be Mycenean but the voice is the voice of the Aryan.

But the general parallel between Homer's Achaeans and the Aryans of the Rig-Veda need scarcely be laboured here. It has only recently been summarized again by an outstanding authority on the ancient peoples,[1] who, after dwelling on the social organization, methods of warfare, religion and funeral rites of the Homeric heroes, continues:—

> "The points of resemblance with Indo-Iranian society, and of contrast both with later Greek life and with what we know of the Minoan [including Mycenean] culture that preceded the 'heroic', are obvious, even if Minoan luxury gilds the picture, and if the ruder traits of 'heroic' behaviour have been softened in telling the story among the Greeks."

He adds: "What is remarkable is that so different a state of society should have been so wholly accepted as the canon of actual behaviour.

[1] J. L. Myres in *European Civilisation*, vol. I, pp. 205, 206.

In this sense indeed Homer may be called the 'Bible' of the Greeks." But this success was no accident. It was the result of the sureness of the poet's judgment in his selection of a model for the society of a "heroic age" presented as a nation's childhood. He had, on a much larger scale, the same kind of success as attended the eighteenth-century advocates of a return to "natural liberty" when they painted a portrait of "the noble savage" for the citizens of an artificial era.

III

Finally, one is bound to ask, where did Homer find his model? Myres, in the passage just quoted, seems to suggest that tribes of Indo-Iranian (that is, Aryan) stock did actually pass through Greece in the Mycenean age, occupy the Mycenean cities and Troy as well, and between them, fight the Trojan War (in Homer the Greeks and the Trojans speak to each other with no need for an interpreter, though some of the allies of the Trojans cannot be understood without one).

Now, it is certainly true that the names of some of the gods of the Rig-Veda have been found on tablets in the heart of Asia Minor dating from perhaps the fourteenth century B.C. Nor is there anything improbable—quite the contrary—in the supposition that the ancestors of the Achaeans of the Mycenean age were, if not Aryans in the strict sense of that much misused term, at least an Indo-European people, closely related in race, religion and language to the Indo-Iranian tribes. But the whole archaeological problem arises from the virtual certainty that the governing class of the Mycenean age, whatever their ancestry, were almost completely assimilated to the much higher Mycenean culture in everything except language. To return to the old idea that the warriors who fought the Trojan War were themselves in the Rig-Veda stage of culture is to render the archaeological problem finally insoluble.

But if the mysterious "Dorians", who have never yet been satisfactorily explained, were descended (as their own traditions asserted) from the stock to which the ancestors of the Achaeans belonged, we should have all the elements of a solution. We should begin with a near-Aryan people, ancestors of both Achaeans and Dorians, speaking Greek, or proto-Greek, and closely resembling in culture and religion the Aryans proper, farther east. We could suppose them living on the semi-mountainous grass lands on the fringe of the Minoan culture of the Greek mainland. Then one branch of them—the ancestors of the Achaeans—begins to percolate into the Minoan culture world, not so violently as to destroy its culture but in sufficient numbers to create a new governing class in the districts they occupy and to give the older civilization the fresh stimulus that caused it to give birth to what later Greek tradition knew as the Heroic Age. At the same time they retained their own language and imposed it upon the subject peoples. (All this is a process of a kind that has been witnessed again and again in history.)

5*

The beginnings of this percolation can be dated close to 1400 B.C., if we make the assumption that the points at which the genealogies of the Achaeans of Homer, and of other Greek princely families, recede into semi-divine founders of dynasties represent the points at which Achaean families entered the Mycenean world as capturers of its cities. Moreover the two centuries between this date and the Trojan War witness the appearance in Hittite and Egyptian records of names that have been plausibly identified with Homer's names for the Greeks, the name "Achaean" among them. On the same archaeological evidence we should be justified in making the further conjecture that another branch of the same near-Aryan people crossed the Hellespont, occupied and refortified the already ancient settlement at Troy and penetrated Asia Minor.

Archaeological corroboration of another type seems to be afforded by the increasing prevalence during the same two centuries of what has been called (by H. T. Wade-Gery, in the *Cambridge Ancient History*, vol. II, chapter xix) the protogeometric pottery, described by Wace (*loc. cit.*, p. 470) as a blend of degenerate Mycenean and intrusive northern elements. By about 1200 B.C. the results of this percolation had become widespread and manifest (*ibid.*, p. 523). In other words, the percolation of this pottery type has the closest possible chronological association with the Heroic Age, for 1200 B.C. is approximately the traditional date of the Trojan War, in which that Age reached its climax.

Meanwhile, the near kinsmen of these invaders of the Minoan world, the ancestors of the so-called Dorians, continued to live on its fringe in their original state of culture, making only occasional intrusions into it. (One Greek tradition tells of the defeat of an invading host of Dorians just before the Trojan War and a promise on their part not to come again for a hundred years, a promise which they faithfully kept, retiring north-ward in the meantime from their original home in southern Thessaly.) The situation would be not unlike that which obtained in the later phases of the ancient Roman Empire. Then, some of the Teutonic peoples beyond the Rhine-Danube frontier infiltrated into the Empire, where they con-tributed many leaders to the governing class, while their kinsmen remained outside the frontier in their original tribal and Teutonic phase of culture, making only occasional and sporadic intrusions, but often entering into treaties with the imperial power.

Then came what the later Greeks knew as the Dorian invasion. Accord-ing to the usual interpretation of the traditional chronology, it should be dated about three generations after the Trojan War; it should be perhaps five generations according to the archaeological evidence, consisting chiefly of the sudden flooding of Mycenean sites by a true geometric pottery (*ibid.*, p. 523). Then at last these unassimilated near-Aryans beyond the frontiers broke in and overwhelmed and expelled their long assimilated kinsmen. It was not a gradual and constructive infiltration like that of the Achaeans but a mass movement and immensely destructive, a difference due largely (no doubt) to the fact that the Mycenean world was no longer capable either of offering effective military resistance or of stamping its culture upon its conquerors. (Again there are striking, though admittedly only partial, analogies with episodes of the last days of the ancient Roman Empire in the West.)

This invasion had three consequences that concern us here.

First, it precipitated a series of migrations to the Aegean islands and Asia Minor. There had been (according to Greek traditions) a drift of population to the coast of Asia Minor long before this—as early, in fact, as the expedition to Troy, which in one aspect may be regarded as part of the same movement. But these new emigrations had, in the main, a new character in which they resembled the mass-movement of the British, under pressure from the invading Anglo-Saxons, across the Channel to the peninsula called after them Britannia Minor, or Britanny.

Several elements of the population of Greece took part in them, including even some of the Dorians themselves, but the most important element in these, as in the earlier, movements to Asia Minor was drawn from the people called by the Greeks Ionians. In the narrower sense of that term they can be identified with the population of Attica, the peninsula about the size of Essex that is dominated by the city of Athens. The name may be loosely used, however, to denote the whole of the civilized element in the basic, pre-Achaean, population of the Mycenean age, an element that, though now thoroughly Hellenized in language, was distinguished by a mentality very different to that of their Greek-speaking conquerors but destined, nevertheless, in the outcome, to be regarded for the rest of time as the pre-eminently Greek thing. We might say "paradoxically regarded" were it not for the fact that the trend of recent scholarship has been to insist more and more on the essentially composite character of the Greek people and Greek culture. (It is the whole burden of the lectures by J. L. Myres published in 1930 under the title *Who were the Greeks?*)

This, then, was (for our present purpose) the first notable consequence of the Dorian invasion, to establish across the Aegean Sea Greek-speaking colonies which included some founded by the most intelligent portion of the basic population of the Mycenean Age. And this consequence draws much of its importance from the second consequence, namely that the invasion brought upon Greece proper a Dark Age to some extent paralleled by the Dark Age brought upon most of western Europe by the raids of the Vikings.

Thirdly, this invasion brought into the ancient and long decadent Mycenean world what might well appear to be living specimens of the Heroic Age. Speaking virtually the same language as the Myceneans had learnt to speak and claiming kinship with them, the Dorians nevertheless represented a wholly different stage of culture, the simpler and less sophisticated, semi-barbarous culture of the highlands that the Achaeans had discarded centuries earlier. Moreover, since there was now no vigorous Mycenean culture to absorb and civilize them, they long retained, albeit in a mitigated form, these rougher ways and this simpler outlook—long enough, at any rate, to provide the poet Homer, writing more than two centuries after the invasion, with models for his picture of the heroic childhood of his race. And the Achaeans of his epics, in their appearance, their manners and their beliefs, are in fact in the main an idealized portrait of the Dorians of his own generation.

IV

Such, at least, is the hypothesis put forward here. It will be well, however, before ending this Note, to add a few corroborative details.

To take first the Homeric religion, pre-eminent among its gods are Zeus and Apollo, with shrines at Dodona and Delphi respectively, and it is known that the worship of these two gods at these shrines was conspicuously a Dorian trait in later times. Mount Olympus, moreover, is the home of the Homeric gods; and Mount Olympus, situated at the extreme northern point of the Mycenean world, was the natural focus for the Dorians encircling that world and in point of fact was close to the centre of distribution of the Dorian tribes during their migrations. Again, Homer's Achaeans cremated their dead and so, usually, did the Dorians, but the Myceneans did not.

Then, to take an example from a quite different sphere, the incursion of the Dorians into the Mycenean world is associated, archaeologically speaking, with the sudden prevalence of a type of brooch or safety pin used for fastening loose-flowing over-garments. Homer's Achaeans wear such garments so fastened; the real Myceneans of the Heroic Age wore close-fitting garments needing no such fastening; and the Dorians wore the dress and used the pin of Homer's Achaeans. It is true that this pin had preceded the Dorians, for the Achaeans, their kinsmen, had preceded the Dorians, but its appearances (in graves and so on), like those of the proto-geometric pottery, are sporadic before the invasion, for the incoming Achaeans were quick to adopt Mycenean dress. But in both cases—of pins and of pots—the sudden increases of the eleventh century have every appearance of being the result of a mass-movement.

Furthermore, the hypothesis accounts, not only for the characteristics of Homer's Achaeans when they differ from the Mycenean reality, but also for the affinities in ideals, manners and dress between Homer's Achaeans and the Greeks of the historic age. For on this hypothesis the Dorians were the source of both, in one case as models, in the other as ancestors. For the descendants of the Dorians were the predominant strain in historic Greece (in the terminology of the fifth century historian Herodotus, they are actually "the Hellenes"). And Homer's occasional archaizing also falls into place as accounting for the points at which his Achaeans do *not* resemble the Dorians and do resemble the Myceneans.

Nor is this account of the Dorians inconsistent with the survival into historic times of Mycenean religion (in the form of secret cults) and the reproduction in the Greece of the great age of the uniquely free spirit of

Minoan and Mycenean art. After all, the bulk of the population of the Mycenean period must have survived the wrecking of their civilization, either in Greece proper or overseas. And it was in Attica, which was never Dorianized but was the headquarters of the Ionians, that the ancient religion most conspicuously survived; and it was the Ionian settlements overseas that took the lead in the great artistic revival of the sixth and fifth centuries B.C. and it was to Athens, the capital of Attica, that the flame was passed, to blaze up into a glory that illuminated half mankind. There were always at least two worlds in the Greek nation and it was only in Homer that they became fully one. (See p. 102, paragraph beginning "The Trojan War, then, . . .")

V

THE LAWS OF MANU
AND THE INDIAN CASTE SYSTEM

V

THE LAWS OF MANU
AND THE INDIAN CASTE SYSTEM

I

ON 26th November, 1949, the new Indian Republic adopted its first Constitution. By one of its clauses the status of "untouchability", which has a history of over two and a half millennia, became legally non-existent. The obvious question we are all asking is how long it will be before untouchability becomes non-existent in the practice of everyday life.

It is one of those questions to which it is possible for quite intelligent people to give quite different answers. It will become clearer (it is to be hoped), as this chapter proceeds, why it is not only the sentimental optimist who thinks that untouchability may disappear quite soon, and why it is not only the cynic who thinks that it is likely to endure for a long time yet. It is not sentimental optimism, for example, even if it is an error, to think that the religious basis of untouchability is collapsing and will carry untouchability with it in its fall. Nor, on the other hand, is it cynicism to point out that untouchability has never depended to any important extent on enforcement by the civil law, and to draw the inference that what was not being perpetuated by legal enactment will not be ended by legal abolition.

Nor is it an act of cynicism to recall the impression made by untouchability on a shrewd American visitor to India, Miss Katharine Mayo, less than a quarter of a century before the Constitution for India was adopted, and recorded in a much abused but never refuted book, *Mother India*, published in 1926.

133

She is speaking of the plight of the people variously known to
the British in India as Pariahs, outcastes, or untouchables and
numbering some sixty millions, or nearly a quarter of the
population of the sub-continent. There is nothing in her
description to suggest an institution on the eve of collapse.

"The tasks held basest are reserved for them; dishonour is
associated with their name. Some are permitted to serve only
as scavengers and removers of night soil . . . to all of them
the privilege of any sort of teaching is sternly denied. They
may neither possess nor read the Hindu Scriptures. No
Brahman priest will minister to them; and, except in the
rarest instances, they may not enter a Hindu temple to worship or pray. Their children may not come to the public
[that is to say, the state] schools. They may not draw water
from the public wells. . . . They may not enter a court of
justice; they may not enter a dispensary to get help for their
sick; they may stop at no inn. In some provinces they may
not even use the public road. . . . Some are permitted no work
at all. . . . They may only beg, and even for that purpose they
dare not use the road, but must stand far off, unseen, and
cry out for alms from those who pass. If alms be given it
must be tossed on the ground, well away from the road, and
when the giver is out of sight and the road empty, then, and
not till then, the watcher may creep up, snatch and run.

"Some, if not all, pollute, beyond caste men's use, any food
upon which their shadow falls. Food, after such defilement,
can only be destroyed."[1]

Such has been the lot of those below the caste-system, as seen
through American eyes, and apparently through their own, if
we may judge from the urgency of the plea made by those who
claimed to speak in their name, that the British should remain
in control in India and not leave them at the mercy of the
Brahmans. Even the lowest of those within the caste-system
stand far above this level.

Nevertheless the gulf between the highest and the lowest
levels of the caste system is also very great. The Hindu scale
of values in this regard is clearly expressed in the scale of

[1] *Mother India*, chapter 11.

punishments for the murder of men of different castes, as laid down several centuries before Christ in the Bhagavatas and still regarded by believers as good theology, though the century and a half of British rule brought considerable modifications of the scale so far as temporal penalties were concerned.

If anyone kills a Brahman, a member of the highest caste, he is "condemned at his death to take the form of one of the insects that feed on filth". Being reborn long afterwards as a Pariah, he will continue to be reborn as one, and blind, "for four times as many years as there are hairs on the body of a cow. He can, nevertheless, expiate his crime by feeding forty thousand Brahmans". But if a Brahman kills a Sudra (a member of the lowest caste, now much sub-divided) "it will suffice to expiate the crime altogether if he recites the *gayatri* [a certain prayer] a hundred times".[1]

A more moderate tariff from the Laws of Manu prescribes fines of 50, 25 and 12 panas to be paid by a Brahman slandering respectively a Kshatriya, a Vaisya or a Sudra. (The Kshatriyas and the Vaisyas formed the two intermediate castes of the original four, of which we shall be speaking presently.) But fines of 200 and 100 panas respectively were to be paid by a Kshatriya and a Vaisya slandering a Brahman, while a Sudra was to be whipped. As for crimes of violence, the person and property of a Brahman were not to be touched, whatever he might do to a member of a lower caste; but whoever struck a Brahman, even with a blade of grass, would become a quadruped for twenty-four transmigrations.

We are not being fair, however, either to ourselves or to the Hindus, if we look upon a collection of such regulations merely as a museum of curiosities and incongruities. After all, we are dealing with a living system with, as we have already said, more than two and a half millennia behind it. (It is true that the Laws of Manu, in which the essence of it is embodied, cannot be traced back earlier, in written versions, than about A.D. 200, but those versions certainly represent very much older originals.) A system by which Hindu India has allowed itself to be almost totally formed, which it has perpetuated for that immense period and which it still maintains for the most part with great

[1] *Mother India*, chapter 11.

vigour, for all its cult of Western ways, must mean a good deal more to her than it does to Western sightseers. A serious enquiry, both into its history and into the ideas behind it, is necessary if we are to estimate at all intelligently the position of the Laws of Manu among the supremely formative books of history.

II

Most educated people know that somewhere in the second millennium B.C. north-west India was invaded across what we now call Afghanistan by tribes speaking an Indo-European tongue—a language, that is to say, belonging to the group of which Latin, Greek, Lithuanian and the Slavonic, Germanic and Celtic languages are all members. The particular Indo-European language spoken by these invaders was very closely akin to Persian and related not very distantly to Greek; and from it are derived by different lines of descent the Sanskrit of India's most ancient books and the modern colloquial Hindi.

They called themselves Aryas, meaning "nobles", from which comes our word "Aryans", a word used in a great variety of inaccurate ways, last and most fantastically by Hitler's propagandists. It is used in this book to denote the twin peoples who simultaneously invaded India and Iran at the time we are speaking of, and any other peoples who appear to belong to this Indo-Persian family by language, culture and blood.

These Aryans, then, descended into India with their herds, and horses and chariots, patriarchally organized under chieftains called rajahs (the Latin *reges*) and a military nobility, and worshipping deities grouped around a Sky-father, Dyaus-piter (Zeus-pater, Juppiter). In these and other ways they recall the description Homer gives of the Achaeans (though, as we have seen reason to think,[1] his picture of them was not taken from the Achaeans who besieged Troy, but from later occupants of prehistoric Greece).

These Aryans were by no means the first inhabitants, or even the first politically organized inhabitants, of India. In the Punjab they were preceded, as recent excavations have shown,

[1] See the Note on Homer's Achaeans appended to chapter IV.

by a partly urban civilization of great antiquity, showing affinities to the Sumerian. It is a matter of dispute among archaeologists whether this civilization was destroyed by the Aryans, or by flood before the Aryans came. In any case the Aryans set up kingdoms of their own in its place. But many of them, reinforced by a later wave of invaders, pressed on eastward into the basin of the Ganges and there certainly they found powerful kingdoms. These they conquered; and then this vanguard of conquerors, bringing but few of their women-folk with them, inevitably mixed their blood with that of the earlier inhabitants, whom they described as being, by contrast to themselves, a flat-nosed and dark-skinned race.

The religion, manners and social organization of these in-vaders is known to us through the ancient collection of hymns known as the Rig-Veda, which, in spite of later editing, reflects them fairly closely. (The earliest of these hymns is commonly dated about 1200 B.C.[1]) Like Homer's Achaeans, these Indo-Aryans worshipped as personal deities the greater and brighter powers of nature, but under names such as Indra, Mitra and Varuna that occur, not in Homer, but on tablets of the four-teenth century B.C. discovered in Asia Minor. To these gods they attributed somewhat vague and overlapping functions and offered sacrifices which, when they first entered India, were performed by the chiefs or kings, or by fathers of families. They had the same tendency that we find in Homer and Hesiod to represent their gods in increasingly anthropomorphic fashion and to systematize their beliefs about them. As usual in poly-theism, there was a good deal of magic mixed up with religion. Of an after life, these Aryans had at first no clear or consistent ideas.

III

Here, however, a factor entered that caused them to diverge very far in the end from their western counterpart. The work of systematizing beliefs, which was done for the Hellenic world by two poets, came to be done for the Aryans of India to a large extent by a professional priesthood. Furthermore, the mono-theistic strain that existed in their religion, as (after a fashion)

[1] This date is adopted by *The Cambridge History of India*, but see the Note on Chronology appended to chapter I.

in the Homeric, began to be developed on metaphysical rather than on theological lines, that is to say, the speculations of the priests sought the ultimate unity in impersonal being, rather than in a personal Creator.

In the end they arrived at the conception of a universal, self-existent world-soul, comprising all reality, to which they gave the name Brahmă, a word significantly enough neuter in gender. By it they expressed the oneness of being and at the same time the ultimate power behind all magic. This is a form of monism, the doctrine that there is ultimately only one substance, sometimes called "spirit", sometimes "matter", sometimes "God", it matters not which, for the only honest term is "it". For a philosophy that admits no distinction between spirit and matter or between God and creatures cannot use any of these terms with meaning, even though a genuinely religious mind will sometimes rise above a monistic philosophy and find God even in the bottomless pit called pantheism.[1]

In the face of these philosophical tendencies, popular religion, by a kind of compensation, became increasingly polytheistic and anthropomorphic, or sub-anthropomorphic, and absorbed innumerable pre-Aryan divinities and cults. The priesthood tolerated and even encouraged this tendency among the common people and thus contrived to keep a hold on them without foregoing their own esoteric speculations.

During the same period, perhaps between 1000 and 800 B.C., the priesthood was developing also the ritual of the sacrifices, which they made more and more elaborate as time went on. In this way they made themselves indispensable to the performance of them. They carried this process still further when, perhaps about 800 B.C., they acquired, probably through merchants, from Semitic sources, the art of writing and used it to enshrine religious lore concerning the sacrifices and their inner meaning.

In the course of these activities the priesthood itself became a more homogeneous body. In its earlier days it had been organized in several groups but, as time went on, a group

[1] The word "pantheism" is strictly speaking a contradiction in terms, for, if God is identical with the universe, no room is left for creation or for a God distinct from His creatures. But in that case "atheism" is a better term than "pantheism". If I am God, there is no God, and my only worship is self-worship. Some, it is true, have questioned the strictly monistic character of Brahmanism, misled, perhaps, by their admiration for mystics who have been raised above it.

originally consisting of controllers of magic, and known as Brahmans, came to the fore and eventually acquired a virtual monopoly in the religious world as a professional and hereditary priestly caste.

Parallel with this development, and closely bound up with it, came the ousting of the Kshatriya class, the military aristocracy, from the day-to-day work of civil administration. This step, which was first taken in the central region of northern India known as "the middle land", was made easier for the priesthood by two causes. One was the progressive shrinking and weakening of the military class as a result, not so much of the wars against the pre-Aryan peoples, as of the unceasing wars of the Aryan states among themselves. The other cause was the growing complexity of these states, which required more elaborate regulations, written and unwritten, and more expert administration, than illiterate warriors could supply.

The overthrow of the Kshatriya as an effectively governing class is dated by some as early as 1000 B.C. None of the dates proposed for this period, however, can be very much better than guess-work, for the early writings of India pay no sort of regard to chronology, and archaeology can give no help.[1] One can do little more than adopt some self-consistent scheme. In any case, by 800 B.C. the Brahmans were in control. It is important, however, to recognize that they did not replace the Kshatriya, and did not attempt to replace them, as temporal rulers. They were too shrewd to set themselves up as theocrats.[2] Instead of this, they used their position of vantage in a highly religious society to plan the organization and way of life of society in all its details according to their own ideas; and they employed spiritual penalties and threats to ensure that their regulations were carried out by all classes concerned.

It was in these circumstances that the Laws, or Institutes, of Manu (Mārava-dharmaśāstr) came into existence. The word *manu*, it may be noted, means simply Man, the Adam of the Brahmans, and a divine origin was claimed for the code. Originating in the "middle land", some think about 800 B.C., it spread over the peninsula, even into the south. It made the Hindu, considered as "a social animal", what he is today.

[1] See Note on Chronology, section iv, appended to chapter I.
[2] For this term, see chapter I, section i.

IV

The Laws of Manu fill a large volume,[1] for they comprise a more or less complete legal code for an already complex society. Of its twelve books, one (the tenth) is wholly devoted to caste; and incidental references to caste, with regulations for maintaining it, are scattered freely through the remainder.

There is nothing tentative about this caste-legislation. We find the essential elements of the caste system set out quite definitely and firmly as part of a fixed order of society. We find also what the compilers believed, or at least what they wished those subjected to the code to believe, concerning the origin of caste and of the graded scheme of degradations that it involved. They teach that it was intermarriage between the naturally higher orders of society and the lower orders and, again, between the higher orders and the offspring of mixed marriages that brought into existence castes in the proper sense of the word, with its suggestion of degrees of inferiority and of ceremonial impurity. Nor does it seem that their teaching was wrong about this, so far as it went, but it certainly over-simplified the matter.

It is certainly true (as can be seen from the earlier hymns of the Rig-Veda) that in the first days of the Aryan conquest there were no castes in the sense of social groups made mutually exclusive by rigid marriage regulations, graded in an order of honour and dishonour, and protecting their distinguishing characters by religious sanctions—a description that may serve as a definition of caste proper. There had, of course, been classes among the Aryans—the warrior nobility, the priesthood, and the cattle-breeders and free peasants, in that order; but inter-marriage was possible and no degradation was attached to the practice of any particular occupation. It was all quite natural. The only taboo on intermarriage between groups was related to race rather than to class. This was the taboo on marriage with the non-Aryans, and some think that was enforced by the non-Aryans at least as much as by their conquerors, as a measure of religious self-protection.[2]

[1] See " The Laws of Manu," translated by G. Bühler, in Max Müller's *Sacred Books of the East*, vol. XXV.
[2] See Majumdar, Raychaudhuri and Datta, *An Advanced History of India*, p. 33.

But the Brahmans changed all that, and inculcated the new outlook from which were eventually derived the startling practices illustrated at the beginning of this chapter. Somehow or other they managed to create, during the so-called Brahmanic period that followed the overthrow of the Kshatriya, a complex of sentiments and taboos of such power as to set up *within* the Aryan and semi-Aryan community a system of dividing lines carrying something of the rigidity and abhorrence hitherto only associated with the dividing line between Aryan and non-Aryan; and the problem is to discover what those feelings were that made these lines.

For few now hold that everything can be accounted for by an original mixture of blood between Aryans and non-Aryans, followed by crossings of half-breeds with pure Aryans on the one side and with pure non-Aryans on the other, all accompanied by a jealous reckoning of the proportions of the two strains such as is expressed in the terms quadroon, octoroon and so forth in the southern States of America today. Something besides racial prejudice certainly entered, even if we extend that term to include the jealous exclusiveness in the matter of religious rites that is associated with heredity among most early peoples.

As a first step towards an explanation, we must note that occupation played a considerable part in the shaping and consolidation of the caste-system—occupation on a family basis, that is to say. That, after all, was what had made the lines of demarcation between the original natural classes of the Aryans. So in the earliest castes, the Brahmans claimed first place as priests, scholars and teachers; the Kshatriyas came next as fighters and temporal rulers; and last came the Vasiyas, farmers and cattle-breeders for the most part, though later they came to include merchants.

That classification, however, made no provision for the handicrafts, and it is generally supposed that it was extended to include them when the non-Aryan aborigines, instead of being killed or driven into the forests, were partially admitted into the Aryan communities to ply their crafts or act as servants. This admission, like inter-marriage with non-Aryans, must have been practised in an ever-increasing degree as the more enterprising of the fighting men pushed farther and farther eastward and felt increasingly a shortage of retainers, as well as of women, when the time came to settle in the conquered territories.

It is certainly the case that the name of the fourth main caste in the Laws of Manu, the caste within which various kinds of craftsmen form sub-castes, is the Sudra caste; and "Sudra" was one of the names given by the Aryans to the aboriginal peoples. It is also the case that the Sudras stood in a peculiar relation to the other three castes, in that they were (and are) at the same time within the caste-system (they are not Pariahs), yet separated from the other three castes in the vital matter of their religious status. The three superior castes constituted the so-called Twice-born (an allusion to a certain ceremonial investiture on admission to the religious community). Each had its proper sacred rites and all might participate in the official Brahmanic worship and read, under the Brahmans' guidance, the sacred books. The Sudras, whose function it was to serve the Twice-born and especially the Brahmans, were only to a very limited extent admitted into Hinduism, though it was supposed that, for great merit, they might be reborn as Twice-born. They were denied, for example, all religious instruction, even in the laws of expiating sin. Nevertheless the gap between the Twice-born and the Sudras was not, and is not, as great as that between the Sudras and the outcastes. All this makes the traditional origin of the Sudras very probable.

Up to this point, then, we have a comparatively simple scheme in which both race and occupation play a part. In actual fact, however, the scheme that appears in the Laws of Manu is already broken up by a complex system of sub-castes, each with its special occupation. Some twenty of these sub-divisions are recognized by Manu and provision is made for their multiplication, which has proceeded throughout Indian history.

Many of these sub-castes have arisen in the manner presupposed by the code, namely from breaches of the rule forbidding castes to intermarry. Others have arisen from changes of occupation by a whole group. But there are other factors again which have added to the complications. Thus, the entry into Hinduism of a fresh tribe of aborigines has sometimes created a new caste; occasionally a religious sect has arisen and formed its own caste; and so on.[1] As a result, the system now contains, it is said, between three and four thousand social units, among which the Kshatriyas and Vaisyas have virtually disappeared (though there are a few groups still claiming descent from them[2]). Indeed, the complexities of the modern caste-system are such that, as has been well said by a leading authority on it,[3] any writer on it is confronted with the dilemma that a full account of it would occupy volumes and a short account is necessarily misleading.

V

So far we have been trying to account for the origin of the caste-system and, in general terms, for its complexity. But even when we have done all this, we are very far from having accounted for its hold on a huge population for so many centuries. It has been pointed out by writers on caste that an equally complex and rigid system of occupational castes existed in the fourth and fifth centuries of our era in the Roman Empire, in which nearly everyone had to follow his father's trade; but it could only be kept going by severe legal penalties and, though the tradition of it may have been one of the ingredients of the serfdom that followed it, it ceased to exist in the West as a system when the administrative machinery of the central government broke down towards the end of the fifth century. But the caste-system of the Laws of Manu survived several long periods of administrative chaos and a century and a half of administrative discouragement.

What has given the Brahmanic social scheme its extraordinary tenacity is the union of the occupational element in it with a family system made almost indestructible by being in itself a religious system. The family in Brahmanic Hinduism is not merely a social unit sanctified by religion; it is itself a religious unit. The old Aryan idea (and, indeed, much more than merely Aryan) was that the chief of the clan or the father of the family was the rightful person to offer sacrifice and prayer for his people; and though it made way in India, as it did not in Greece,

---

[1] See Dunbar, *A History of India*, vol. I, p. 18.
[2] See J. Eggeling on Hinduism in the *Encyclopaedia Britannica*, 11th edition.
[3] Sir Herbert Risley in *The People of India*.

for a professional priesthood performing the chief religious functions, nevertheless it left its enduring mark in this fact, that the normal religious unit in Hinduism is the family and not, as in most religions, the congregation.

This fact at once gave a strong religious sanction for a doctrine taught by the Brahmans, the doctrine of *sva-karma*, that there is a sacred obligation upon every man to fulfil the duties of the state of life into which he was born. No man may leave that state, or, by marrying outside his caste, cause his offspring to leave it (though he must marry outside his family) and normally he must practise the hereditary trade of his caste.

This simple religious sanction pervades the whole system, but it has been developed by the Brahmans in two ways, first, in a philosophy that provides it with a basis in metaphysics, secondly in a strictly enforced scheme of penalties, spiritual and temporal.

To take first the philosophical justification, it is to be found in two basic metaphysical doctrines of Brahmanism, first its monism, and secondly the doctrine of the transmigration of souls, that was being developed at the very time when the caste-system was crystallizing.

Monism, as we have seen, denies the reality of the distinction between spirit and matter and it denies also a real multiplicity of individual objects. The appearance of duality (of spirit and matter) and of multiplicity, in the world we see around us, is held to be illusion (*maya* in late Brahmanic terminology). Brahmanism teaches that those who are enlightened will endeavour to penetrate this veil of illusion and arrive at the motionless reality underlying it, and at self-identification with it, and so at what Buddhism was to call Nirvana, the "blowing-out" of the candle flame.

To reach this it is necessary to escape from passion and from material activity of any kind, so far as this is possible. The means to this end are self-mortification and contemplation. All occupations tend, therefore, in Brahmanic thought, to be graded according to the degree in which they approach perfect tranquillity; and the inference is made that it is the duty of the lower castes to render to the higher the menial and bodily services which make this contemplative tranquillity possible.

This theory provided for thinkers a philosophical justification for the caste-system, which to the ordinary man was presented as being of divine origin. It was also the soil in which, perhaps between 800 and 600 B.C., there grew up the doctrine of transmigration, which eventually replaced the earlier and vaguer, but on the whole happier, Aryan notions of an after-life. According to this new doctrine, if bodily death comes to a man with the passions and the desire for material activity still unexhausted in him, the unspent activity has to be worked out in a form either more remote from motionlessness or less remote, according to whether the individual of the preceding life has receded from the motionless unity or has advanced towards it.

The conception of a law of Karma ("the deed") entered here and coloured all this with the notion of moral retribution. As a man had sowed in his previous lives, so must he reap in the present and in future lives. Those born in low castes or beneath the caste-system were to be regarded as paying the penalty of offences (perhaps against the higher castes) committed in previous lives, and were taught so to regard themselves and to humble themselves accordingly.

Here was a sanction immensely powerful, among a people given to a morbid religiosity, for the subordination of the lower castes. Men were made to feel that the subordination must be accepted with resignation as a punishment earned in a previous life, and must be accepted with no less resignation because that previous life had been forgotten.

Not many, however, could be expected to grasp these doctrines fully; and a great part of the formative power (politically speaking) of the Laws of Manu came from the fact that they provided a plain dogmatic statement of the practical implications of this philosophy and of the penalties for offending against them. A few extracts will be illuminating.

"On account of his pre-eminence, on account of the superiority of his origin, on account of his observance of certain restrictive rules, and on account of his particular sanctification, the Brahman is the lord of the castes."[1]

---

[1] *Laws*, X, 3. Based on the translation by G. Bühler in **Max Müller's** *Sacred Books of the East*, vol. XXV.

"The service of the Brahmans exclusively is declared to be an excellent occupation for a Sudra; for whatever else besides this he may perform will bear no fruit." (X, 123.)

Here is the law relating to the Svapaka caste, otherwise known as the Kandalas. The origin of the caste is first accounted for as follows: If a Kshatriya begets offspring by the daughter of a Sudra, that offspring is an Ugra (a caste described parenthetically as "ferocious in manners and delighting in cruelty"). A Svapaka is the offspring of the union of a Kshatriya with an Ugra. For these Svapakas or Kandalas the following regulations are laid down:—

"The dwellings of the Kandalas and Svapakas shall be outside the village . . . and their wealth shall be dogs and donkeys. Their dress shall be the garments of death; they shall eat their food from broken dishes; black iron shall be their ornaments and they must always wander from place to place" (X, 51, 52). Among their occupations, they must "carry out the corpses of those without relatives" (X, 55) and act as public executioners (X, 56). Among the duties of a good householder of the higher castes is to place gently on the ground at a distance from his house some food for "dogs, outcastes, Kandalas or Svapakas, those afflicted with diseases that are the punishment for former sins, crows and insects" (III, 92).

The code goes on to enforce these inequalities in social life (if so mild a phrase will serve) by prescribing a systematic inequality of the castes before the law. Hammurabi's Laws had prescribed heavier penalties for certain offences when committed against nobles than when committed against ordinary freemen but, to set against this, the nobles themselves were liable in certain cases to heavier penalties than other men, somewhat as on the European principle of *noblesse oblige*. But the Brahmans, making full use of their professional monopoly of religious learning and of the administration of the sacred rites, punished offences committed by themselves against lower castes with remarkable clemency and made the punishments inflicted for offences against the higher castes more and more inhuman the lower the offender stood in the social scale.

How inhuman they could be is shown by the examples of this inequality given in the first section of this chapter. Even getting the better of a Brahman in an argument involved a penance. In general, it may be added, offences against caste were penalized more heavily than robbery or murder. Correspondingly, a benefit conferred upon a Brahman could expiate much; feeding a Brahman and saving the life of a cow (a sacred animal in Hinduism) were both highly meritorious acts. The one-sidedness of it all is (to Western eyes) shameless and crude almost beyond belief, but it was by provisions such as these that the Laws of Manu provided the rigid framework for a social system that lasted longer than any other that has arisen among the historical peoples of the world.

VI

Even now we have not fully accounted for this permanence. We can only do that if, in addition to all the causes already adduced, we give due weight to the positive side of the caste-system in virtue of which it is actually acceptable even to those to whom one would have thought it least acceptable. As a very recent writer has said:—

"The restrictive side of the caste-system has been the stock-in-trade of travellers, publicists and missionaries for generations. It is important to remember that these restrictions are merely the reverse of the positive Hindu duties" conveying "the feeling of rightness and propriety to the Hindus" and causing the system to be valued even by those in its lower grades.[1]

For one thing, unprejudiced observers have quite often found in members of the lower castes an entirely genuine reverence, almost amounting to worship, for the Brahmans. There is the case of the Sudra who would not eat in the morning until he had drunk water which a Brahman had sanctified by dipping his toe into it. And if this is regarded merely as evidence of the success of the Brahmans' methods of psychological suggestion, and material benefits to the lower castes are looked for, here is

[1] P. Spear, Ph.D., *India, Pakistan and the West*, 1949, p. 64.

a description of the practical virtues of the system, written by an Englishman and highly idealized, but not without a foundation of truth:—

"It provides every man with his place, his career, his occupation, his circle of friends. It makes him at the outset a member of a corporate body; it protects him through life from the canker of social jealousy and unfulfilled aspirations; it ensures him companionship and a sense of community with others in a like case with him. The caste organization is to the Hindu his club, his trade union, his benefit society, his philanthropic society."[1]

If social stability is now a little valued ideal, the vogue of social security may help some to appreciate some of the points made in this panegyric. We may add one other on the same plane. One of the products of the system has been an extraordinarily high standard of craftmanship in certain trades.

Unhappily, in the absence of Christian charity, fallen human nature in an atheistic priesthood and a polytheistic people found out infallibly the vice opposed to every virtue in this catalogue, incorporated each of them separately in the system and tinged the whole with an indescribable malevolence. The response of the Brahman to the veneration of the humble is the contempt that springs from a quite diabolical pride. The counterpart of the mutual helpfulness of fellow-members of a caste came to be their collective abhorrence for members of other castes. The religious sanctions of the social grading were translated into a morbid sense of pollution from contact with a lower grade, particularly in connection with eating, and the preparation of food.

This last characteristic of the Hindu caste system was not originally fundamental to it; food pollutions are not mentioned in the Laws of Manu as a source of the loss of caste. But the spirit of the Laws is readily expressed in terms of them if the disposition to do so is there; and it was undoubtedly there, and the observance of these and similar pollutions grew with the passing of the centuries until it became the feature of the caste system that most struck the first European observers.

[1] Sidney Low in *A Vision of India*, 1906, ch. xv., p. 263.

It was ubiquitous, and frequently bizarre in its manifestations. Sometimes it had some kind of physical basis, or could be represented as having one, as when those who plied a particularly dirty trade were kept at more than arm's length or when the use of two separate mouthpieces for the same hookah was deemed sufficient to allow men of two different castes to smoke together. At other times the explanation would a ppear to be metaphysical, or else lost in some remote historical cause, as when the cleanly but laborious trade of the carpenter is held to be polluting. The developed system had, indeed, almost incredible intricacies of contaminations. But running through them all was, and is, one common feature—every contact with an inferior class is felt to be a degradation.

There lies the cause of that weight of disgust and contempt that has pressed, and still presses, through layer upon layer, upon all but the highest castes in the Hindu world. And those who cherish the contempt suffer a greater penalty than its victims. No other cause has done more to blind Hindu India to the vision of a divine brotherhood in Christ.

VII

It must not be supposed that the caste-system, given definitive form so long ago in the Laws of Manu, passed unchallenged through all those centuries. On the contrary, it met with three most powerful threats, and survived them all.

The first sprang up in India itself. It came from Buddhism, founded in northern India in the sixth century B.C. by Gautama, known as the Buddha (or "enlightened one"). It was intended to provide a way of renunciation for the attainment of Nirvana to be followed by an Order of ascetics, in independence of the Brahmanic priesthood. It was soon popularized as a polytheistic system of belief, which eventually included the Buddha himself among the deities. It was more ethical than Brahmanism, for it emphasized right conduct as a means of escaping from suffering. The Buddha himself seems not to have wished to abolish caste, but the religion he founded struck an immense blow at the system by ignoring caste in the reception of converts.

6

At first it spread rapidly. It actually became the official religion of the Mauriyan Empire, founded in north-eastern India a little before 250 B.C. by Asoka, who himself became a Buddhist monk. Wherever it flourished, it practically eliminated caste. But eventually the system proved too strong for it, except in the outlying lands of Ceylon, Burma, Nepal and Tibet; and the Moslem invasions of India from the eleventh century onwards finally swept Buddhism from India proper.

But the Mohammedans, with their doctrine of the equality of all believers, proved a still more formidable foe to caste, and their victories created great blocks of population to which caste, once eliminated by the sword, has never returned.

Nevertheless, two-thirds of the vast population of the subcontinent remained either within the caste-system, or under it as pariahs. Moreover, the system kept on growing more complex with the passing of the centuries, and was even, in some respects, made more rigid. In the fourteenth century, for example, commentators on the Laws of Manu promoted rigidity deliberately as a protection against proselytization by Islam.[1] The chances of rising to a higher caste by education were diminished by additional restrictions, and spare-time occupations that might lead to the same result were frowned upon. Only the Brahmans, as the highest caste, had considerable latitude in the matter of occupations. Within certain limits they might take up other than the priestly or educational professions, without losing caste, including even certain manual occupations. Scavenging, of course, was forbidden, but not crime, the hereditary occupation of certain Brahman clans.

The British conquest was the third great threat to the caste system, but proved innocuous to it to a surprising degree. Any adequate treatment of this curious topic would swell this section to a fantastically disproportionate length. One can only note the typically British blend of imperviousness to any non-British point of view when presented to the mind and a benevolent tolerance of "native" customs regarded as a matter for the administrator. In the eighteenth century Warren Hastings had the Laws of Manu translated into English for the guidance of his officials but, in the nineteenth, Macaulay made sure that it

[1] See *Advanced History of India*, p. 403.

was British Law that was studied in British schools. But more efficacious against caste than any disparagement of it by British moralists or disregard of it in British courts was the impracticability of observing many of its taboos in British offices and British trains.

But caste survived all this and survived even a phase when to be British was all the fashion. No doubt certain deep affinities to it in the English class system operated, though unconsciously, in restraining the English from bearing too hardly upon it. Moreover caste seemed to be in the very air in India, and the British, while loudly proclaiming their disdain for its distinctions, themselves reproduced them to an extraordinary extent in their own attitude to Indians, even to those of high caste and social rank, to whom they took up much the same attitude as the ancestors of those same Indians had done to the dark-skinned non-Aryan inhabitants of the land at the time of their own conquest of it. Until the last years of their occupation they formed a fresh caste themselves, with its own social and physical taboos recalling those of Manu. Their attitude was accurately caught in a famous novel, E. M. Forster's *Passage to India*: "Remember", says a seasoned memsahib to a newcomer from England about to meet some Indian ladies, including some queens of Native States, "remember you are superior to all of them except a few Ranees, and they are your equals."

VIII

The analogy must not, however, be pressed very far, for there is no religious element in the Englishman's colour-bar and, whatever the origins of Hindu caste, religious sanctions have been bound up with it for more than two millennia. And it is just this feature of the Hindu caste-system that makes its future so unpredictable today.

On the one hand it makes for its perpetuation, for it gives it a support that is independent of political change or legal enactment. It was with a reasonable distrust of political promises that the representatives of the sixty million untouchables petitioned the British Government, when it was preparing to quit, not to leave them to the mercies of the Brahman

Congressmen. But those plausible oligarchs, by posing as oppressed democrats, had gained the ear of that most gullible of human beings, the British Parliamentarian abroad, and the really oppressed people got very little consideration.

A more serious threat to the Brahman ascendancy during the same period lay in the fact that by far the most popular nationalist leader was a member of the lowly money-lender caste, Mohandas Karamchand Gandhi, who, moreover, made the emancipation of the untouchables one of the principal planks in his platform; and his popular canonization in his own life-time seemed at one time as if it might undermine the religious basis of Brahmanism. But whatever view we may take as to Gandhi's sanctity, it is certain that he remained to the last far too astute a politician to break with his Brahman colleagues, and the Brahman ascendancy was never directly attacked by him.

It was, in fact, not his unorthodox propaganda, but the manner of his death that eventually forced their hands. For at the very time when the administration was being transferred to a self-governing State of India, with Brahmans in all the important offices, Gandhi was assassinated by a fanatic for Brahmanism, and the halo of martyrdom that he thus acquired impelled his former colleagues for very shame to insert in India's Constitution the clause abolishing untouchability to which reference was made at the beginning of this chapter. And, though this clause did not directly affect the caste-system, it struck at a sentiment that from the first has been closely bound up with it. Not for the first time, violence defeated its own ends.

It is not unlikely, however, that the association of caste with orthodox Hinduism was in any case due to become, no longer a strength, but a weakness. The very fact that the nationalist agitation had attained complete success meant that the Indian politicians were no longer required by the exigencies of nationalist propaganda to stress their Hinduism in opposition to an allegedly tyrannical Europeanism; and this meant that whatever internal weaknesses Hinduism had developed in recent years were certain to come to the surface.

Thus, in the economic sphere the Brahman leaders felt free to resume with far fewer tactical inhibitions the process of

Westernization to which most of them had long been strongly attracted; and they no longer felt it necessary to pay lip-service to such eccentricities as Gandhi's spinning-wheel and the other economic vagaries of his Hindu Sinn Fein movement. Moreover, the pressing economic and administrative problems of the new Indian state quickly compelled them to make full use of this psychological release; and the effects of this in making many caste taboos impracticable cannot be substantially different to those experienced when it was the Westerners themselves who were introducing the same Westernisms in the same spheres.

Even more profound effects of the changed tactical situation may be looked for in the sphere of religion itself. Esoteric Brahmanism, the Brahmanism of those initiated into Brahmanic philosophy, though often dressed up in religious terminology for Western consumption, has always tended to atheism, except for a few chosen souls to whom God has spoken, for that is the ultimate logic of its metaphysics; but popular Hinduism has suffered from an excess of gods. Against this polytheistic Hinduism, often degenerating into mere fetish worship, the materialistic brand of Western education so avidly absorbed by Indian progressives of all castes has been operating for many years with devastating effect; but the nationalistic politics that were one of the by-products of this Western education operated to conceal in part its religious effects. The mask can now be thrown off by those of the lower castes who have been affected in this way; and the Brahmans for their part can hardly keep their own religious pretensions once their bluff has been called by the other castes.

In fact, they soon struck at the religious character of the Republic of India by the agreement signed on 8th April, 1950, with the Moslem State of Pakistan providing for the safety of their respective religious minorities. For that agreement laid it down that the allegiance and loyalty of the religious minorities is owed, not to the state that is predominantly of their religion, but to the state of which the line of partition happens to have made them citizens and in which they are to enjoy complete equality of citizenship with those of the majority religion. The ultimate implications of this for the Hindu caste system will be obvious to such intelligent men as the Brahman leaders; and they will be the first to see that the struggle for supremacy within their state will, under the new conditions, have to be waged with new weapons.

It is not impossible that the means to re-establish their ascendancy on a new basis will be found in a movement greater than Indian nationalism and, like it, a by-product of the culture of the West in its decay. It is worth remembering that the spiritual forerunners in Russia of the Communist Party were not class-conscious proletarians or peasants but an atheist intelligentsia, the product of the philosophical Nihilism of the last third of the nineteenth century. An avowedly atheist Brahman class might prove equally receptive to Marx's materialistic philosophy of history. It has already shown itself capable, when given a political objective, of pursuing it with an intensity and a tenacity supposed to be alien to the Oriental; and many of its members, now that the nationalist movement no longer fills their political horizon, are in search of a new objective.

Thus Communism in India has now its first real chance of appealing successfully to the politically-minded educated atheist. The intellectually more agile among the Brahmans now enjoying their first spell of political power in a self-governing Hindu India may soon be seeing a more enduring future for their oligarchy in the establishment of a Communist bureaucracy. They will call it a dictatorship of the proletariat in deference to Marx, but they will entrench themselves even more elaborately than their Russian counterparts in a system of privileges strongly reminiscent of Manu.

VI

THE SAYINGS OF CONFUCIUS

VI

THE SAYINGS OF CONFUCIUS

I

IN the course of the nineteenth century, China came for the first time fully under Western eyes. When the first excited marvellings at the curiousness of her manners were abating and more serious observation was taking their place, the characteristic that struck the observers perhaps more forcibly than any other was the essential uniformity in social character throughout her vast area and her teeming population.

There were, it is true, great diversities of dialect, practically amounting to differences of language; there were striking differences of physical type and of temperament, as between, say, the Cantonese and the northerners; occupations naturally varied from area to area in a country which geographers, with some reason, term a sub-continent. But, for all that, social organization and the administrative system, the accepted ideas and conventions, the written language and even the method of holding public examinations were virtually uniform all over China proper, although she roughly equalled both in square miles and in inhabitants the combined totals of the dozen or so nations that make up the continent of Europe apart from Russia.

On further investigation it appeared that these uniformities might be brought, broadly speaking, under two heads. Everywhere society was dominated by the family system in an intensified form, with all that that implies; and in every locality down to the smallest country-town the administration was in the hands of an all-pervading but centralized bureaucracy, which the famous examination system was designed to recruit.

On looking still further into the matter, enquirers found that both these institutions were very old and, moreover, by their nature promoted stability and their own self-perpetuation. Take, for example, the family system as it worked in China. In the economic sphere it tied sons to their father's land and occupation (the overwhelming majority of the population were, of course, small farmers). It discouraged them from ventures far afield where they might not be within reach of ageing parents; and it was capable of bringing back emigrants from the ends of the earth. It required the eldest son, when the parents were dead, to stay at home to tend the parental shrine.

In the political sphere, this same family system discouraged, not only the innovating spirit that characterizes all younger generations, but all individualistic self-assertion. It fostered a submissiveness to be practised in every unit of society. In the family, which might include three or four generations living together, submission was owed to its venerable head. It was owed to the clan, which served the purposes of a benevolent society and, in particular, might finance the education of its promising youngsters. It was owed to the village elders, who carried the weight of local self-government in lesser matters and, in emergencies, in larger matters. Beyond all these, this filial submissiveness was directed to the supreme father, the sacred Emperor, who in his turn was the Son of Heaven.

It is true that certain elements of instability were latent in this system. Under the pressure of over-population, repeated divisions and subdivisions of the family-plot among sons, and among their sons in their turn, sometimes made the holdings entirely inadequate to support their cultivators. A case is instanced of an area in which 88 per cent. of the family holdings were of less than one and a half acres. In such cases many were squeezed out of the peasantry and took to brigandage. So, too, in the political sphere, intense preoccupation with the family and the clan left little room for patriotism or for consideration for national interests.

But these things were not enough to destroy the family system. The brigands had their own code, and preyed upon those rash enough to travel rather than on the family that stayed dutifully at home; and floods, famines and epidemics on a gigantic scale kept the population fairly constant in the long run. In the long run, also, loyalty to the family made for political permanence more than loyalty to the state would have done, in an Empire in which breakdowns in the central administration were frequent, and corruption continuous.

If we turn to the Chinese bureaucracy of the same period, we see an institution possessing, if possible, even greater rigidity. It was "a bureaucracy of literati", a civil service, that is to say, consisting of men with a literary training, and forming a distinct class. It ranked highest among the four recognized social groups, namely scholars, farmers, artisans and traders in that order, with soldiers not ranking at all, unless perhaps with the brigands. A very few titled families and princes of the blood alone took precedence of this civil service, which was in effect the only aristocracy of China (which presumably accounts for the fact that China has never been reckoned among the aristocracies).

In theory this class was not hereditary, for anybody might enter it if he could pass, by fluency or fraud, a very stiff competitive examination in the Chinese classics. In practice, however, it was very largely hereditary, thanks to the advantages under both heads possessed by the sons of civil servants. Moreover, once admission to the service had been secured, there were other ways of avoiding a clash between the two loyalties owed respectively to China's two great institutions. Since the system of examination in the classics was defended on the ground that no one obtained office who had not a thorough knowledge of the principles on which the Chinese social system was based, and since the family principle ranked first among these, not only was paternalism the proper disposition of the magistrate as an administrator, but nepotism in promotion could also be represented as a pious duty; and the claims of two potentially discrepant systems could thus be brought into harmony.

Such was the ordered picture of Chinese society and administration presented to the fascinated eyes of the diplomats, traders, missionaries and custom-officials who flocked to China from Europe as soon as British naval guns had obtained from the always polite Chinese permission for them to pursue their several activities in that country. And these visitors learnt one more fact, that this social and administrative order, which was certainly very old, was based on the teachings of the philosopher Confucius, who was active as a teacher about five hundred years before Christ. They proceeded to do a simple sum in arithmetic and concluded that China had been Confucianist for a good deal more than two thousand years.

There, however, they were wrong. The teachings of Confucius had had by no means an easy or a rapid victory, nor an uninterrupted reign when victorious. The story of their successive advances towards the political formation of China is worth telling, for history presents no more instructive example of the triumph, through sheer persistence, of an inferior mind.

II

The earliest official religion of China was monotheism, practised, however, with the restriction that worship might be offered by only a single official, the Emperor. He acted for the whole people, so that there was no official priesthood; and the only other worship of which the imperial government was officially cognisant was the worship paid, according to a well-established ceremonial, by all other persons to their dead ancestors. With this went naturally a belief in an after-life but, among a respectful people, not in a Judgement or Hell. Morality tended to be identified with conformity to the precepts of parents and governors and to be cultivated for the sake of pleasing them. All this, according to many scholars, was in existence under the Shang dynasty, at least a thousand years before Confucius, when the Empire was confined to little more than what we now call north-west China.

Unofficially, superstitious beliefs and cults of all kinds, including the forms of nature-worship characteristic of an agricultural people, flourished amongst all classes, from the Emperor downwards. The remoteness of the supreme God left room for fatalism, with a host of magical practices as its accompaniment, including divination, in which the magnetic compass found its earliest use.[1] Divination, indeed, for the purpose of deciding between alternative courses of action, was in universal use, by governments as well as by private persons. Moreover, a

[1] See F. Hirth, *The Ancient History of China*, pp. 126–136.

whole world of spirits, anthropomorphically conceived, filled the popular imagination; and ancestors came to be regarded as able to intervene, both for good and for evil, in the affairs of their descendants.

The disintegration and diversifying of belief was accelerated by the collapse of the Empire into a sort of feudal anarchy from the eleventh century B.C. onwards, under the Chou dynasty. (We may compare the collapse of the Egyptian monarchy at the end of the Sixth Dynasty.) Moreover, the feudatory states that thus emerged filled a much wider and more diversely populated area than the original China. Not only was the whole basin of the Hoang-ho (the Yellow River) now Chinese, but the most southerly provinces lay along both banks of the middle Yangtze-kiang, extending as far south as the Nanling range into the modern Hunan.[1]

In the latter part of this period of decadence arose two men, completely opposed to each other both in views and in temperament, who stand at the head of the two main streams of Chinese thought and feeling. If it is true that every philosopher is necessarily either a Platonist or an Aristotelian, it might also have been said until very recently that every Chinese who thought at all, thought either with Lao-tze or Confucius, even if he had never heard of either.

Lao-tze, pronounced something like *lowdze*, means simply "the old philosopher". It was the name given to Li Ir, who was born in 604 B.C. in the vassal state of the so-called "Man barbarians" in the Yangtse valley and may reasonably be supposed, both on this and on other grounds, not to have been of purely Chinese descent. K'ung Fu-tze (that is to say "the philosopher K'ung", Latinized as Confucius), was born in 551 B.C. in the Shantung peninsula and died 72 years later. He belonged by descent to the class of the Ju, experts in the ceremonial of the temples and of divination, and keepers of records, who in virtue of their ability to read and write became indispensable to the feudal rulers as administrators, besides acting as advisers on religious rites and tutors to the young nobility.[2] In all this the young K'ung perfectly represented his

---

[1] See Hirth, *op. cit.*
[2] E. R. Hughes, *Chinese Philosophy in Classical Times*, Introduction.

class, surpassing his fellows only in the seriousness with which he took its traditions and the conscious analysis to which he subjected them.

A story is told, of the only meeting between these two men, that would appear to be entirely characteristic of both. K'ung at the outset of his career had already decided to reform the life of the nation on the ancient principles and paid a visit to the very much older man in order to learn from him what these principles were. It appears that he was severely snubbed by the aged Lao-tze, who hinted not very obscurely at "haughtiness" and "licentious schemes".[1] For Lao-tze, whose thought has remarkable affinities with that of Brahmanic, or even Buddhist, India, by this time believed himself to have discarded all ambition. Like Gautama (and possibly taught by him, but the question of priority is clouded by chronological doubts about the Buddha) he had formulated a doctrine of the Way (*tao*, rhyming with "cow", in Chinese), the goal of which was "No Action". "Do nothing, and all things will be done", is a saying attributed to him; "the weak overcomes the strong" is another. "Keep behind and you shall be put in front"; "recompense injury with kindness" are other sayings found in early Chinese literature attached to Lao-tze's name and receiving their confirmation in the Gospels.[2]

Certainly there was nothing in all this to appeal to K'ung in his youth, or indeed at any age, for he was always an intensely ambitious politician, intent on reforming others. Already at the age of twenty-one he had established a school of political morality for young men. His great desire was to find a ruler who would give him an opportunity of applying his precepts in actual government; but this was only fulfilled once, and for a few years, when he was fifty-one. He died a disappointed man because in all the states of the Empire there was no ruler intelligent enough to make him his mentor.[3]

[1] See his speech as given by Hirth, *op. cit.*, pp. 240, 241.

[2] These sayings are taken from the collection in the Introduction to H. A. Giles, *Chuang-Tzi, Mystic, Moralist and Social Reformer*, quoted by Hirth, *op. cit.*, pp. 300, 301.

[3] See Bonsall, *Confucianism and Taoism*, p.10. I follow here the general opinion of the aut! ᵛrities, but according to Waley (*The Analects of Confucius translated and annotated*, p. 14) there is not the slightest evidence that Confucius obtained a position of political authority even for a few years.

There was, moreover, an even deeper difference between the minds of the two men. Lao-tze was a true philosopher with a highly speculative mind, who wished to clear all old beliefs out of the way and start afresh. K'ung was not made for thought that was either speculative or abstract, and he was entirely agnostic about God, though a firm believer in divination and fate. His pious aim was the restoration in all its completeness of the fabric and manners of the ancient state. The precepts of its sages and the details of its ceremonial constituted the sole object of his researches and the texts for all his teaching. "I am a transmitter," he said of himself, "not a creator."[1] His purpose, moreover, was essentially practical. "For him", it has been said, "everything is concrete, everything looks to the formation of a practical governing and a submissive governed class. His motive was twofold : a reaction against the administrative abuses of the feudal princes, and the repulse of the theories propounded by contemporary innovators."[2]

Nor was he a writer. So noticeably did he lack literary gifts that the chief composition to which his name is attached is attributed by the more pious of his disciples to another hand. If anything of his is included among the decisive books of history, it is because his aphorisms and conversations were recorded by his disciples, in *The Analects, The Doctrine of the Mean* and *The Great Learning*. We are reminded of Socrates and also, at some distance, of the Gospels.[3]

III

An obvious difficulty in presenting the teaching of Confucius arises from the fact that there is nothing systematic in his thought. Indeed, he condemned in set terms any reduction of principles to a system, either of thought or of action. "A fixed

---

[1] *Analects*, vii, 1 (Hughes' translation).

[2] L. Wiegler, S.J., *The Religion of China*, p. 11.

[3] As regards the authenticity of these sayings, scholars differ considerably as to the number that should be accepted. Waley (*op. cit.*, p. 24) takes the extreme view that the *Analects* contains very few sayings of K'ung and possibly none at all, though he then proceeds to quote its sayings with considerable freedom in building up his portrait of Confucius. Happily the controversy is not of the first importance to the present chapter, which is primarily concerned with the political influence of the book as actually handed down and received. H. G. Creel's *Confucius, the Man and the Myth*, appeared too late to be used in this chapter.

and definite statement of what is right and what is wrong is a stupidity"; "Every preconceived plan, all taking of sides in advance, is an evil"—these are two summaries of his teachings.[1] Nevertheless, if we use this self-same antagonism to systematic thinking as a centre around which to group his teachings, we shall find in them a very real consistency of a sort.

Take first his approach to his fixed political purpose, which was to establish once and for all the correct relations between ruler and ruled: we cannot fail, with the above-mentioned clue in mind, to be struck by the small amount of mental activity he demanded on either side. In the first place, the proper form of the relationship was not to be ascertained by reasoning. It was one of a fixed set of five relationships in which all social ties are comprised, the others being those of father and son, husband and wife, elder brother and younger brother, friend and friend. The family was in fact the model for the state. On one side there was to be paternal government by a pious and therefore virtuous Emperor, on the other, reverence modelled on filial piety, the supreme virtue, and giving rise to loyalty. This patriarchal pattern should be reproduced also throughout the whole hierarchy of the government; and in actual fact under the Confucian bureaucracy of later times the district magistrate was known to the people as the "father and mother official". Problems arising out of the fact that the state is larger and more complex than the family were simply ignored.

Confucian ethics, therefore, so far as the governed were concerned, consisted essentially of the instruction of the people in their political and family duties of loyalty and kindness on a well-known and accepted pattern. Only precepts and maxims should be used in their instruction; no proofs or reasons should be given them; all other than this official teaching should be kept away from them.

Here we have one of the reasons why ceremonial played so pre-eminent a part in Confucianism. A relationship conceived on this narrow, rigid pattern could be reduced to still lower terms as a fixed code of actions; and when it had been so reduced men would more easily learn it and more unquestion-

[1] J. Mullie, *Studies in Comparative Religion*, " China ", p. 9; and Weigler, *op. cit.*, p. 13, quoting the disciples Li Chi and Chung Yung.

ingly conform to it.[1] "The ritual exists in order to make a tradition which is handed on."[2]

The paternalism of the ancient state had already been embodied in innumerable ceremonial acts and phrases, many of them written down and codified. Confucius sought these out unwearyingly, revived them and elaborated them. He practised them himself and (when he could) enforced them on others with almost inconceivable pedantry. Not only did worship have its rites; the most ordinary recurring situations of life had their appropriate ritual of speech and gesture as complex as a court's and all designed to inculcate and fix the five relationships. In the end all ethics, for the governed, could be reduced to them; as a modern commentator has summed up the position: "people have no higher rights or further duties".[3]

This political pragmatism had a different application to the governing and educated classes. For them Confucius laid down the rule of "reciprocity": "what you do not wish done to yourselves, do not do to others".[4] If, even in this negative form, the Golden Rule in which (we are authoritatively told[5]) pre-Christian morals are summarized, had really been a summary of Confucian teaching and had been made to stand out clearly as such, some sort of ordered ethical structure might have been built up; but it is precisely this condition that is never fulfilled for any rule in Confucianism. Over all hangs Confucius' almost pathological reluctance to commit himself to any absolute statement of abstract morality or truth. Even his favourite virtue of *jen*, rendered variously by the translators as "benevolence" ,"philanthropy", "social good-feeling", "human-heartedness" and "goodness", is never defined in general terms. So much did he love, in speaking of it, to hedge his replies about with evasions that on one occasion when asked about it he actually replied: "The human-hearted man is cautious in what he says", and when his questioner not unnaturally asked

---

[1] Compare *Analects*, ii, 3.

[2] Li Chi (*T'an K'ung*, i), quoted by Hughes, *op. cit.*, p. 31, gives this as a saying of Confucius.

[3] From Mullie, *op. cit.*, p. 10 on which the preceding paragraphs are partly based.

[4] *Analects*, xv, 23; see also xii, 2 (Hughes' translation).

[5] Matthew vii, 12.

whether this was really meant as a definition of human-heartedness, he would only say: "Since doing is so difficult, can a man be otherwise than cautious in speaking?"—a completely typical piece of Confucian dialogue.[1]

And what was caution or agnosticism in the teacher was not unnaturally taken as a cover for an unprincipled opportunism by those who in after years imbibed it as part of their professional training. It is but a short step from the discouraging of all plans laid down in advance to the reduction of right conduct to a judicious picking of one's way between all clear-cut courses. It was K'ung himself who said: "The cautious seldom err", and two of his disciples, Li Chi and Chung Yung, thus epitomized the Master's views in this regard: "One must go forward with a determined intention to embrace nothing with passion and repulse nothing with antipathy, but to do whatever appears fitting at the moment and in the given case, in due measure and proportion."

"These words", says a writer who quotes them,[2] "have made Confucian China the China of the literati. They inculcate an inert and apathetic opportunism which has no place for the ideal, for patriotism, plan, programme or politics, love or hatred. Their message is rather: 'Dip when the wave comes, breathe again when it has passed, and so on for ever'." The same writer speaks of K'ung's historical commentaries as displaying "that art of calculated concealments, of resolute disguises and delusive euphemisms, which remained the pattern imitated by all the literati".

But there is a ritual for this too. The poor are praised "who are cheerful, and the rich who love the rules of propriety";[3] and out of this studied opportunism Confucius builds up his picture of "the superior man", "the true aristocrat". "He is dignified but does not wrangle, social but not a partisan."[4] And in this balanced decorum he must be self-sufficient. As one

---

[1] *Analects*, xiv, 2. The verbatim quotations are from the translation by E. R. Hughes, who, unlike some translators of Confucius, always does his best for him.

[2] Wiegler, *op. cit.*, p. 13.

[3] *Analects*, i, 15. Legge's rendering, in the *Encyclopaedia Britannica*, 11th edition.

[4] *Analects*, xv, 21 (Legge).

translator has it: "What the superior man seeks is in himself; what the small man seeks is in others."[1]

The note of self-sufficiency, all too often suggestive of a rather stupid pride, comes out even in the quality of K'ung's agnosticism. The "superior man" is taught not to look beyond himself to a spiritual world either for knowledge or for support, still less for judgement upon himself. Confucius assured him of a future life but was silent when asked whether there was a judgement to come. It was one of his own pupils who complained to him: "The Master's views on the fine externals of culture we often have the privilege of hearing, but not his views on man's nature nor the ways of heaven."[2] It is true that another rendering of this saying[3] suggests that Confucius reserved the subjects in question for private teaching to an inner circle; but this interpretation meets with the double difficulty that nowhere in the Confucian tradition handed on by the inner circle is there any indication that Confucius had anything to say on the ways of heaven and, secondly, that he is recorded as having more than once declared that nothing could be profitably said concerning them.

The most that can safely be affirmed of his beliefs in a world of spirits is that he seems to have accepted it as a reality towards which some sort of prayer was possible and from which a prudent man would not allow himself to be altogether cut off but with which he would be chary of trying to establish familiarity and concerning which he would be even more chary of committing himself to any definite opinion.[4] "To give one-

---

[1] This is Legge's rendering of *Analects*, xv, 20. But Jennings (in Lubbock's *Hundred Best Books*), Waley and Hughes all give a different turn to this saying. Hughes has: "The man of honour makes demands on himself: the man without a sense of honour makes demands on others." His rendering of *Analects* iv, 11, may be compared with both versions of xv, 20: "A man of true breeding sets his heart on spiritual power in himself: the man of no breeding sets his heart on land." (Waley is in substantial agreement with both these renderings by Hughes.) The Chinese original would appear to give the translator considerable liberty in building up his picture of Confucius. Those unversed in the language have to try to compile a self-consistent picture from this far from self-consistent material.

[2] *Analects*, v, 12, as translated by Hughes, in substantial agreement with Waley.

[3] By Jennings, *loc. cit.*

[4] See *Analects*, iii, 12; vii, 20; xi, 11, etc.

self to the duties due to men and, while respecting spiritual beings, to keep aloof from them, may be called wisdom."[1]

IV

This mentality, so uninspiring and so pedantic, eventually imposed itself upon the whole Chinese nation—surely the greatest triumph ever won by unoriginality. It was a victory all the more striking because the Taoist school of philosophers (the school of Lao-tze) offered to the strong artistic sensibilities of the Chinese race an alternative outlook, intuitive and imaginative to a high degree.

Part of the explanation may very well lie in the very nature of those artistic sensibilities. Broadly speaking, the history of Chinese art has shown the Chinese to be more appreciative of the niceties of harmony and balance and duly graded proportions than of the audacities of imagination or intuition or of the searching gaze into the human soul (one cannot imagine a Chinese Rembrandt). Confucianism appealed to this particular form of sensitiveness.[2]

A more obvious cause of the victory of Confucian teaching is that it was based on historical research into those precepts and practices that had, in the not very remote past, given the bulk of the Chinese their most characteristic social traits, so that in K'ung's maxims they heard calling to them what was already in their system, exaggerated no doubt to the point of grotesqueness but essentially the same. For that reason even his shallowest sayings struck many of his hearers as profound and they recorded and embellished them in a group of memoirs that, together with the works of the Confucianist philosopher known as Mencius (372 to 289 B.C.), constituted for future generations a kind of Confucian Canon. Moreover, the ruler

[1] Quoted by B. S. Bonsall in *Confucianism and Taoism*, apparently rendering *Analects*, vi, 20. Waley (*op. cit.*, pp. 31–33) comments on these passages from the *Analects* that they do not imply agnosticism but are intended to give priority to the material needs of life over expenditure on offerings to the spirit world. But if this is true, our impression of K'ung's materialistic indifference to the spirit world will be all the sharper.

[2] Waley (*op. cit.*, p. 37) makes a not dissimilar point very bluntly but very neatly when he says that the success of Confucianism "was due in a large measure to the fact that he contrived to endow compromise with an emotional glamour".

of his native state is said to have built a shrine to his memory after his death, at which sacrifices were offered.

Nevertheless the Confucian cultus was showing no great signs of vitality when in 213 B.C., 266 years after the philosopher's death, an act of violence was perpetrated which had the unexpected and quite unintended result of giving the Confucian literature a new importance. China was under the rule of the great Shi-huang, of the T'sin (or Ch'in) dynasty, who put an end to the so-called feudal system, united almost the whole area of modern China under one rule, and styled himself the First Universal Emperor. This potentate, being perpetually censured by Confucian scholars for his enmity to the ancient ways, fell into a rage and ordered the destruction of all books relating to ancient times and the execution of four hundred of the scholars. He then transferred his patronage to the Taoists.

But the Confucianists who escaped the purge had been quick to hide copies of their Canon, whereas other writings relating to ancient times had no such zealous guardians. Consequently the only lasting result of the holocaust was the very opposite of what its perpetrator had intended. When it became safe to produce the condemned writings from their hiding places, it was found that the Master's selections from the ancient records and his interpretation of them had a virtual monopoly; and the early history of China has been viewed by the Chinese through Confucian spectacles from that time almost to our own.

What is more, when in 206 B.C. a usurper founded the great Han dynasty, the new Emperor made a point of visiting the grave of Confucius and sacrificing there a pig, a sheep and an ox. Fifty years later a temple dedicated to the philosopher was erected on the same spot; and the worship conducted there acquired in due course an elaborate liturgy embellished by music.

But it was another institution created by the Han Emperors that was destined to do more for the Confucian formation of China than any quasi-deification of Confucius. In their concern for the administration of their vast Empire they founded a system of examinations for entry into the Civil Service, and in the existing situation in the literary world the Confucian writings inevitably took a prominent place in the syllabus.

v

Thus at the beginning of the Christian era the three great instruments for the creation of a Confucian China were in existence. The Confucian corpus of writings practically represented antiquity in the eyes of a conservative people; their author and inspirer was in receipt of quasi-divine honours; and his teachings held the first place in the training of the administrators of the country. But, instead of the period of uninterrupted progress that we might now expect to be able to record, we enter upon an era of ebb and flow, in which the predominance of the Confucianists was challenged by powerful forces both from outside and from within the country, and more than once seemed in danger of extinction.

Before the Han dynasty had run its course (it lasted from 206 B.C. to A.D. 220) a new and seductive religion had entered the country. This was Buddhism, by which (in this connection) is meant, not the severely atheistic monasticism founded by Gautama, but the popular quasi-polytheism into which it had developed in northern India, the only form in which it ever made a wide appeal in eastern Asia, beyond the monasteries. It had established itself by this time in Chinese Turkestan (now known as Sinkiang) and an official mission of enquiry was sent there from China. This reached Khotan, from which it returned in A.D. 67 with writings, images and a priest.

For some time the progress of Buddhism in China was slow, but it kept its footing in the country and its chance came during the civil wars and barbarian invasions of the fourth and fifth centuries of our era, when it was propagated for political purposes by some of the barbarian conquerors, first in North China, then in the south. In A.D. 472 public prayers to Confucius were prohibited (though, apparently as a kind of compensation for his loss of divinity, he and his descendants were in the following year granted patents of nobility). By the end of that century all China was made officially Buddhist. Nor would we be right in inferring that the triumph of Buddhism was merely political. Mahayana Buddhism (as this form of it is called), for all its many and gross faults, did at least give the Chinese something that their own public cults had never provided, least of all the Confucian cult, namely a private, personal religion.

During the sixth century Confucianism, which had fallen almost out of sight, experienced a revival as a semi-religious cult, and temples of Confucius were built in all the most important cities of the Empire.[1] But again it had to meet competition in the form of imported religions, one of which was Mohammedanism, which was well established in Central Asia, not far from the frontiers of China, by the middle of the eighth century. Then came the most dangerous crisis of all, when it was divided against itself.

This came about during the Sung dynasty (A.D. 960–1280) as a result of a combination of causes. The first of these was the striking of yet another blow at Confucianism by the entry of yet another foreign religion. This was Shintoism, from Japan, which was readily taken up by the Sung Emperors, partly (no doubt) because they were flattered by its Emperor-worship. Once more Confucianism almost disappeared from the north. But presently an invasion of the nomads beyond the northern frontier drove the Sungs themselves southward for a time and, during their sojourn in the south, they studied the now almost forgotten Confucian texts.

These were now undergoing a process of reinterpretation by some Confucianist scholars whose very un-Confucian occupation it had been to study the philosophical writings of Indian Buddhism. These had inspired them with the desire to systematize the scattered maxims of Confucianism into a coherent body of philosophic doctrine. Thus arose a school of Confucian Progressives, led by Chu Hsi, who lived from 1130 to 1200, and was thus an almost exact contemporary of Averroes, the Spanish Moor, the greatest of those Mohammedan commentators on Aristotle who prepared the way for the Christian Aristotelianism of St. Thomas Aquinas.

It was natural enough, in view of the influences under which

[1] Giles, *Religions of Ancient China*, p. 42.

it had been formed, that his philosophical scheme should be monistic (as indeed was that of Averroes) and it was monism of the crudely materialistic type associated with the nineteenth-century German, Haeckel. It, of course, denied the existence of God and of an immortal soul, though it allowed for some sort of temporary survival after death (influenced here also, no doubt, by its Indian antecedents). It drove the more conservative Confucianists into a strong demand for a return to the letter of the ancient texts; but, though they were greatly disturbed by this attempt to systematize the Master's mind, it would be a mistake to think that the atheism of the system made them concerned to maintain a belief in God. Confucius himself had deliberately used the vague, impersonal term "Heaven" as a substitute for the divine name, which appears nowhere in the *Analects*.

Between the two schools a see-saw struggle now took place, the aim of which, however, was not so much logical victory as official favour. Chu Hsi himself died in official disgrace; but in A.D. 1241 the Progressives obtained the recognition of his system—China's first systematic philosophy—as the true and original Confucianism and the approved syllabus for the examinations. (This did not, of course, prevent the annual sacrifice to Heaven by the Emperor from continuing to be an essential rite of the Confucian state.)

The victory of the Progressives, however, remained precarious until the Sung dynasty was overthrown by Kubilai, Khan of the Mongols, who in 1280 established himself as Emperor with Peking as his capital. True to their dislike of principles, the Confucian literati hastened to offer their services to the Mongol conqueror and his successors and manned his civil service, keeping their hold on the examinations and on the public offices to which they led. They were rewarded by the building of Confucian temples and, since the Progressives had Kubilai's ear, by a decree endorsing the Sung edict, to the effect that "in public examinations the matter of the compositions, which was always taken from the classical books, should be, besides, in accordance with the commentaries of Chu Hsi".[1]

---

[1] Wiegler, *op. cit.*, p. 21.

VI

Now at last, more than 1,750 years after the death of Confucius, China entered upon that wholly Confucianist phase in which she was found by the Westerners in the nineteenth century. When in A.D. 1368 the Mongols gave way to the Ming dynasty, the Confucian literati maintained their position, although the founder of the dynasty was a Buddhist. It was under the Mings that a kind of *summa* of the neo-Confucianist philosophy was prepared as a text-book and officially promulgated in 1415. Then in 1642, the Manchus, another Tartar people, replaced the Mings on the throne and the literati once more played their favourite role of props of a foreign rule and the recipients of its favours. Then, indeed, began their golden age, which lasted for something like 250 years. The mandarins of whom the Westerners heard and talked so much in the latter half the nineteenth century were these Confucian bureaucrats at the end of five hundred years of unbroken and increasing prosperity.

As late as 1894 their position was reaffirmed by an Imperial Edict ordering all official examiners "to conform scrupulously to the established law, to venerate the commentaries of Chu Hsi equally with the text of Confucius, and to accept no dissertation containing opinions differing from his".[1] But the end was near. The very year of the Edict saw the defeat of China in a war against Japan. It was an event which shook the complacency of the Empire to its depths, for Japan had been regarded as no more than a kind of cultural dependency of China. It threw also a new light, for those in a position to know, on the practical consequences, when brought to the test of battle, of the traditional corruption of the bureaucracy, as when (as told in the Life of Li Hung Chang) a consignment of shells for Chinese naval guns was found to consist entirely of dummies.

There followed in rapid succession the so-called Boxer Rebellion of 1900, which was only suppressed by European troops, and the sensational victories of the modernized Japan over Russia in 1904 and 1905. At last the Imperial government

[1] Quoted by Wiegler, *op. cit.*, p. 22.

realized that a purely classical and literary training for its administrators was insufficient under twentieth-century conditions. In September, 1905, it abolished at a stroke the old system of examinations and a rush for Western learning began. As a sop to the still immensely powerful and honoured Confucianists, the Master was, by another Edict, raised to an equal rank with Heaven—a happy substitute for deification in an atheist state in which the measure of all things was precedence. His descendants continued to be almost the only hereditary nobility in the country.

Then, in 1912, the Empire itself fell and, with it, the old relation between the state, through the Emperor, and Heaven. Confucianism ceased to be in any sense a state system. During the troubled years of the Chinese Republic it strove with varying fortunes amid a welter of ideological novelties to establish itself as one of China's unofficial cults. Finally, with the coming of the Communists the Confucianists were faced with the severest test they had ever experienced. For they had nothing in common with them except atheism and even that they did not take seriously, and they were faced with people who took seriously both their atheism and their economics.

VII

From the Communists' point of view, indeed, it may well have seemed that it was they who were faced with the harder task. A sect essentially doctrinaire, rigid, ruthless and fanatical was confronted with a class with no fixed principles, yielding and temporizing; for Chu Hsi's metaphysical systematizing came far too late to affect the Confucianist mentality, least of all in the sphere of conduct and character. Indeed, it soon became apparent to the shrewd leaders of Chinese Communism that "the older generation in China, grown up in the atmosphere of Confucian ethics, of individualist *laissez faire*, of give and take compromise", had to be written off as hopeless material.[1]

There was, moreover, a special ideological reason why the survivors of the great mandarin caste and those brought up in its tradition were likely to prove quite useless to the Communists, who in the other countries that they have captured

[1] From an article in *The Tablet*, 7.1.50.

have been able for the most part to make use of the bureaucracies they found there. The difficulty lay, not in the possession
of an idea by the mandarinate, but in the absence of an idea.
Bureaucracy in its Western forms is commonly and rightly
regarded as the normal instrument of the totalitarian state,
almost its very essence. But that is because its members have
all been brought up with the Western idea of the State, an idea
of which the Confucianist corps of mandarins knew nothing
at all. Civil Service though it was, there was always something
curiously private and personal about it. Here are two quotations that are particularly instructive because they are from two
writers who are wholly opposed in their sympathies and who
paint the mandarinate in quite different colours, but are nevertheless agreed on the absence from it of what the French
conveniently call *étatisme*.

The first writer[1] claims that the Confucian literati were
never properly speaking a public institution at all. "In every
age they have been a private coterie of retardatory and reac-
tionary politicians, a closed caste, almost a secret society,
perpetuating their order by the education of the young, by
co-operation, and by intermarriages." The other writer[2] is
insisting on the personal aspect of their relation to their em-
ployer, the Emperor.

"The Emperor", he says, ruling as a benevolent patriarch,
"was assisted by the officials recruited from the people on the
basis of a civil examination in the classics. They were arranged
in ranks, each possessing certain right and duties, and were
bound together and to the Emperor by a rigid ceremonial. The
Emperor and the officials united all the functions of government, being the priests, executives, the law-makers and the
judges. The government was one of men rather than of laws. . . .
The conception of the State as an abstract entity was never
allowed to develop." And to this admirable summary of what
Confucianism was meant to be in administrative practice, we
may add an epigram by the same writer that will remind us
also of the absence of any true political thought or theory from
Confucian paternalism. He describes the body politic ruled on

---

[1] Wiegler, *op. cit.*, p. 23.
[2] Dr. Legge, in the *Encyclopaedia Britannica*, 10th edition.

Confucianist principles as having "the size of a giant while it retains the mind of a child".

Not of such are Marxist bureaucracies made. We may add one other disqualification, that is really an aspect of this personalism but so outstanding that it deserves separate mention. The Chinese mandarinate was corrupt even by bureaucratic, and even by eastern standards. Some sentimentalists imagined that all that would end with the passing of the old Imperial régime. But few things are more tenacious than the vices of a civil service and it was the corruption of the Republican civil service under the Kuo-mintang that ultimately lost Chiang Kai-shek American aid and brought about his fall.

For all these reasons Mao Tzetung and his colleagues were soon by-passing the older generation and concentrating their efforts on forming a Communist youth. In this process they began by striking, with an unerring precision only possible to Communists who are themselves Chinese, at the two elements in the Confucian tradition that, however grotesquely they may have been exaggerated or distorted in it, were fundamentally sound, respect for the family and respect for a liberal eduation.

Here is an item from *The Times* of 7th January, 1950 :—

"The inhabitants of a village, without exception, are made to attend almost daily meetings for political indoctrination; the younger peasants are urged to throw off the parents' control and even inform against them. Sons and daughters are encouraged to choose their wives and husbands without any regard to their parents' wishes, and any parental interference in this matter is treated as a sign of counter-revolutionary leanings."

As for education, here is an extract from *The Tablet* of the same day:—

"The new régime had to take over educational establishments, as they stood, and at first merely added indoctrination courses. Simultaneously, however, they established 'People's Revolutionary Academies', open to everybody, workmen, students, boys and girls in their teens. Four months' training in such establishments suffice to qualify men and women for army, administrative, educational and factory posts: and last July the first batch of 12,000 was thus turned loose on the nation. No wonder there is a slump in university candidates—who would waste four years to get his objective, a job, when he can now get it in four months? No doubt this is a transitional measure, but it emphasizes the fact that Chinese Communists have a profound contempt for the ancient Confucian respect for culture and its professional exponents, the literati. Half-educated themselves, the Communist leaders only aim at producing a half-educated rank and file—the mental rampart of doctrinaire cock-sureness, devotion to party clichés and ruthless intolerance of criticism. The result, of course, is an admitted general incompetence in the services, which, however, is to be put right as soon as possible. In Manchuria there exist already ten 'industrial institutes', to train technicians and engineers; in Peking an establishment to turn out a really efficient Ogpu is in full blast. But for scholarship and research as such there is no more money available."

With the younger generation thus cut off from the two sound things in Confucian China, the Communist leaders could calculate with some reason that they would be aided in their positive teaching by the psychological effects of what was unsound in Confucianism—most of all by its denial of absolute values and absolute truth.

"Hitherto" (I quote again from *The Tablet* article), "Chinese millennial tradition has neither known an absolute Creator in its religion, nor the concept of an absolute truth in its philosophy, nor that of absolute rights in its law. . . . The great force and fascination of Communism is just this, that for the first time in history the Chinese people are now exposed to a *mystique* which tries to sweep them by mass-suggestion off their feet into the passion for a cause. . . . Communism at all events does claim to be the ultimate answer to all problems . . . its claims are absolute—and that very claim is something completely new to Chinese thought."

There is only one other institution making such a claim, the Catholic Church, and that, so far as China was concerned, they reckoned to have well in hand.

It is a strange picture. Confucius died in 479 B.C. More than 2,400 years later there was still in existence a nation of four hundred millions which many centuries ago accepted him as their educator and whose ideas and mentality were in fact mainly formed by him, particularly in the case of their educated class. These were at last confronted with a system opposed to his in the most vital matters. As a direct result of their formation by him they found themselves without the intellectual equipment to meet this challenge and also with a sense that it was the first time they had met a body of teaching offering intellectual certainty on these same vital matters. Could there be a greater testimony to the magnitude of the formative influence, through the ages, of Confucius as a teacher or a more deadly indictment of him as one who was not qualified to teach?

VII

PLATO'S *REPUBLIC*

VII

PLATO'S *REPUBLIC*

I

WITH the *Republic* of Plato we enter upon a new series of books. The six books of our first group, in so far as they directly moulded states, did so in the main by formulating precepts addressed to particular peoples, precepts according to which the rulers of those peoples were adjured to plan and to administer, and their subjects to live obediently. Those books of the group that did not directly mould states—the Book of the Dead and the Epics of Homer—were politically influential because each impressed upon a particular people a particular outlook and attitude of mind in accordance with which they lived as citizens or attained consciousness as a nation. None of them laid down universal political principles applicable, and intended to be applied, to all states and state-building in all places and periods. None of them, setting out from first principles, used them as the starting-point for logical deductions concerning the proper form of states.

The Ten Commandments were, indeed, a formulation of the universal moral law and several of the moral aphorisms of Confucius had a general form; but neither Moses nor Confucius formulated political first principles and deduced their consequences. With Plato and Aristotle, however, pure political speculation enters the field and achieves simultaneously what is almost its beginning and what is something very like its consummation. Their treatises are the first of their kind in the history of the world and they have been followed by a long series of works of abstract political theory, not one of which has escaped the stamp of one or the other of them and which between them supply a high proportion of our remaining decisive books of history.

7   181

Both writers were Greeks, both spent the greater part of their lives in Athens and one was the pupil of the other, even if in some sense his opposite in intellectual temper. Such a tremendous conjunction of genius stands outside the range of profitable speculation. It is not, however, difficult to explain why the genius of each should have occupied itself to a notable extent with political philosophy. They occupied themselves with philosophical speculation because true philosophical speculation had begun with the Greeks and the time had come, after a period of sterile reaction against it, to return to it and show that it could be fruitful. They speculated upon politics amongst other subjects, not only because any list of subjects requiring philosophical treatment must include politics, but also because the same period that had seen the birth and first ventures of philosophic thinking had seen also throughout the Greek world, and at Athens in particular, a series of political developments that had raised all the fundamental political questions.

A sketch, therefore, of the philosophical and political antecedents of the two great political treatises we have now reached is required if we are to form an intelligent estimate of their place and influence in the political history of the world. (The allusion to these antecedents made in the chapter on Homer's epics was too brief to serve this purpose.) It will be convenient to begin with the political developments since Homer, for these provided a forcing-house for the flowering of the philosophic mind as well as problems for its first political solutions.

II

When the Greek world emerges into history after its Dark Ages, the Homeric monarchy has almost entirely disappeared. It was not violently overthrown. Its functions were transferred, first in one city-state, then in another, but mostly during the second half of the eighth century B.C., to elected magistrates, drawn from the little circle of nobles that had formed the King's council and responsible to this circle. If we are to attribute the passing of the hereditary monarchy to any one prevailing cause, we should probably not be far out if we put it down to loss of glamour, for it is on that elusive but very real appeal that hereditary monarchy so much depends for its acceptance.

Nor would it be difficult to assign causes for this loss. There was the squalor and poverty of the Dark Ages themselves, brought about by the destruction of the Mycenean civilization by the Dorians. There was the passing of the "heroic age" in which the kings were warrior chiefs. The very smallness of the kingdoms must have played its part, for it is difficult for royalty to retain its magic when the king and the royal family and the bulk of his subjects all live together in what would now be called a little country town. At any rate, at the period in question the monarchy had come to be reverenced for little more than its religious functions; and these, when republics came, could be separated from the political headship of the state and transferred to a city official specially set apart (for it will be remembered that the Greeks had no priests for their public religion).

Nevertheless, this undramatic transition, for all its unexciting character and its petty scale, was of great significance for the political history of the world. For one thing, nothing quite like it had happened anywhere else. The states of Asia had known periods when existence was squalid and humdrum; and they had seen many usurpers without ancestry ascend the throne; but it had not occurred to the peoples of Asia to abolish monarchy as an institution. But it did occur to the Greeks; and the change, when they made it, sharpened their political consciousness in two ways. It sharpened that sense of themselves as politically different from the Asiatic that came to fill so great a place in their national outlook. It suggested also to their minds the idea that the form of the state was something that to some extent rested with themselves to determine and could be a matter for deliberate choice. And in this notion was implicit the whole question of where the ultimate sovereignty in the state lay.

Not that a jealous clique of decayed chieftains was capable or desirous of discussing such large matters; but, if one class in the little community could make a change in the form of the state to its own advantage, another class might attempt to do the same and, if the prestige of the monarchy had fallen too low to enable it to resist change, the prestige of the oligarchy was virtually nothing at all. In point of fact, it was their own greed and selfishness that brought it about that their initial tampering with tradition was the first of a long series of revolutions that (since the people concerned were Greeks) did not end until all political institutions had been put in the melting-pot and all the fundamental political questions had been asked.

For the hereditary nobility of chieftains that had formed the king's council had suffered from the same general decay that had undermined the monarchy. They were little more than a close corporation of landowners—as often as not, land-grabbers—supplementing their rents by freebooting and piracy. The miserable peasantry on their lands sank lower and lower— the solitary voice of the poet Hesiod, writing in this same half century, told of their sufferings. But a new and less helpless class was arising. It was the great period of Greek colonization (as distinct from the migrations that had taken them to Asia Minor) and this meant the establishment of trading stations along the Mediterranean and Black Sea coasts. About the year 700 B.C., moreover, the use of coined money entered the Greek world from its hinterland in Asia Minor, where it had been invented. As a consequence, a bourgeoisie of traders entered the competition for political power, and rival factions of the nobles sought alliances with them.

Here was an opportunity for the ambitious political adventurer, who might put himself at the head of some combination of discontented groups, achieve popularity with the proletariat by overthrowing the oppressors of the moment and establish himself as despot of the city. He might even found a dynasty, but he would be careful not to call himself "king" (the Greek term for him was *tyrannos*) and would sooner or later have to fall back on naked force, often employing foreign mercenaries. Even so, he often continued to be acceptable to the majority, who might prefer strong rule to no rule; and the "age of the despots", as it has been called, lasted for nearly a century and a half. From about 650 to 500 B.C., that is to say, these despotisms were established frequently if intermittently in the majority of the Greek cities on both sides of the Aegean Sea.

The greatest contribution of the despots to Greek life was as patrons of the arts and sciences. Under their rule, particularly in the Ionian cities of Asia Minor, men first speculated philosophically about the nature of the physical world and conceived the idea of fixed laws of nature, poets wrote in the modern vein about their own emotions, and sculptors treated realistically the human form—all very much as men did under the despots in fifteen-thcentury Italy. To the intellectual and emotional ferment was added an economic and social ferment, for crafts and manufactures were developed and slave-labour, hitherto mainly in domestic use, was introduced into the new factories.

Finally, the very nature of the despot's power, resting as it did on no traditional loyalties, inevitably provoked questionings in such minds as the Greeks. It roused in them, not only repugnance to rulers who put themselves above the law, but also speculation as to what the ultimate sanction of the law was and who, in the last resort, was to enforce it. Moreover, such speculations, once started, could not stop short at any section of the citizens and this fact, together with the frequent need of the despots to appeal to the populace for support, brought democracy for the first time into view as a possible political form.

One absolute limit, however, was imposed both on political speculation and on political experiment. All the Greek city-states were states of slave-owners. Even the freest community of free citizens held another community, not much smaller than itself, as property, rigidly excluded from even the most elementary political rights. No constitution-making dared cross that boundary. Within that boundary it might democratize to the last man.

III

It could do one other thing, made impossible in modern states by their very size: it could make democracy a reality to the last man. It could give every adult male citizen active political work to do that would occupy him for a substantial number of hours a day on a very high proportion of days in the year, in addition to the days spent in serving in the citizen-army, in training or in the frequent inter-civic wars. (It was one of the effects of slave-owning that it made this practicable.) The time came, indeed, when this constant busying of himself in politics came to be regarded by the average Greek citizen as the characteristic mark of Greek democracy—far more characteristic and essential than any constitutional provision concerning the counting of votes and the like.   We shall never understand either the political ideals or the political reasonings of Plato or Aristotle unless we get this fact firmly into our heads at the outset.

Once we have done that, we shall grasp also the vital importance to the Greeks of the size of the state; and by that they would not have meant, as a modern politician would mean, the importance of the state being large enough. They would have meant the importance of the state being small enough to allow a proper political life to all free citizens. And, broadly speaking, their idea of a suitable size was on the scale of one small town with its countryside to one state. In fact, this equation was so much part of the very texture of their political thought, that in their great period they had no other word for a state, properly so called, except one ($\dot{\eta}$ $\pi\acute{o}\lambda\iota s$) that also did duty for "city". The modern nation-states, consisting of political aggregations so large that the ordinary citizen's political functions can amount to a very few at the most, exercised at very long intervals, were excluded from Greek political thought by its very vocabulary. The Greek had no political word for them.

So vital is this point to an understanding of the books we are about to discuss that it will probably be helpful to give some actual figures[1] and some twentieth-century equivalents.

The population of the state of Athens, when it was at its maximum and larger than that of any other Greek state, numbered perhaps 320,000 in all. Of these, rather less than half were resident in the city of Athens itself, giving it the population of Brighton in 1931. The remainder were distributed over Attica, a region about the size of Essex. (This was during the

[1] Taken from A. W. Gomme's essay on "The Greeks" in *European Civilisation*, vol. I, pp. 564, 644, 645. They are, of course, only approximate estimates, but were made with care.

city's greatest period, the Periclean age, of which we shall be speaking presently.) Of this total, perhaps 115,000 were slaves and 30,000 resident aliens and their families, leaving between 160,000 and 180,000 as the number of citizens and their families, of whom about one-third lived in Athens. The adult male citizens over eighteen numbered between 43,000 and 45,000. (The figures for area and population for Aberdeenshire and Aberdeen respectively, though not an exact equivalent, are near enough to the figures for Attica and Athens to be helpful to the imagination.)

That was the largest state. "Most of the states were much smaller: many had not more than 2,000–4,000 citizens"—adult males, that is to say; which gives a range, in terms of Great Britain and the 1931 census, of from Hythe and St. Andrews to Sheerness and Llandudno. Many states were smaller still, citizen armies of from 500 to 1,000 strong being quite common, giving a range, say, from Fowey to Launceston and Oakham. The huge and politically formless states of Asia were simply not states in the Greek sense of the word and, in general, an increase in the size of the state was considered by the Greeks something to be avoided, since it tended to diminish (in the words of the authority we have been quoting) "the only kind of political life they cared for, where every citizen had the opportunity to take a personal part in public affairs and did not delegate his functions [to representatives] . . . because politics, like philosophy, letters, music and games, was part of the good life".[1]

And let no one apply to the past the criteria of a materialistic age and suppose that, because the Greek states were no larger than modern country towns, they were insignificant for political history. It was very largely because they were small (since smallness meant for the Greeks fullness of political experience) that Greek political life was able to run through almost the whole gamut of political experiment in a few generations; and it was largely for the same reason that the Greek political mind was able to probe into almost all the fundamental political questions within the same period. That, in fact, is how the two books which we have now reached came to be written then, and to be readable today.

[1] Gomme, *loc. cit.*, p. 564.

IV

All this ferment had begun among the Ionian Greeks in Asia Minor but it was not there that the process was to be worked out. The wealth and luxury of the Asiatic hinterland that the Greek moralists had always feared had just the influence they predicted for it. When in 560 B.C. King Croesus of many tales ascended the throne of Lydia and embarked on a career of conquest, the Greek cities of the coast put up no effective resistance to him; and when in 546 B.C. Croesus in his turn fell before the expanding Persian power that was soon to capture Babylon, the same cities passed with no serious struggle from Lydian to Persian rule. A more valiant struggle thirty-six years later came too late to be effective. It, too, was suppressed and presently the passion for new ideas subsided. It was left to the Greeks of what we now call Greece, and particularly to the Ionian Greeks of Attica, to keep the heady liquor fermenting; and, more than ever, they thanked the gods of their cities that they were not as the Asiatics were.

Athens, Attica's capital, had passed through much the same political phases as the other capitals, her most notable addition to the normal pattern being that her first written constitution was frankly plutocratic. This was Solon's, published in 594 B.C. and creating an interlude in the age of the despots. Certain of its provisions, however—for an elected Senate, for regular mass-meetings of the citizens and for their service on juries—subsequently proved capable of being made the framework of a democracy. Another of its features, also carried on into the democracy, was the minuteness with which it regulated the lives of the citizens. The readiness with which this regimentation was accepted by the citizens is even more interesting. Totalitarianism was an accepted fact long before Mussolini and Stalin.

The last of the despots was expelled from Athens in 510 B.C., two years after the armies of Darius the Persian had made their first expedition across the Bosphorus. An essentially democratic constitution, that of Cleisthenes, was established, by which citizenship was granted (on that occasion but not again) to resident aliens and emancipated slaves; and every adult male citizen, irrespective of hereditary or social status, was given an active share in the government in one way or another, particularly in local government and on the juries. The power of the nobility was broken by substituting for the old clan system a new method of sub-dividing the people, based upon locality. The elected Senate took over many of the functions of the old hereditary Senate and a beginning was made in making the mass assembly of the citizens a real power in the state.

The immediate effect of this revolution was to arouse in all citizens of Athens a strong pride in their civic privileges and an equally strong Hellenic patriotism. This led them first to give support to the revolt of the Greek cities of Asia Minor and then, when that had called down upon Athens and all Greece the avenging expeditions of Darius, to take the lead in throwing back the Persians in the never-to-be-forgotten battles of Marathon and Salamis (in 490 and 480 B.C.). The further effect of the new constitution was to open the way, on the one hand, to the most concentrated display of literary and artistic genius the world has ever seen and, on the other hand, to further a still more radical constitution-making.

Thus, in 487 B.C. a beginning was made in filling important offices by lot, as a check against tyranny by an experienced official class with a monopoly of administrative technique. A quarter of a century later, a young man named Pericles overthrew the existing government and began to carry a series of constitutional reforms which made it possible for any citizen to be chosen by lot for almost any office in the city-state, and enrolled them all on panels from which were chosen by lot paid jurors by whom anyone, official or private citizen, might be tried for almost any offence.

Moreover, he formed from these juries committees (known as the *nomothetae*) armed with such extensive legislative powers that, in conjunction with the mass assembly of citizens, they gave the *demos* (or populace) almost absolute political sovereignty. The total effect of all this political machinery was, furthermore, to give almost every individual member of the *demos* enough active political work to fill between a quarter and a half of his working life, beside providing him with

7*

political topics of conversation sufficient to fill the greater part of the remainder. This personal activity was in one sense an enhancement of the sovereignty of the *demos*; it was also, perhaps, some safeguard against its arbitrary use.

For some thirty brilliant years Pericles used his unrivalled political talents to ride the whirlwind he had roused. After him came a quarter of a century of oscillations between demagogy and reaction, during the whole of which (truces apart) Athens was engaged in a bitter war with the Dorian state of Sparta. At the end of it, in 404 B.C., she surrendered from military and political exhaustion. By this time Plato, the Athenian, was a young man of twenty-four.

This struggle between Athens and Sparta, the Peloponnesian War made immortal by Thucydides, considered as an episode in inter-civic power-politics does not concern us here. But Athens and Sparta were not opposed only as heads of rival confederacies; they were the symbols and the active champions of opposed political ideologies. During the three and a half centuries since the extinction of her monarchy, Athens had pursued the logical consequences of that first step, right to the very bitter end. For the same three and a half centuries Sparta had retained with no substantial change the constitution traditionally attributed to Lycurgus and to the year 774 B.C., the first of the written constitutions of the ancient world.

It was a constitution, moreover, that imposed upon the citizen body a régime of a rigidity abnormal even for Greece. In this case the citizen body consisted of a tiny ruling class (not more than 9,000 grown men in all) descended from the original Dorian conquerors and living practically as an armed camp in the midst of a resentful population of serfs held down only by the sword. Hence the unparalleled state-discipline to which every member of it was subjected from the age of seven until the age of sixty. The strictest physical and mental training was given in the state schools to both boys and girls. From eighteen to thirty the young man lived in regimental camps or barracks. He might not make a home with his wife until after that age and, even then, his meals, consisting of the very plainest food, had to be taken in public dining-rooms. Gainful occupations were left to licensed resident aliens, and foreign travel required the state's permission. Nor was there even any real political liberty. A shadow of the Homeric constitution survived in form but for many generations the ultimate political power had been in the hands of a small Directory of five "ephors" holding indeterminate powers and responsible to no one.

Once cast in this mould, Sparta and the Spartans had for centuries remained culturally barren and impervious to fresh political ideas. But, in the circumstances of Plato's youth, the idea of Sparta must have figured almost as prominently as the ideas of the Athenians amongst the furniture of young Plato's mind; and he admired without reservation, if not all the details of the Spartan state's moulding of the citizen, nevertheless the completeness with which the citizens were moulded by the Spartan state. It is a fact to be noted in connection with what is to come.

V

As for the ideas of the Athenians, they had come to a pretty pass by this time, and the explanation is not far to seek. For nearly half a century almost the only non-technical education available for young men of university age had been in the hands of a body of teachers all of whom took as the starting-point of their teaching the proposition that philosophical truth was unattainable.

This had been the consequence of the declared bankruptcy of philosophy after the first century and a half of its existence. The bankruptcy itself had been due in part to the vagueness and largely imaginative character of the physical science of the day and, even more, to the absence of any clear distinction between physical science and the science that deals with the nature and validity of physical science and its phenomena, namely metaphysics. Those who wish for a further elucidation of the collapse may turn at this point to the Note on the Bankruptcy of Early Greek Philosophy appended to this chapter.

This failure of the philosophers to answer ultimate questions had been brought home to the Athenians by two men, Protagoras and Gorgias, who had been trained in philosophical schools in the Ionian tradition and had come to settle in Athens about the time when Pericles began to rule there. The immediate result was a rush on the part of teachers of philosophy, headed by Protagoras and Gorgias themselves, to cash in on the new situation by giving lectures that assumed at the outset that the truth concerning the subject of the lecture could not be known. This was soon after 450 B.C., at the peak of the Periclean age. Pericles himself, who was very much of a free-thinker, risked such reputation as was left to him among conservative Athenians by openly associating with some of these lecturers.

Thus the Sophists came into existence as a body, or several bodies, of professional travelling lecturers, offering the nearest equivalent to a university education available at a time when no stationary universities had yet been founded.[1] One group of them professed to fill the gap left by the philosophic collapse by teaching civic virtue; but this, in the circumstances, meant no more, and hardly could mean more, than teaching civic virtuosity, or the conduct most likely to ensure a successful career for the professional politician. Others gave popular technical expositions of artistic or scientific subjects. Others, again, branched off from this into the art of arguing, being careful to explain that they were not concerned with the truth or falsehood of the case presented but only with how the argument could be won. In the same way, the art of politics gave rise to the art of "rhetoric" or oratory; and this in its turn led to the discussion of political principles, always, however, on the understanding that the ultimate truth of these matters could not be known.

Among the Sophists who taught in Athens during the last quarter of the fifth century B.C. was a squat and ugly man who resembled his fellow Sophists in being an educator of young men, in teaching them civic virtue and the art of disputation, and in repudiating philosophical systems. He differed from them, however, in refusing to take fees for teaching (he preferred to keep his independence, he said) and also in another way, less obvious but in the long run more disturbing.

---

[1] The account of the Sophists in the 11th Edition of the *Encyclopaedia Britannica* is by a master hand, the late Henry Jackson, O.M., and since it could hardly be bettered has been made the basis of the present section.

He seemed to think that "civic virtue" should be the concern, not only of the political careerist, but of every citizen and that it should consist of real moral conduct, the morality to be expected of a man as a man. Moreover, when it came to arguing, he evidently believed that his method, which was a peculiar one, ought to be followed, not because it led to victory, but because it led to the discovery of truth. Absolute philosophical truth, he would admit, was unattainable, but there were such things as right opinions and, what is more, you could only get right action if you allowed conduct to be shaped by them.

This teaching was almost as odd, in that generation, as the man's appearance; but young Plato found something very attractive in both. Since his childhood this unusual Sophist, whose name was Socrates, had been a familiar figure to him; and at about the age of twenty he attached himself to the group of young men who formed Socrates' regular, if informal, audience. The association lasted for eight or nine years, at the end of which, in 399 B.C., the Athenian democracy, which found it too difficult to distinguish between the common Sophist and the uncommon one, mistakenly put the uncommon one to death for impiety and Plato, now nearly thirty, was left to continue his intellectual journeying alone. But the association had done its work and the survivor of it presently took the most gigantic step in pure thought ever taken by the human mind.[1]

VI

Plato knew very well that the great adventure of philosophy had come to a dead end before he had been born. But he could see equally clearly that the reaction against it had come to a dead end also (if, indeed, it had ever had any real intellectual life) and, if he had learnt one thing rather than another from Socrates, it was that disputes about words were of no importance at all unless the words stood for realities; and then they could assume a great importance. Therefore he very much

[1] Experts differ widely as to the respective shares taken by Socrates and Plato in the formation of the theory of ideas. Fortunately the solution of this problem is not of great importance to the present discussion and, with the help of an occasional "probably" or "possibly" we shall carry on without further reference to this controversy.

wanted to probe into realities and their natures, for only in that
way would it be possible to arrive at general truths, truths valid
for all times and circumstances, which the Sophists said could
not be known and which were the only kind of truths ultimately
worth knowing.

He was particularly concerned to probe into the realities
of political life. "His original aspirations", says a great authority
on him,[1] "had been those of a social and legislative reformer,
not those of the thinker or man of science. . . . It was not until
the actual execution of Socrates opened his eyes once for all
that he gave up his original intention of taking up active
political life as a career." Even then he remained intensely interested in the fundamental questions of politics, concerning
the ultimate purpose of the state and the ultimate norm of
political action.

All this made him look back to the philosophers, who had at
least asked ultimate questions concerning the nature of things
He called for a "return to Parmenides", meaning by that a
return to the problem of the one and the many discussed, as
Parmenides had been one of the first to discuss it, in terms of
abstract thought.[2] If the relationship of the plurality of changing
objects to the unchanging unity believed to underlie them could
be cleared up on these lines, a road to the understanding of the
ultimate nature of these objects would surely be opened. But
it was a necessary condition of this that the knowledge of the
One and the knowledge of the many were not treated as
Parmenides and his disciples at Elea had tended to treat them,
as mutually exclusive objectives between which a choice must
be made. They must be sought together without denying the
reality of either. But that meant that a link must be found
between them.

Plato's famous theory of ideas was an attempt to meet this
challenge. But it met it indirectly. It approached the problem
of the nature of things through the question of how we know
things and showed how the many and the one could be linked
in reality by showing first how they are linked in our minds.

---

[1] A. E. Taylor in *Plato: The Man and his Work*, p. 4.
[2] See the Note on the Bankruptcy of Early Greek Philosophy at the end of this
chapter.

Plato pointed out that if we are to know the nature of a changeful, transient object such as a particular tree or horse or fellow-citizen, we have first to make some sort of definition of it. Indeed, we have to do this if it is to become an object of thought or discussion at all. Without definition it is no more than an object of the senses, as it might be to a dog. But once this definition or idea of the thing has been provided we pass from the realm of change and appearance into a world of permanence and universal propositions, for it is of the nature of a definition to be unchanging and eternal, unlike the particular object that exemplifies it, which may be a poor specimen of the type or may change or be destroyed at any moment. We pass also, when we define, from the multiplicity of the individuals of any type to the oneness of the type itself.

It seems likely enough that Socrates had spoken frequently of the ideas of things in this sense, using for the purpose the term "form" (εἶδος), which the young men around him had perhaps picked up from the Pythagoreans. But, if we are to believe Plato's great pupil Aristotle, it was Plato rather than Socrates who took the next and immensely significant step. So far, we have been given no guarantee that in passing from sense-objects to ideas and general propositions we have done anything more than pass from things that are at least realities of a kind to a world of mere words and word-play. Plato's great hypothesis was precisely this, that it is the world of ideas that *is* the world of realities and that it is only by embodying, that is to say, being an actual exemplification of an idea, that an individual object exists at all.

That is where we cross the gulf between psychology and metaphysics. We have seen how an object of the senses, by being defined in general terms by an "idea" or "concept" and by being henceforth regarded as an example of that concept, becomes an object of thought. Plato added that it is by embodying or (in his terminology) participating in an idea or universal thought-form that the object in question possesses real being. The "form" of an object (in this sense of the word "form") not only makes it the kind of thing it is; it is also the deepest cause of its existing at all. The most that mere physical causation can do (as in the act of generation, for example) is to make it *possible* for something to exist. Actual existence only comes about when that "possible something" receives into itself, as it were, the idea or form of itself; we might say "when it takes form", but to make our modern phrase express Plato's thought we should have to spell the "form" in it with a capital F.

Now, it is clear that, if all this is true, our discussion of things in terms of the "ideas" they embody is no mere word-play but is a discussion of realities, that should lead us to the unchanging unity of the truth of things. But it is equally clear that the theory raises an enormous question as to the way in which these ideas themselves exist. Do they exist at all when they are not being embodied in any individual examples or retained in anyone's memory? To put it crudely, suppose that a disease had wiped out all horses, and everyone had died out who had ever seen a horse or heard of a horse, would the "form" of a horse exist and, if so, where?

Plato had no doubt at all about the answer, and it was not the answer that most people would now give. He believed that ideas (in his sense of the word) existed independently of their embodiment in physical objects or their retention in human memories. He believed, indeed, that they existed in a much more complete and real way than physical objects exist. For they are things of the mind, not subject to the imperfections, mutability and decay of physical things, and exist in a world of their own, an eternal world of ideas.

Before dismissing this theory as fantastic, let us note that it was only necessary for St. Augustine to identify this world of ideas with the Divine Mind, which St. John called the Logos, to make Plato's notion credible and satisfying. But Aristotle, who knew nothing of the Divine Trinity or of St. John, had some justification when he criticized and even ridiculed his master's teaching on this point and propounded an alternative view as to the way in which ideas exist, of which we shall have to say something when we come to his theory of the state. For his theory of the state was profoundly influenced by his views about ideas, just as Plato's was, which is the reason why we have spent so long on these metaphysical issues. And it is not only Aristotle's opinions and Plato's that are in question but practically the whole subsequent history of political thought.

For the great debate between them has gone on in one form or another ever since.

But their deep differences as to the manner in which ideas exist should not cause us to overlook the extent to which they were in agreement. On the root notion of objects becoming objects of knowledge in virtue of their "forms" and existing in virtue of their participation in these forms, Aristotle and Plato thought alike. We may add that the relatively short period during which European philosophy has tried to do without this notion has been one of philosophic anarchy and progressive disintegration.

VII

Such, then, was the background, political and philosophical, of Plato's treatises on the state and particularly of the first of them, the *Republic*, the greatest and most seminal of them and, at the same time, the most intimately bound up with the theory of ideas. It was written probably about 390 B.C., when Plato was not far from forty years old and about to found the *Academeia*, or Academy, which became a kind of university for Athens that lasted until it was closed by the Emperor Justinian more than nine hundred years later. It may be added (to have done at last with biographical matters) that some twenty years later Plato embarked upon the one great adventure of his life in the sphere of practical politics, when he was invited to Sicily to train in the art of government an inexperienced and incompetent young man, Dionysius II, who had just succeeded his father as despot of the Greek settlement at Syracuse. We may note the parallel with what are commonly supposed to have been the experiences of Confucius and also that neither on this nor on subsequent visits was Plato as successful as Confucius is said to have been; but, finally, that this need not necessarily have been wholly, or even mainly, Plato's fault.

The treatise in question is known, as we said, as the *Republic*, a title which has nothing to do with republicanism.[1] It takes

---

[1] The English term "Republic" is not a translation of the Greek title, 'Η Πολιτεία but a stupid transliteration of the Latin word *respublica*, which means something quite different. The Greek word is used by Aristotle to mean balanced constitutional government. Plato uses it in this very treatise (IX, 591*e*) for the interior, intellectual and moral "constitution" of a wise man and some thirty lines earlier speaks of the importance of forming a πολιτεία or "polity" in a child "as in a state". Perhaps "constitutional régime" would be as accurate a rendering as any, but heaven forbid the use of such jargon in a title!

the form of a discussion between Socrates and his young friends. The first Book consists of a somewhat heated argument about the nature of justice but presently Socrates convinces the company that justice will be more easily seen in its true nature when seen on a larger scale, namely as it works out, not in the individual, but in the state. They then proceed to construct a state from first principles, that is to say, starting from its primary purposes. Eventually Socrates shows that "justice" or "righteousness" is an essential element in the pattern of the state and that this must have far-reaching political implications. For, if righteousness is to be the formative principle or "idea" of the state, it must work itself out in the institutions and arrangements of the state, and how it is to do so is the next question considered.

Now, it is of the first importance to the understanding of Plato's book to grasp at the outset the fact that it does *not* set out to portray an "ideal" state in the ordinary sense of that term. Unless we grasp this, we shall completely miss the secret of its age-long and still active influence on political thought and construction. We shall, on the one hand, be distracted by particular features of Plato's commonwealth, some of which are quite impracticable as he himself admitted,[1] some even grotesque, and nearly all of which are limited by the horizon of the tiny political unit that, as we have seen, constituted in Greek eyes the state properly so called. We shall be distracted by all these details, which certainly disqualify it from being what *we* mean by an ideal state, and miss the all-important sense in which it might, in philosophic jargon, be called an "ideal" state, namely that its construction follows the procedure of all Plato's thinking, political or otherwise, his method of thinking in terms of formative ideas.

His "Republic" is not an ideal state in the modern sense of a state fulfilling our highest aspirations and containing no flaws. It should rather be called an "idea-ed" state, a state "informed" or shaped by an idea or concept and owing its very existence to the fact that it is thus "informed", just as any individual man or cat or tree exists as such in virtue of the fact that it is "informed" by the universal idea or concept of "man" or "cat" or "tree".

[1] E.g. V, 472, 473; IX, 592.

It is not, therefore, the details of Plato's state, it is not even the general character of the concept that it embodies, that has constituted the essence of Platonism in politics for more than two thousand years. It is the bare notion that a state should be shaped by a concept and derive its authority from that shaping, together with the fascination of watching it in the process of being thus shaped and perhaps taking part in it—these are the things that have caused a picture of a largely impracticable and slightly ridiculous garden suburb to be a fountain-head of inspiration for political thinkers for longer than any other piece of reasoned constitution-building in the world. And they have made it also the ultimate literary source of all reasoned absolutism in politics; for, unless the "idea" contains in itself the antidote to absolutism, all idea-ed states must be absolutist.

For if a state is to be consciously and completely shaped by an intellectual thing, such as a universal idea, it must embody that idea throughout its constitutional forms; it must possess administrative organs capable of giving effect to that idea in all its activities; its administrators must be imbued with, and trained in, that idea; and its subjects must be "conditioned" so as to be receptive to that idea, or at least to be amenable to a rule of life shaped by that idea. No other idea can be allowed to dispute the sway of the dominant idea and, unless the idea itself demands it, no political safeguards or individual liberties can be allowed to stand in the way of its application. For political absolutism on an intellectual system, which is the kind that matters most, is the transposition of the compelling power of logic into compulsion by the will, exercised upon a whole community. Therein, indeed, lies its terrible power of fascination.

Furthermore, if the builders of the idea-ed state are pagans or atheists, then the idea will be to them something ultimate, as no merely political idea ought to be. There will be no appeal from it to a personal God transcending all political ideas conceivable by man; for there will be no belief in a God who is the Creator and Father of men and the source of the moral law by which a man must live if he is to be fully a man (or, for that matter, fully a citizen) and on which his moral and ultimately his political rights are based.

Not only so, but in these circumstances the idea will almost certainly trench upon the sphere of moral conduct, in which case (since it is conceived as having no God above it) it will be given the rights of God, as the ultimate source and criterion of all human rights and morals, with authority to mould the consciences of citizens to its pattern. This is something much more than political absolutism, which is the rule of the sovereign —king or Parliament, as the case may be—unchecked by constitutional restraints. It is moral absolutism, which is the rule of the sovereign, be it despot, Parliament or people, unchecked by the moral law, and is the ultimate absolutism. To it gravitate all atheists—and all theists too, unless they are active-minded and intelligent theists—when their goal is the shaping of the state by an abstract idea. Such is the pull of the abstract idea upon the abstract thinker; so readily do an absolute idea and an absolute logic claim all human affairs as their province; so surely do they communicate an absolutist temper to the will.

That is why Plato, though he would have repudiated many of his children, has been the father of absolutism whenever his method of thinking has gripped the minds of political thinkers. Nor has he ever been excelled as a gripper of minds.

VIII

So important is it to grasp the fact that the key to Plato's extraordinary influence upon political thought lies in his theory of "informing" by ideas rather than in the particular character he gives to the idea of the state, that I have so far done no more than allude to the particular character. Obviously, however, that character is going to bear to some extent upon the issue, if only because, as I have just said, the degree in which the state-shaping idea trenches upon the sphere of moral conduct determines the extent to which absolutism passes into moral absolutism.

For example, on what used to be called the "low" view of the state, the state's functions are minimized; the state may even be reduced to a mere policeman keeping a necessary minimum of order amidst a go-as-you-please individualism, or to a mere insurance company guaranteeing to its members a certain minimum of social security. In that case there will be no direct and positive effort by the state to impose a moral code or to form consciences. Indirectly and negatively it may be operating in the moral sphere, as when it tacitly condones unlimited acquisitiveness and competition as beneficial to society as a whole, regardless of their effect upon individuals, or persuades the community that a set of merely material benefits are worth the sacrifice of economic and social self-determination by the recipients; but it will not avowedly play the moralist. But Plato, true to the Greek tradition which the Sophists had disparaged, took the "high" view of the state, regarding it as essentially the promoter of the moral life as well as of economic well-being. The "idea" of the state in his thought, therefore, was bound to be concerned with morals, so that any absolutism that it directly inspired was bound to be moral absolutism.

As a matter of fact, his state-shaping idea was nothing less than the idea of righteousness itself. It will be remembered that Socrates, in the dialogue, proposed to show righteousness in its true character by displaying it embodied in something on a large scale, not the individual man, but the political society of men. From that point he proceeds deductively to show just what the political implications must be of righteousness as he conceives it. (That is how the dialogue, which begins with righteousness as its topic, becomes a dissertation on the state.)

Now, in nothing that has been said so far, have I intended to suggest that it is a bad thing to take a high view of the state and to attribute to it a moral purpose to be achieved by action in the moral sphere. The state certainly does exist for more than economic purposes. It certainly should help men to live together rightly, and on a higher moral plane than the natural man can attain in isolation, practising virtues that a man cannot practise alone. Moreover, in fulfilling this purpose, the state must itself act righteously and it must provide a framework so designed that within it a citizen may readily be trained in righteousness and practise it with no unnecessary obstacles. All this is sound political doctrine; and the weakness of nineteenth-century Liberalism, and its failure to meet the challenge of Fascism and Nazism, was due precisely to the fact that it had emptied the idea of the state of almost all positive moral meaning.

But Plato meant a great deal more than this. If his state had taken for its function the administering of the natural moral law; if it had admitted that that law had originated outside and before the state; if it had allowed it to be formulated and expounded, and its truth guaranteed, by a teacher other than the state and possessing (in the sphere of morals) an authority higher than the state's, then his state would still have embodied a moral idea and acted on the moral plane, but it would not have been morally absolutist, whatever it might have been politically. For it would not have been the source of its own morality. But in actual fact it *was* the source of it.

It was not merely to have the duty of administering the moral code; it was to be the visible embodiment of that code. Nor is that phrase to be taken in the loose sense in which we say, for example, that a man is the embodiment of good taste, meaning that he habitually displays good taste in his judgements. The phrase "embodiment" is to be taken literally. The state was to be the heavenly idea of righteousness made visible on earth, a sort of Logos incarnate. Moreover, it was to be, for itself and its citizens, the *only* incarnation of the idea. It was to be itself the revealer to itself and to its citizens of its own moral dogmas, the sole instructor and guide of its own conscience and its citizens', the sole judge of its citizens' causes and its own.

Nor, in all this, was Plato saying anything shocking to a Greek. In Acton's famous phrase: "The vice of the classic state was that Church and state were one." But it had the excuse that there was as yet no Church.

IX

How, then, in Plato's picture, is the incarnating of righteousness in the state to be brought about? How is the true idea of righteousness to manifest itself in the state and be diffused through it, so as to become the norm of public and of private conduct? The question leads us directly to the most characteristic and notorious institution of the Platonic state.

Plato starts from the fact of the division of functions in a community. This division is, in a large community, somewhat elaborate but can be simplified (he says) into a broad distinction between producers on the one hand and those who direct and protect the activities of the commonwealth on the other. The latter class, the Guardians, can conveniently be subdivided into the Guardians proper, who constitute the governing class, and their auxiliaries, the citizen-army, which fights the commonwealth's wars against other states and enforces the Guardians' plans and orders at home.

To each of these classes he assigns its appropriate virtues, for these virtues, being part of the idea of the state, must, like the idea itself, enter the state through its members and, in each case, through the members whose duties particularly call for the virtue in question. Thus, if the state as a whole is to be wise, it is the governing class who must possess the wisdom. If the state is to be brave, it is the citizen-army who must possess the courage. If the state is to display self-control, its better part must control the lower, as in the individual man, which means that the desires of the common herd are to be controlled by the desires and wisdom of the cultivated few. And the master virtue of distributive justice, which keeps all classes and individuals in their proper places, must permeate the whole.[1]

We should note here that Plato, consistently with his declared intention of ascertaining the nature of righteousness in the individual by showing it in action on a large scale in the state, pictures the state on the analogy of the soul of a man. In the threefold division of the state, the Guardians correspond to the intellect, the auxiliaries to "the spirited element", that is to say, the will, and the producers to the irrational appetites.

Plato then enlarges on the selection and training of the Guardians. He insists that both the Guardians proper and their auxiliaries must undergo a long course of mathematics, harmonics and gymnastics. It would take us too far afield to explain the position held by those subjects in the Greek scheme of education; but Plato was certainly being very Greek here; and one example may be adduced to show that the Greeks were not being as silly as perhaps they sound. They had a well-founded belief in the characteristic effects of different kinds of

[1] Book IV, 428-434.

music on character and the emotional life. Their ideas on the subject may have been as primitive as, from the twentieth-century point of view, their music was, but at least they were not such utter fools as to allow whole populations to be saturated from youth upwards, first with the subtle and limitless complexities of classical music, and then, still more extensively, with the titillating inversions and discords of jazz and swing, without conducting a single public scientific enquiry (in an age of enquiries) into the mental, emotional and physiological reactions to be expected from, and actually set up by, these overwhelming invasions of the sub-conscious.

The training, then, of both Guardians and auxiliaries must be mental, moral and physical, and rigorous in all three departments, even from childhood. The music must be of the simplest and severest type (in any case, it would have amounted to little more than a form of plain chant). The nursery stories must include nothing derogatory to the gods or to great men. The poets, and particularly Homer, must be excluded both because of their unedifying pictures of the gods and because of their tendency to dramatize the emotions, thereby weakening us by arousing too much sympathy with the troubles of others.

Furthermore, both Guardians and auxiliaries, in order that they should not acquire private loyalties and ambitions, are to be forbidden to possess either families or private property. They are to have communal meals, and their wives and children are to belong to all of them. The women of these classes are to be educated in the same way as the men and perform the same functions, being allotted to the class of Guardians proper or to the auxiliaries according to whether they show an aptitude for philosophy or for war. The children of the Guardians must be bred eugenically and are to be brought up in state nurseries and schools, so that parents and children may be unknown to one another. Thus the Guardians will have no private interests; the whole body of them will be animated by a single public purpose.

There is much in all this that recalls either in its details or in its spirit the constitution of Sparta, on which, as we have seen, Plato had long looked admiringly. Some features will remind us also of the Church's laws for her priesthood; others of the discipline imposed in Soviet Russia upon the Communist Party, whose function in the U.S.S.R. resembles that of Plato's Guardians in many respects.

X

Thus we come to the highest and most important element in the training and occupations of the Guardians proper, namely philosophy—for the state must be ruled by philosophers. We must put out of our minds that figure of fun, the stage-philosopher, the depraved and eccentric philosopher of carica-ture and, all too often (as Socrates admits), of real life. The true philosopher is something quite different. He acquires wisdom by contemplation and he contemplates, not the passing ap-pearances of things, but absolute and eternal ideas, such as constitute the realities of things. He contemplates, above all, the idea of the good, in which is to be found the essence of the state. Philosophers, therefore, are the natural rulers. Plato's state is an aristocracy.

From this point he is led to survey the other forms of state known to the Greek world, a subject we can study more scientifically in Aristotle. Plato admits that aristocracy is liable to degenerate into what he calls "timocracy", which means government by those animated primarily by a love of honours and prestige; and timocracy in its turn degenerates into an oli-garchy of wealth (what we should call a plutocracy), with ex-tremes of riches and poverty as its trade-mark in the society it governs. To this phase the natural reaction is an armed rising of the people and the establishment of an egalitarian democracy marked by an extravagant love of liberty, degenerating into licence. Then the political champion who has led the *demos* against the oligarchy becomes a despot and a tyrant, and the most wicked and miserable of all forms of government has been reached.

So Plato returns to the notion of the true aristocracy, which (he thinks) will endure if its members seek happiness in the right place. The very word "philosopher" means "lover of wisdom", and the pursuit of wisdom is the highest pleasure, and inseparable both from virtue and from happiness, for what is most reasonable is also the most lawful and the most orderly. "The man of understanding", says Plato,[1] "will direct all his energies throughout life to this one object", namely the formation of his soul according to the most perfect pattern. It is with this object in view that he will shun, not only vices, but even legitimate private advantages and honours—anything, in fact, that might disturb his moral harmony and the serenity of his contemplation of the truth.

"But if that is his chief concern", says Glaucon, the chief interlocutor of Socrates in the dialogue, " he will not concern himself with politics."

"But indeed he will", replies Socrates, "in his own city, at least; though perhaps not in the land of his birth, unless by some providential accident."

"I see what you mean", replies Glaucon; "he will concern himself with politics in the city we have just been planning, and which exists only in the realm of ideas; for I do not believe it is to be found anywhere on earth."

"Perhaps in heaven", says Socrates, "there is laid up a pattern of it which he who desires may gaze on and, in gazing, plan himself on the same pattern. As to whether that city exists or ever will exist on earth, that is of no importance to him. For in any case he will adopt its practices himself to the exclusion of any other."

"I think he will", says Glaucon.[2]

Thus ends the dialogue on the state, for Book X is a kind of Appendix on poetry. Plato has returned to the question asked at the beginning: what is the pattern of virtue for the individual man? To answer it he has gone round by way of the pattern of the state and sought that in the realm of pure thought. He who finds it there, if he is wise, will organize his own conduct in accordance with it, in so far as the state in which he lives allows, and, in so far as he is given the opportunity, will organize, also in accordance with it, the state in which he lives.

And it is through the philosophers alone that the pattern laid up in heaven can be introduced into the state on earth and made the effective principle of its formation and perpetuation. That

[1] *Republic*, IX, 591.
[2] IX, 592.

is why the class of Guardians, each individually moulded by the Idea and collectively moulding the state by the Idea, is the pivotal organ of Plato's politics, linking earth to the absolute. It is this aspect of Plato's political thought that more than any other has gripped and fascinated political thinkers and administrators of all subsequent ages—the thought that the perfect state can only come into existence if it embodies an absolute and unchangeable Idea, which it can only do if it is completely controlled by a selected group of persons who have completely grasped the Idea and live themselves in accordance with it.

That this ideal involves political and, in most circumstances, moral absolutism has enhanced rather than diminished its fascination for those likely to pursue it. For who, seeking to establish the idea-ed state, will cast himself for any rôle but that of Guardian? And who, having so cast himself, will agree with Socrates that, provided he lives by the Idea himself, it is of no importance whether or no he succeeeds in forcing the mould upon others?

NOTE ON THE BANKRUPTCY OF EARLY GREEK PHILOSOPHY

(To Chapter VII, section v; see p. 191)

I

This note aims at giving the reader a sufficient idea of the causes and extent of the bankruptcy of philosophy in Greece in the second half of the fifth century B.C. and, thus, of the magnitude of Plato's task when he entered the field and of the historical significance of his own remedy for the situation. It is based upon a number of accounts, of which the last to come into the writer's hands (after his chapter on Plato was completed) may be recommended to the general reader who would like to follow up the subject further in a short and easily accessible book that, in spite of the strange omission of all reference to Zeno of Elea, certainly makes it come alive to the twentieth century reader (*The Greek Philosophers*, by W. K. C. Guthrie, Public Orator at Cambridge, Home Study Books, 1950).

First, then, it is as usual important to get our chronological perspectives right and to realize that the man whom the Greeks with good reason looked upon as the father of philosophy, Thales, the Ionian of Miletus, was in his prime just about 200 years before Plato, in his prime, wrote *The Republic*, and that before him no one who has left any record of himself had asked the fundamental questions of philosophy.

Secondly, it is equally important to realize that neither Thales nor any of his immediate successors would have known in the least what was meant if anyone had told him that he was asking the fundamental questions of philosophy. Nor, indeed, did they ask them in a form that would be regarded today as bringing them under that description. They did not, for example, make the formal distinction between appearance and reality and ask what was the ultimate reality behind the visible universe. They did, however, speculate on what was the unchanging and permanent element in the visible universe itself.

In this respect they have something in common with the nineteenth-century physicists with their quest for uniformities, in the shape of a material substance common to all physical objects and of natural laws deducible from observed phenomena but in no way transcending them. But if their speculations went no further than the physical universe, it was not because they were materialists. That term implies the rejection of the spiritual, and that rejection, in its turn, only becomes possible when the material and the spiritual have been expressly distinguished. But that is another distinction that these first Ionian philosophers had not made; and in point of fact they ascribed to the physical universal properties that would now be called spiritual and that they termed divine.

They were regarded by the Greeks as philosophers because they looked for an underlying uniformity and a basic substance in a universe hitherto regarded as subject to the caprices of the deities of the Homeric pantheon; but in their quest they took it for granted that in the physical universe they would find all the spiritual values, such as they were, of the polytheism that they rejected—a reasonable assumption, since anthropomorphic polytheism does not itself transcend the physical universe. A school of materialistic atheists only arose among the physicists when the universe had ceased to be regarded as an indivisible whole.

When, therefore, Thales identified the underlying basis of the universe with water, or moisture, he intended by that (if Aristotle is right) to account not only for all purely material objects, but also for all the phenomena of life, including the human soul. "Everything", he is reported to have said, "is full of the divine."

Thales, however, is best known today for his prediction of a solar eclipse, commonly supposed to be that of 585 B.C. But he could have accomplished this feat on the basis of Babylonian astronomical records, which he had certainly studied; and its significance in the history of philosophy depends entirely on how far it led him towards the conception of natural laws, a question on which we have not enough evidence to pronounce. Of one thing we can be quite sure, that it would be a huge anachronism to attribute to him the nineteenth-century idea of a law of nature as a kind of compulsive behaviour pattern deducible from measured observations. Less doubtfully he can be regarded as the founder of abstract geometry—the geometry of universally true propositions concerning geometrical relations, as distinct from the geometry of mensuration that he had learnt in Egypt. Thus he formulated and proved the far-reaching theorem that the angle inscribed in a semi-circle is always a right angle. The bearing of this on the story of philosophy will appear presently.

His pupil and fellow-citizen, Anaximander, went considerably further in his speculations on the essential basis of the physical universe. He inferred from the variety and conflicts within it that a clash of opposites had been latent in it from the beginning and this led him to formulate what had been called an anticipation of the nebular hypothesis. He spoke of an indeterminate mass from which were separated, on the one hand moisture and cold, condensing into water and earth at the centre, and on the other hand dryness and heat, from which came air and fire. Out of these elements all natural objects, including the beasts and, through them, men, were supposed to have been evolved by a series of mutations. But, though he supported his ideas with much shrewd observation of nature, there was no question of quantitative measurements or demonstrations. Another Milesian, Anaximenes, who postulated vapour as the primary substance, connected its condensation and rarefaction with cold and heat respectively, and the most rarified form of air with the human soul and the divine principle in the universe—all this again without quantitative verification.

Meanwhile a wholly new approach to the problem of the basis of the universe had been inaugurated by that strange and almost mythical genius Pythagoras, working among the Greeks of Southern Italy, to which he had migrated from Samos about 530 B.C. He was both the founder of a religious sect and a mathematician of such originality as to rank high amongst those pioneers of the science who have gone "voyaging through strange seas of thought, alone". It is in this second aspect that he chiefly concerns us here, on account of the inferences that he drew from his discoveries concerning the relation of numbers to the physical universe.

For he and his many disciples were led by them to see the basic principle of the universe, not in any of its material constituents, as the Ionians of Miletus had done, but in the reduction of a primordial indeterminateness to determinate relations and harmonies, from which its order and beauty were derived and of which numerical ratios were the most perfect expression. His astonishing discovery that the harmonious intervals of the musical scale can be expressed by simple arithmetical ratios and the overwhelming impression that it made, both on his own mind and on his contemporaries, caused his way of approach to the philosophical problem to have an immense vogue and raised it almost to the mystical level. More than a century later the young Plato felt the thrill, and his own even more original and far profounder philosophical invention never quite shook itself free from the fascination of the Pythagorean theories of numbers.

II

Thus by about 500 B.C., two wholly different approaches had been established to the fundamental question of physical philosophy, concerning the basic and unifying principle of the universe, and two different types of answers had been given. But both types of answers inevitably raised a further question. The permanent and unifying element in the universe might be identified with some material substance within it or with some form or structure imposed upon it, but neither answer accounted for the universe as it is now—neither for its multiplicity nor for its variety nor for its movement—for neither of them gave any reasoned account of how what was originally uniform and motionless could have come to assume these features. Unity and permanence might have been made intelligible but at the cost of presenting philosophy with the far more difficult problem of change and differentiation.

The problem was less pressing for those who took the Ionian way of approach to it through matter than for those who approached it through form, for, as already remarked, their physics were all-embracing in that they included the vital principle, and even the divine. It was, in fact, met about 500 B.C. by Heraclitus of Ephesus with an embarrassing readiness, for he was prepared to deny any underlying permanence and to identify the basic substance with something that is the very quintessence of change and movement, namely fire—manifested in all the phases of combustion and extinction, in sticks and stones, in the divine mind and in the souls of men. But we must not press this identification too materialistically, for the fire of Heraclitus was, in part at least, a symbol of the fundamental flux, or becoming, which was his substitute for fundamental being.

Thus he saved the universe from immobility, but only by stultifying the Ionian attempt to find a core of unchanging substance in an indivisible universe. For he had had to equate intelligence with combustion and to postulate change unrelated to a framework of permanence.

But once again the philosophical question of the day was answered in a wholly different manner at the other end of the Greek world, in Southern Italy, this time at Elea, some seventy miles from Naples. There Parmenides, about the middle of the first half of the fifth century B.C., appealed to pure reason to show that change was impossible. His argument ran something like this: Nothing can both be and not be. But if that which is becomes other than what it is, it is not itself; in other words, it is not. Therefore that which is, can never be other than what it is. Therefore change is impossible and, with it, motion. The only reality is the unchanging One; all the rest is illusion, whatever the senses or experience may say.

Surely the world has produced no more notable example of faith in pure reason.

The fallacy is concealed in the second of the above propositions, in the use of the word "is" in two different senses. But grammarians had not then been at work on distinguishing the uses of words, and the fallacy remained undiscovered for a century. Meanwhile the demonstration was reinforced by the novel dialectic and the famous paradoxes of Zeno, also of Elea. One of them is the proof that Achilles can never catch the tortoise, which is still argued among schoolboys. But no one could answer Zeno in his day.

III

The effect on the world of philosophy was paralysing, for the Greek genius for abstract thought, now thoroughly roused and on its mettle, could not but respect a logic that it could not refute. It touched even the physicists, for it seemed to sterilize the underlying substances of the older school and even to quench the fire of Heraclitus.

However, the physicists did at least put up a fight, which is more than can be said for those whose approach was through "form". They made what, from their point of view, was the only possible answer. They abandoned the postulate of unity in the universe, saying that if the One can never become many, then, since many things do in fact exist, there must have been plurality from the beginning. (The fact of motion they tried to save in other ways, none of them very satisfactory but all too technical to be worth pursuing here, since the developments essential to our present historical enquiry can be sufficiently explained without them.)

In the West, Empedocles, from Sicily, concluded that the four elements known to Greek physics—earth, air, fire and water—were all real and primary substances and that from their interactions, motivated by love and strife (both conceived as having physical dimensions) all natural

phenomena had arisen fortuitously. A theory of natural selection helped
to give this theory an air of plausibility, but it is not altogether surprising
that the chief reputation of Empedocles in his own day was gained as a
magician and, after it, as a subject for poetry.

Altogether different was the destiny of the ideas of Democritus, a Greek
from Thrace; for he carried materialistic pluralism to its logical extreme
in a materialistic theory of atoms that in one form or another has played
will-o'-the-wisp to the human mind ever since. Nor was its materialism
accidental. The thorough-going physicist of the original Ionian school had
been able to treat his universe as the heir to the spiritual content of the
polytheistic scheme because it was an indivisible whole, but no one could
suppose *fragments* of the physical universe to be spirit, or divine. Already
the Ionian pluralist Anaxagoras, atheist though he was, had drawn a
definite distinction between matter and mind and had recognized that,
in so far as mind was needed to explain material phenomena, it had to be
brought in from outside them. Democritus, however, equally sure that
there was nothing spiritual about matter, looked to nothing beyond his
atomism, and relied on it to explain, not only the vast variety of physical
objects, but also the mechanism of sensation and (invoking the smallest
and roundest atoms) the souls of beasts and men.

I say "explain", but the reader must once more be cautioned against
supposing that precise quantitative calculations played any part in the
physical hypotheses of the ancient Greeks. It is true that all sorts of shapes
and sizes were postulated by Democritus for his atoms (which were
indivisible particles, all of one substance). There were sharp atoms to
explain acid tastes, hooked atoms to explain coalescence, thin skins of
atoms drifting through the air, to explain vision, and so forth. But all
these were essentially qualitative differences, and the product of the
imagination. The idea of arriving at the shapes of atoms by measuring
effects in controlled experiments was simply non-existent.

This inability to adduce experimental proof of the existence of atoms
(all supposed to be below the level of visibility) or to demonstrate the
connection of their imagined properties with any actual objects or events,
or to harness them to any physical mechanism, was no doubt part of the
reason why the theory left the Greek mind unconvinced. If these practical
tests had been met, the complete absence of any explanation of the existence of the atoms, or of their motion, would probably have been ignored,
as it is today. As it was, the ordinary man was left with the feeling that
the ordinary objects of sight and touch were still unexplained by any
physical philosophy. As for the logic, apparently so convincing to the
logicians, that proved these objects to be illusions—well, the everyday
objects were there every day, and the very plausible inference could be
drawn that it was the philosophies that were illusory—the abstract and
the physical alike.

IV

This was the impasse that Greek philosophy had reached by the middle of the fifth century B.C., in the spring-time of the Periclean age, and the stage was set for drawing the further inference that knowledge of the ultimate nature of things was impossible. This was done by two men. Protagoras, born about 480 B.C. at Abdera in Thrace but brought up in the Ionian school of philosophy, came to Athens during the ascendancy of Pericles and published a book on *Truth* in which he claimed that the physicists, with their theories of flux or change, had made it clear that absolute knowledge was impossible—"Man is the measure of all things", of being and of not-being. His contemporary Gorgias of Leontini (in Sicily), who also settled in Athens, used the dialectic which Zeno had used to demonstrate the non-existence of the many to demonstrate also the non-existence, or at any rate the unknowability, of the One.

The only thing for philosophers to do in these circumstances (so it seemed) was to acquiesce in these conclusions and confine themselves to practical problems in which ultimate questions could be shelved. This is where the Sophists came upon the stage, and they held it for more than two generations, till Plato was ready to take up the problem of the One and the many where Parmenides had left it, or rather, where Parmenides had taken it up, before his disastrous logic had made it insoluble. He would return to it with Parmenides' determination to find a solution in terms of pure thought exempt from the preoccupation of the physicists with objects of sense, and with the faith of Parmenides in human reason. But he was also determined to hold on to both elements in the problem, the many as well as the One, the changing as well as the unchanging; for the very essence of the problem was to find a place for both. Thus was born the Platonic doctrine of ideas.

(See section V of the foregoing chapter: " This failure of the philosophers . . .", p. 191.)

VIII

ARISTOTLE'S *POLITICS*

VIII

ARISTOTLE'S *POLITICS*

I

OVER the gateway of Plato's Academeia at Athens was an inscription to the effect: "No entrance except for geometers." The young Aristotle (he was seventeen when he applied for admission) had too good a brain to have been ploughed in matriculation at any University, whatever the compulsory subjects, but the fact remains that geometry was definitely not his speciality, and he was never altogether at home at the Academeia. That is no doubt why, when Plato died, he was not appointed to succeed him as President, although he was in his intellectual prime and admittedly the ablest mind of his day. (This was in 347 B.C., when he was thirty-seven.)

He did, it is true, achieve supreme greatness in one abstract science, namely logic, in which he created almost from its foundations the system that served as the framework for almost all philosophical thinking in Europe down to quite recent times and is far from having been superseded today, in spite of Bertrand Russell and his successors. Nevertheless, his real bent was for the biological sciences. He was the son of a doctor and, when he left the Academeia after his disappointment over the Presidency, one of the uses he made of his freedom was to spend some years in collecting and studying biological material abroad. It was no less a biologist than Charles Darwin who said of him: "Linnaeus and Cuvier have been my gods, but they are nothing to old Aristotle."

With Plato, by contrast, geometry was a ruling passion, and he wrote also on so abstract a topic as the theory of numbers; indeed, he laid his theory of "ideas" open to criticism on the ground that he reduced the "ideas" to little more than numbers. But the difference between the two men was much more than a difference in their favourite subjects. It went deep down to the whole mode of approach to the intellectual life. What is more, it was not merely a difference between two individual philosophers. Plato and Aristotle represent respectively two types of the human mind that have ever since divided the Schools of philosophy between them. As someone said, parodying Gilbert and Sullivan:—

> "Every little philosopher that's born into this world alive
> Is either a little Platonist or else a little Aristotelian."

The fact is all the more significant because, as remarked in the last chapter, in their central philosophical technique the two philosophers are at one. Aristotle equally with Plato expressed both the way in which we know individual objects, and the way in which they exist, in terms of "informing" or shaping by universal thought-forms. Aristotle, like Plato (though in his own very different manner), applied this technique to the special case of the theory of the state. Moreover, in this particular department of philosophy, an external and accidental circumstance added its quota to the mental furniture that was common to both thinkers. For they were subject to the same limitations of political horizon, and made the same assumptions about the kind of political life most desirable and about the small scale on which alone the desirable political life could be lived. Nevertheless, in no field more clearly than in political theory did the two men exhibit within their common mental framework the great gulf that lies between their use of it.

It was suggested in the last chapter that between the two philosophers who both thought in terms of "informing ideas", the root difference lay (so far as it was of a kind capable of intellectual formulation) in their views on the question of how the ideas or universal thought-forms existed. Plato thought of the idea as pre-existent and eternal in a spiritual and truly real world of ideas and as constituting the reality of every individual object to which it gives "form". In Aristotle's hands the pre-existent idea becomes a manufactured concept, universal and abstract certainly, but derived by the human mind from individual objects. In the process of observing objects, the mind notes what they have in common and formulates the aspect or characteristic or complex of characteristics in which they can be said to be essentially alike, and that formulation is the concept. For Aristotle, the individual objects from which these concepts are thus derived are the primary realities and the derived thought-forms are but abstract figments of the mind.

Nevertheless, for him as for Plato, these thought-forms do really "inform" and give their character to the individuals; and, for him as for Plato, to be thus "informed" is necessary to the individual, not only if it is to be known but also if it is to exist. Nothing can exist that is wholly formless.

There is the same community in philosophical technique and the same radical difference in its application when they come to speculate on the purpose of things. This is a speculation to which the theory of ideas inevitably leads, for we cannot explore intelligently the nature of a thing or arrive at a satisfactory definition of it unless we can form some notion of, at any rate, the immediate ends to which its characteristic activities or properties are directed. Ultimately, therefore, Plato and Aristotle ask the same question about everything, including the state, namely: for what purpose does it exist? But two men could hardly differ more in the way they set about answering it. Plato speculates upon ultimate values laid up in heaven and deduces, from his notion of them, how the thing that is to embody them and fulfil them must work. Aristotle starts by examining the actual mode of life or working of the object under discussion and deducing from it the purpose it serves.

We have already seen how, in the particular case of the state, Plato, though living in the same Greek world as Aristotle, with all its variety of political experience and experiment, speculates with a mind radically detached from any actual experience or even possibility and produces a picture of a heavenly state that can fairly be said to be like nothing on earth. It is true that in his old age, after his unhappy experiences of the practical politics of Syracuse, he came nearer to actual and possible Greek political construction in his treatise called *The Laws*, but he never ceased to be at heart an *a priori* and deductive thinker.

Aristotle, on the other hand, is always descriptive and inductive. He sets a body of research students to work at collecting particulars of some hundred and sixty Greek city-state constitutions, not passing over even the most insignificant cities, and sows the *Politics* thickly with selected examples, after studying the lessons they convey. And we may note in this connection a fact that throws much light upon his mind and upon the limitations both of his mind and of his method. Not only was he unable to conceive of any state-forms as being politically valuable or worth philosophical consideration except those of his little Greek world of city-states; he was so little conscious of the limitations of that world as to be unable to conceive of the passing of those forms or to realize that, partly as a result of the conquests of his own pupil, Alexander the Great, their day was actually passing even as he quoted them. No book that has lasted for the rest of time went out of date more quickly in certain passages than the *Politics*.

Of Aristotle, then, as a political thinker, we may say summarily two things. First, he represents, for the whole human race, one side of the great dichotomy in political thinking of which the other side is represented by Plato. Secondly, on his own side of the great dividing line, there are two Aristotles. There is the walking encyclopaedia of the actual Greek political experience of his day, already out of date, like most Encyclopaedias, before publication is completed. There is also the profound philosophical student of political humanity, dealing with man as a being political by nature, and with the state as an organ necessary to perfect his nature; dealing in thoughts as universal as Plato's, but generalizations from nature, not speculative principles. In the introductory Chapter 2 of the *Politics*, consisting of less than forty lines, the Greek word for "nature", with its cognates, occurs twenty times. "And", says he, "nothing contrary to nature is right."[1]

II

It must be admitted that, as a book, the *Politics* suffers much from this duality in its author, which frequently causes the train of thought to be broken or obscure. Even more tiresome is his inability to forgo any opportunity of criticizing his master, Plato, fairly or unfairly. He is particularly critical of the

[1] *Politics*, VII, iii, 6.

Republic, which he takes in the very way that its author repudiates in the book itself, namely as a manual of proposals for actual and immediate execution.

Apart from all this, there is in the *Politics* no systematic and logical development of the argument such as would cause each section to depend on what precedes it and introduce what follows it. The book, short though it is, was many years "on the stocks" (some say from 357 B.C., when Aristotle was not quite thirty, till 322 B.C., the year of his death);[1] and like some of his other writings, shows signs of being little more than fairly continuous notes for a course of lectures. It may well have been that it was a course that he was constantly giving and that he worked over the notes year after year, arranging them sometimes in one order, sometimes in another, and that they were finally pieced together and written out in full by one of his students after his death. It is certainly a fact that there is no agreement among modern editors as to what the proper order of its sections should be.

It was not, therefore, without reason that the late H. W. C. Davis used to insist that "the *Politics* should be treated as a quarry of arguments and theories, rather than as an artistically constructed piece of literature". (In this respect, also, it is in marked contrast with the *Republic*, which is generally regarded as Plato's literary masterpiece.) But few quarries have provided richer ore for subsequent thinkers. Indeed, its thoughts have been so much quoted and have sunk so deep into the literary and political tradition of mankind, that the twentieth-century reader's appreciation of them is necessarily dulled. His case is like that of the man in the story who came away disappointed from a performance of *Hamlet* because the play was all made up of quotations.

Here are a few examples, some (in quotation marks) substantially from Jowett's translation, others paraphrased.

"A state is not the growth of a day."[2] Only the most platitudinous speaker would venture to introduce that remark into a speech today, but the thing badly needed saying amidst the

[1] Ernest Barker, in his edition of the *Politics* (Oxford, 1946), suggests 335 B.C. as the year when it was begun.
[2] *Politics*, V, iii, 11. Here and elsewhere, for convenience of reference, I have used the traditional numbering of the books, and not Jowett's.

8*

kaleidoscopic changes of Greek democratic politics and the even more facile radicalism of the sophist lecturers. In another passage (II, v, 16) we read similarly: "We should not disregard the experience of the ages."

Again, "the state is a creation of nature and man is by nature a political animal " (I, ii, 9).

"The individual when isolated is not self-sufficing" (I, ii, 14); the state is essential to the completion of human nature.

"The state is by nature clearly prior to the family and to the individual, since the whole is necessarily prior to the part" (I, ii, 12, 13). Aristotle is, of course, speaking here of priority in nature and in purpose, not of priority in time.

"The state is made up, not only of so many men, but of different kinds of men; an aggregation of similar persons does not constitute a state" (II, ii, 3); and a few lines further on he recurs to this notion of unity in diversity.

Almost at the outset the "high view" of the state is enunciated.[1] The state is a unit "originating in the bare necessities of life and perpetuated for the sake of a *good* life" (I, ii, 8), and for the practice of the distinctively civic virtues.

And this is Aristotle on law:

"The rule of law is preferable to that of any individual" (III, xvi, 3); and, only a little further on: "He who bids the law rule bids God and reason rule, but he who bids man rule adds an element of the beast" (III, xvi, 5). By "law" here Aristotle means, of course, something much more than the laws made from time to time by the state's legislature. He has in mind, in the first place, the natural moral law, then the customs and tradition which men have accepted as binding in the past and, finally, such laws enacted by the state's legislature as conform to the first two, or to the common reason of mankind. "The law", he says magnificently, "is reason unaffected by desire" (*loc. cit.*).

In the same vein he condemns as perversions all forms of constitution that override the laws, or the law. He is referring here to his famous classification of constitutions into six types of which three are primary types and the other three are respectively perversions of the first three. We shall be speaking of these later.

[1] See chapter VII, section viii.

The *Politics*, then, is a quarry from which may be obtained pure gold, but this must not be taken to mean that no more can be got from it than can be comprised in an anthology of its aphorisms. Though the book as a whole cannot be edited into order with any certainty, it contains long passages of reasoned argumentation combined with shrewd observation in which Aristotle's conception of the state is built up step by step; and the details of his conception have had far more importance for subsequent political thought than the details of Plato's. By Plato, men have been inspired to plan the state in terms of an idea, but not necessarily of Plato's idea, still less with Plato's elaborations of it. From Aristotle they have learnt to understand the true character of the state as a natural phenomenon, and they would have been influenced quite differently had Aristotle seen its features otherwise than as he did. And it is the ultimate secret of Aristotle's influence on political thought that, for all his limitations as an encyclopaedia of institutions, he was truly great as a political naturalist. He saw further into the type than one would have thought possible from his collection of specimens; and what he saw in it is our chief source of political instruction even today. He would have had an influence at least analogous, if opposite, to Plato's if he had done no more than teach statesmen the importance of the naturalist's approach to statesmanship. As it was, he was such a good naturalist that the first cry to be raised when political thought has lost touch with realities has generally been "Back to Aristotle!"

What, then, did he teach? Defective as is the plan of his book in its present form, it does at least state his fundamental thought at the outset. We are told at once that men are members of political communities by nature, and need these communities to complete their nature. In this one observation, now so trite, Aristotle solved once and for all an infinity of questions and dilemmas by which political doctrinaires of all ages, including his own, have shown on paper that no state which does not violate man's nature can exist for long.

They have, for example, put the question: Has the citizen, by his contract of citizenship, surrendered his political rights to the state? They have then proceeded to argue that if he has not, he can resume them at any time and there is no guarantee against the state's dissolution; but if he has surrendered them in such a way that he cannot resume them, there is no guarantee against the state's absolutism.

But more than two thousand years before Locke and Rousseau, Aristotle's dictum exposed the social contract as the myth it is. There never have been, and never could be, men existing with political rights in a pre-political phase, a so-called "state of nature", and forming a state by an artificial compact between them. Men born and reared outside political communities, the Mowglis and Tarzans of real life, are not noble savages but barely human, and neither possessed of political rights nor conscious of their meaning. The natural place for men to be born is within a political community and within families within the political community; and, when they are so born, their mutual relations within the political community, and the political rights and duties implied in them, are as natural to grown men as those within the family are to children and parents. The political community *is* man's state of nature.

Political rights and duties, therefore, neither exist before the state nor are brought into existence by a contract to form the state. They arise out of the very circumstances in which men are naturally born and from their instinctive response to those circumstances. Political rights and duties are, in fact, natural rights and duties, and no more need a contract to create or shape them than do the mutual rights and duties of parents and children.

It is true that, since man is a rational animal, he can do rationally and deliberately what comes natural to him. Aristotle seems to have envisaged intelligence and will playing a part in the actual construction of the state to which men naturally tend (I, ii, 15). Similarly, men can be conscious of their rights and duties within the state, and formulate them; but if they do this, they will simply be formulating the laws of their own nature. How many thousands of pages have been wasted in doctrinaire disputation through the neglect of this single observation of the first scientific political naturalist!

Aristotle goes on to support this primary observation by

recounting the elementary personal relations that enter as ingredients into the political complex, and the rudimentary needs satisfied by them. There is, for example, the household, comprising the relations between husband and wife, parent and child, and master and slave or servant, and Aristotle (unlike Confucius) is careful to say that the ruler-subject relationship must be distinguished from all these. Bound up with the household is the institution of private property and, furthermore, that of money-making, which may be limited and proportioned to household needs or else unlimited, as in trade, in which case it is not (according to Aristotle) a natural necesstiy.

From the union of households is formed the village and, from the union of villages, the state, usually the smallest union capable of being economically self-supporting. But that which originated in satisfying merely material needs is continued for the satisfaction of man's higher needs and the perfecting of the moral side of his nature, a process which (like his economic activities) can ordinarily only be carried out in the state.

IV

Such are the foundations of Aristotle's natural history of the state, all comprised in the twenty or so pages of Book I. But when he comes to the question that naturally follows upon the conclusion of Book I, the question of what precisely is this higher activity, this something beyond economic self-sufficiency, that distinctively makes the state to be a state, he passes temporarily from the standpoint of the naturalist to a series of theoretical discussions frequently recalling Plato's.

A state properly so called is, according to Aristotle, a community in which citizenship can be fully practised; and this definition leads him to elaborate the Greek ideal of citizenship and to analyse and classify the constitutions of states according to the extent to which they permit this ideal of citizenship to be realized. This part of the *Politics* is neither the most characteristic nor the most influential contribution of Aristotle to political thought. Nevertheless, some of its teachings must be recorded here because, if not characteristically Aristotelian, they are characteristically Greek and played no small part in the Greek formation of the European mind. Besides, some of Aristotle's greatest thoughts are embedded in them.

Aristotle begins his consideration of the essentials of citizenship in Book III. (Book II, as the *Politics* is now arranged, is occupied by a discussion of the ideal states of Plato and others and of some good existing states.) A citizen, says Aristotle, is one "who has the right to take part in the deliberative or judicial administration of the state" and, "speaking generally, the state is a body of citizens sufficing for the purposes of life".[1] And let no one be deceived by the apparently non-committal language of these definitions. Their language is found to commit Aristotle to a great deal when it is realized, first, that there is an underlying assumption that the purposes of life are fulfilled in and through the performance of civic duties and, secondly, that these duties are conceived on a very high and exacting level.

How exacting, is quickly shown in the course of some remarks on the composition of the citizen-body. After pointing out that citizenship will normally be hereditary, Aristotle goes on to say (III, v, 3), though his language is not always consistent, that in the best type of state those who are compelled to work with their hands for a living will not be citizens. They will be the servants of the community, whether as slaves or as wage-earners. And this is perfectly logical on Greek assumptions, as we saw them to be, in the preliminary sections of the chapter on Plato; for even if the manual workers were admitted to citizenship they would normally be debarred, both by lack of time and by lack of the right mental formation and capacity, from practising the higher civic virtues, and particularly those required for the actual work of governing. And, without those, there can only be citizenship on a lower level and Aristotle, though he grants that there are states which have, for one reason or another, at times admitted citizens on that lower level, is obviously not interested in them.

He develops these ideas in Book VII in the course of a discussion, somewhat in Plato's manner, of the best form of state, meaning by that, the form best adapted to promote the highest

[1] III, i, 12. Jowett.

kind of individual life, for the two things are closely inter-connected. He has already decided in his treatises on ethics, to which the *Politics* is really a sequel, that the best life, and the most truly happy one, is a virtuous life, either active or contemplative, "with" (he adds, in the*Politics*[1]) "possessions enough to make good actions possible". His task in the *Politics*, therefore, is to follow this up by showing what effect this demand for the virtuous life must have on the form of the state if that life is to be lived aright in it—and it certainly cannot be lived except as part of the state's life, being (as Aristotle conceives it) essentially a civic thing.

It then becomes apparent, argues Aristotle (VII, iii), that political power and the activity of ruling (which is part of the virtuous life) is only good when exercised by those who are naturally superior in this respect to those they govern. Conversely (section ix), when men are to be found who are really just, they should not have to live the lives of mechanics and tradesmen, which is inconsistent with the practice of the higher virtues as Aristotle understands them (III, v, 5), or those of husbandmen, who have no leisure, but they should have the leisure necessary for the development of virtues and the performance of political duties.

We have reached by another road the position we were at before, that the citizen body should in general consist of persons with leisure to practise the civic virtues, identified for all practical purposes with the performance of the duties of a governing class. Aristotle does not shrink from the conclusion that those whose character fits them for those duties should be endowed with property sufficient to give them the necessary leisure. Thus endowed, they would serve as soldiers and as councillors in youth and in maturity respectively and, in retirement, as priests of the city's shrines. Thus all the citizens properly so called will share in the government, each in his turn, being trained to obey in youth and rule in age.

And leisure, which is the means to these activities, is also their end—leisure and the virtues of leisure, the leisure of the cultivated man who will spend it on the state, on the arts and on political speculation in the company of his fellow citizens.

[1] VII, i, 13.

"Leisure is higher than occupation", says Aristotle, "and is the end to which occupation is directed."[1]

V

This is, indeed, the core of Aristotle's teaching concerning the nature of citizenship—the core, indeed, of all Greek political thought on the subject, even that of Athens in her extreme democratic phase. For Athens under Pericles was extremely democratic in the Greek sense precisely because, thanks to payment of judge-jurors and similar devices, every male adult not a slave or an alien had time to sit in the courts, to attend the mass meetings, to serve in the municipal magistracies if he was drawn for them and, in all circumstances, to talk politics in the city square with all the other citizens similarly unoccupied.

Anyone, therefore, who was endowed, no matter how, with the necessary leisure, possessed in Aristotle's eyes, one of the essential qualifications for full citizenship, the other being the ability to make good use of the leisure. We must be careful, therefore, before we apply to him the ideas of twentieth-century class-politics and accuse him of hostility to the working class as such and of framing political constitutions to give expression to this hostility. His attitude to the working class was a consequence rather than a cause. It was the consequence of the very high conception of political life that he shared with the Greeks generally and of the characteristically Greek absence of sentimentality with which he first perceived and then accepted as a fact that to be wholly dependent for one's livelihood on working with one's hands or in business was incompatible in more ways than one with political life on this level.

It should be added that this perception and acceptance constitute undoubedly a good part of the explanation of the Greek attitude towards slavery. They were probably a contributory cause of the actual development of it, in the Greek world, from a domestic institution confined to a comparatively few prisoners of war into an industrial slavery manning the mines, the factories and the workshops. They certainly go far

---

[1] VIII, iii, 2. Here Jowett's partiality for trenchant vigour seems to have betrayed him and I have thought it safer to quote Barker's carefully precise rendering (Oxford, 1946).

to account for the readiness of high-minded and reflective Greeks to justify the institution and, in particular, for Aristotle's astounding dictum that non-Greeks are natural slaves (I, ii, 2-4).

For the distinction that he makes, in that famous passage, between those fitted only to work with their bodies and those able to foresee with their minds simply gets us nowhere at all towards justifying that dictum. Even if we granted the ethical assumption of paganism that those with superior minds have a right to enslave those only capable of manual work, the distinction would still not fit the actual facts of Greek slavery, in which the fortunes of war played a much larger part in deciding who should be slaves than did any kind of "natural selection". Still less did the distinction correspond to the dividing line between Greeks and non-Greeks, as Aristotle knew perfectly well.

What was in the background of his thought was something implied rather than expressed in this passage. It was the picture of the vast Asiatic states, ruled by despotic monarchies, whose subjects, whether free men or slaves in the economic sense, were alike inert politically, all equally content to leave administration to royal officials, equally uninterested in political discussion, and with no thought of changing the form of government, though an occasional palace intrigue might change its personnel. For such populations the Greeks had nothing but contempt; and, granted their exacting political standards and their pre-Christian ethics, they might naturally ask the question of what use was it for such people not to be slaves. In the intense political life of a Greek state they could have no place except as labourers or clerks. Let them serve as such and set better men free for better things. Let agricultural labourers, in particular, since their work is heavy, be chosen from races lacking in spirit, since they will be better adapted to the work and, at the same time, less likely to revolt.[1]

VI

Such were the views on class questions which flowed from a conception of citizenship as, in a sense, an end in itself and a

[1] *Politics*, VII, x, 13.
8**

privilege whose justification was the practice of the duties and virtues of citizenship in a high degree. They flowed quite logically for the clear-eyed Greek pagan, though quite shockingly (to the point of being barely realizable) for the sentimental pagan of the post-Christian humanitarian age. We must be prepared for the same logic and the same shocks when we come to examine the meaning that this Greek idea of citizenship requires us to attach to the differences in political forms of which Aristotle, and the Greeks in general, had so much to say. For we still use the terms of Aristotle's famous classification (III, vii, *sqq.*), "monarchy", "aristocracy", "democracy" and the rest, but with implications that were quite unknown to him and are cherished in blank ignorance of his presuppositions.

They have come now to denote differences in the extent to which the general body of the population, and (in particular) what is called the working class, control by an occasional vote the policies pursued by organs of government manned mainly by professional politicians or civil servants. To Aristotle, the different constitutions were more like different schemes for passing round the work of the organs of government—legislative, executive and judicial—among the members of a class of politically-minded persons who, in one way or another, were set sufficiently free from the work of getting a living to perform the duties allotted to each, with time over for talking politics. Some schemes would circulate the various public offices more rapidly than others, or round a wider circle; some schemes would go further than others in making artificial provision for the necessary leisure, and so on; but all would take it for granted that there was a limit to the number of persons sufficiently politically-minded to be included on the rota (identified with the citizen-body); and all would treat proposals for delegating the work of the state to elected representatives or to paid civil servants as devices by which the members of the citizen body were deprived of, or could be induced to abdicate, their rights and functions as citizens.

That was the range of choice open to Aristotle or any other Greek of his time when discussing forms of constitution; and the best form of constitution would necessarily be, for him, as we have seen, the form most favourable to a high standard of civic activity and civic virtue. Aristotle himself, though too cautious to commit himself completely, clearly hankered after a high quality rather than a wide distribution of citizenship in this sense. His arguments find an analogy in the discussions that used to go on in England in the nineteenth century (before everyone paid lip-service to universal suffrage) concerning the extension of the franchise. Some preferred a comparatively small electorate of presumably more intelligent and instructed voters; others wished for a larger electorate of persons who presumably knew at least their own wishes and had a right to express them.

But the analogy remains only an analogy because, as we have seen, in the nineteenth century the question was merely what proportion of the population should have, every few years, the last word on national policies conducted by other persons; while for Aristotle the question was what proportion of the free population should be on the rota for conducting public policies and administering the state. We can find a closer parallel to his standpoint if we go back another century, to the eighteenth.

For, until the very end of that century in England, there was no serious question of extending the franchise, and the electorate remained an irregularly distributed but strictly limited body, amenable on all ordinary occasions to the manipulation of the governing class. That class could, therefore, and did, make very much the same assumptions about itself as Aristotle's governing class made. It assumed that a moderate amount of political activity in an atmosphere of cultivated leisure was the most suitable life for a gentleman; and that it ought to be confined as a general rule to gentlemen, that is to say, to those who did not have to earn their living, though suitable members of the professions might be permitted to enter political life as protégés of aristocratic patrons. It held also that political questions were a very suitable subject of conversation and that constitutional issues were open to discussion to the extent that (but only to the extent that) this permitted a certain amount of competition within the governing class for the prestige and perquisites of public office.

Even here, however, the analogy with any possible Greek

constitution is most imperfect; and perhaps it breaks down most completely, not, as some might suggest, over the absence of slavery (for Aristotle and the eighteenth-century aristocrat were at one in regarding the labourer, the craftsman and the trader unsuitable for public life whether slave or free man), but in the matter of size. We have already had a good deal to say about this in connection with Greek political ideas, but it is impossible to keep away from it for long, in discussing them, particularly if the Greek ideal of citizenship is in question. For just as that ideal gave a certain direction to Greek thinking on class-questions and a certain colour to Greek debates on constitutions, so, as we have seen, it set a narrow upper limit to Greek notions as to the possible size of the state. Nor could anyone have been more emphatic on this point than Aristotle himself. There is a revealing passage (II, vi, 6, 7) in which he has been discussing the ideal size for a state and has calculated the population that would be needed to support in economic idleness a citizen body maintaining a citizen army of 5,000 warriors. Finding that it would occupy "a territory as large as Babylonia or some other huge country", he dismisses the suggested figure of 5,000 warriors because "in framing a constitution, though we may assume what we wish, we should at least avoid impossibilities". Elsewhere (VII, iv, 11) he scoffs at the idea of a state so large that a herald cannot make himself heard by all the crowd.

He would have found confirmation of his views in the fact that even in the close aristocracy of eighteenth-century England, in so many respects an approximation to his constitutional ideal, the number of those who thought it worth while coming up from the country to reside in London while Parliament was sitting and the Clubs full was a very small proportion of those recognized as eligible for political life by reason of their wealth and station. As for the huge democracies, so-called, of the nineteenth and twentieth centuries, it is only in managing the affairs of the very smallest units of local self-government that it would be physically possible for them to be democracies in the Greek sense, and then only on condition that local government was freed from the stranglehold of the centralized bureaucracy.

VII

All these logical consequences of the Greek ideal of citizenship do undoubtedly make much of the *Politics* alien and unreal,
and proportionately less influential, for "the modern mind".
That is all the more reason for reminding ourselves that the
sense of strangeness arises, not from the fact that we have pro-
gressed far beyond the Greeks in this matter, but from the fact
that their ideal of citizenship was in most respects much fuller
and higher than ours. It is perhaps even more necessary to
remind ourselves of this when we come to certain further consequences of that ideal in Aristotle's thought, of which something must be said if we are to form a balanced estimate of his
influence.

It is clear, in the first place, that if so much is expected of the
citizens in the way of intelligent political activity and the
profitable use of leisure, their education and training becomes
a matter for serious consideration. The eighteenth-century
English aristocrat realized this and acted on it in his own rather
supercilious way. Aristotle took the matter almost too seriously.
He emulates Plato without Plato's lightness of touch when he
examines what both of them regard as the most important work
of the legislator, namely the provision of an adequate moral,
mental and physical training for the select group who are to
live the full civic life of war, administration, leisure and self-
cultivation.

Moreover, though somewhat less radical and drastic than
Plato in the details of his plan (after all, his governing class are
not so specialized in their functions as Plato's Guardians), he
is as absolutist and totalitarian in his fundamental assumptions.
He is as certain as is Plato that it is for the legislator to condition
the citizens completely in mind and body for the life deemed
by him to be politically virtuous and in harmony with the plan
of the state. "The citizen", he says (VIII, i, 2) " should be
moulded to suit the form of government under which he lives."

Thus the legislator must begin by regulating marriage and the
procreation of children and must then prescribe for the rearing
of them from infancy; here Aristotle's medical training and bent
makes him very detailed (VII, xvi, xvii). Even ante-natal super-

vision of mothers is provided for, and also exposure of infants, and abortion, to eliminate the deformed or the superfluous, for the population must be stabilized.

Still more important is it, in Aristotle's view, that education should be stabilized; for it needed a Christian philosophy, based on a belief in man as a being created by God in His own image and redeemed by being re-made in the pattern of God-made-man, in Whom is every kind of human perfection, to make variety an educational ideal. "Since the whole city has one purpose," says Aristotle (VIII, i, 3, 4), "it is plain that education should be one and the same for all, and that it should be public and not private. . . . Nor must we suppose that any one of the citizens belongs to himself, for they all belong to the state . . . and the care of each part is inseparable from the care of the whole."

It might be Plato speaking of his Guardians. It might be Mussolini, Hitler or Stalin speaking of all his subjects. All the more surprising and impressive is it, in view of the moral absolutism implied by such language in the mouth of a pagan, to discover in Aristotle, what both Nazi and Soviet law-courts expressly disclaimed, a deep reverence for law.

This reverence is in part bound up with the very conception of citizenship that gave rise to these high claims. It was intolerable to Aristotle as (in theory) to any Greek of the great age, that the free decisions of free men arrived at by free and intelligent discussion, should be overridden by political violence. That is why his classification of constitutions arranges them in two groups, the first group consisting of monarchy, aristocracy and the balanced constitution, any of which may be chosen by the wise man, and the second consisting of the perversions of the first three, namely despotism, plutocracy and the rule of the poor, between which three there can only be a choice of evils (III, vii, *sqq.*)

But this is only one aspect of his reverence for law, and perhaps the less important. It is evident, though his terminology is loose here, that by law he means much more than the laws which may be passed by the government of the day, which may be as violently unjust as any act of a dictator, even though passed by the mass assembly of the people (III, x, 1–3). "Customary

ARISTOTLE'S *POLITICS*

laws", he says a little later (III, xvi, 9), "have more weight, and
relate to more important matters, than written laws." And
beyond that again there is "natural justice", based on natural
reason. In the words we have already quoted, "he who bids
the law rule bids God and reason alone rule".

Here Aristotle is once again the great naturalist, who, observing first that men are not fully men unless they are citizens of a
state, then saw that they carry in their own reason the divinely
ordered pattern of their lives as citizens. When this second
truth is held steadily side by side with the first, it is possible
to have the high view of the state without moral absolutism.

VIII

If, after this survey, we are to try to estimate the influence
of the *Politics* on the political thought of succeeding ages, it
will be convenient to speak first of those teachings in it in
which Aristotle appears to us painfully limited by his own
time and nation. We have seen that these relate, first, to the size
of the state, secondly to the size of the citizen-body relatively to
the whole population of the state, thirdly to the complete
conditioning of the citizens and the entrusting of this to the
state.

We have, however, also seen that, in all three matters,
Aristotle's views are related, not merely to the limitations of his
generation, but also to one of his most fruitful political ideas,
his conception of citizenship. If he confined his political
analysis to the little Greek city-states, it was not that he did not
know of any other political committees but that he did not see
the slightest prospect of his ideal of citizenship being realized in
them. It is not unlikely that he would have come to the same
conclusion if he had lived in our own day. Similarly, if he wished
to confine citizenship to a small and specially endowed and
trained section of the population, it was not from any malicious
desire to oppress the proletariat but from a reasoned conviction
that citizenship as he understood it was not capable of being
extended to the proletariat; and again it is quite possible that
his opinion would have remained unchanged if he had been
able to observe the workings of modern democracies. As for

his plan for conditioning a picked body of citizenship-conscious citizens, if we substitute in it (as a fair modern parallel) a picked body of nation-conscious or race-conscious or class-conscious Party men in control of the state, it will at once be evident that he could be quite as modern as we are, and that if we were as much limited as he was by Greek sanity we would be all the better for it.

Certainly it was not for nothing that Aristotle was so very Greek. If he closed his eyes to many non-Greek things in order that he might better contemplate and set down the Greek ideal of citizenship, he did at least preserve for posterity an idea without which it would have been poorer, the idea that political life, the life that the citizen of a state lives in his capacity as citizen, has a distinctive character of its own, something that distinguishes it alike from family life, from economic life, and from membership of a nation that is not a state, something that asks of a man activities that cannot be practised in any of these other lives, and distinctive virtues without which his natural development is incomplete.

It is a truth that particularly needs to be restated in an age when, for ninety-nine per cent. of the population, deliberative and legislative activities are reduced to recording a vote at long intervals in the light of the headlines in a Party newspaper; when the administrative work of the state is left almost entirely to an omnipresent but secretive swarm of clerks, to whom it is not citizenship but a job; and when "the good life" for which the state exists consists of queueing up for material bounties from it. That the distinctively political idea of citizenship did not succumb earlier to this economic and materialistic view of it, is in no small measure to the vigour with which Aristotle expounded it and to the survival of classical studies into the first phase, at least, of the mechanistic age.

But if Aristotle thought politically, to our advantage, as a Greek, he had also, to our advantage, political thoughts that are admittedly world-thoughts and timeless. The most easily formulated of these is his conception of the sovereignty of the law, which comes all the more impressively from one whose conception of citizenship led him so easily to moral absolutism. He insisted that laws, governments and even forms of constitution ultimately derived their authority from their consistency with human custom and with the moral law inherent in human reason and at the same time divine; and that, when any of them was inconsistent with these, it became a perversion or a mere act of violence. This is the essence of all constitutionalism.

The times were not propitious for these thoughts to become politically effective at once. Even before the *Politics* was fully written, the Greek political world had been submerged in a world empire whose legacy was a fusion in which, in the field of politics, the Greeks accepted more from the Asiatics than the Asiatics ever learnt from the Greeks. Then the Romans, when they came, thought in terms of their own republican traditions rather than of a universal constitutionalism, and presently those traditions also vanished and the Roman Empire became the symbol and epitome of absolutism for all time, as we see in Justinian. But thoughts similar to Aristotle's, drawn from various and mostly Christian sources (for all universal thoughts are Catholic), came increasingly to prevail in the political thought of Christendom—we can recognize them in the famous summary of the purpose of Magna Carta, "that the king is, and shall be, below the law".[1] And then, not long after Magna Carta was signed, when Catholic Christendom was at its height, St. Thomas Aquinas was supplied with a close translation of the *Politics*, and the scattered thoughts became part of his own intellectual outlook in a fusion through which Aristotle still speaks in Catholic political speculation and Papal utterances.

But English constitutionalism also owes a debt to Aristotle. Lord Acton, correcting Dr. Johnson, called St. Thomas Aquinas the first Whig. Dr. Barker would correct Lord Acton and make Aristotle the first Whig, because he taught St. Thomas Aquinas. That is only partly true, for Aquinas had other sources, but at least Aristotle reinforced Aquinas' thought and, to use Dr. Barker's own words, "through St. Thomas he taught Catholic Europe". The same writer goes on to trace the line of transmission from the thirteenth to the eighteenth century, through St. Thomas to Richard Hooker, the author of the *Ecclesiastical Polity*, and through Hooker to Locke, who drew

[1] Pollock and Maitland, *History of English Law*, vol. I, p. 173.

largely on Hooker's theory of law and government for his own two *Treatises on Civil Government*, and, again, through Locke to Burke, who had also some first-hand knowledge of both St. Thomas Aquinas and Aristotle. There is thus, says Dr. Barker, "not only an analogy . . . between the climate of Aristotle's *Politics* and the climate of English political thought in the seventeenth and eighteenth centuries. There is also some measure of affiliation".[1]

IX

Finally—and most difficult of all to capture and restate, because it is nowhere explicitly formulated and systematized by Aristotle, and the Greeks had not even a word for it—we derive from the *Politics* the philosophy of what we can now call the "organic" state. It is implicit in Aristotle's biological outlook, and it is only necessary to set out its many facets one by one to see how deeply his thought was permeated by it, even though, for lack of a word, he may never have been clearly conscious of it as a separate and distinctive mode of thought. It may be added that even in our own day the metaphor is applied to politics for two mutually inconsistent purposes, and that both of them can find support in the *Politics*.

In the first place, then, the state is a biological phenomenon, the product of spontaneous growth and not artificially put together. Nothing could be more Aristotelian than that.

Furthermore, the state, like all complex biological units, is composed of members all of which are themselves alive, each with its distinctive form and function and its own contribution to make to the whole. This principle, which is explicitly stated in Book II, chapter ii, underlies the whole discussion of citizenship and non-citizenship and has a further application to the corporate units composing the state—the household and the village, for example—as well as to individual citizens.

Nevertheless, the state, like all biological units, is something much more than the sum of its parts. A heap of stones is simply an aggregation of stones but a swarm of bees has a corporate

[1] Ernest Barker, *The Politics of Aristotle*, Introduction (p. lxii), to which the paragraph preceding this last one is also indebted.

life wholly different from the sum of the lives of the same number of solitary bees ; and the various members of it individually live lives that dovetail into one another, such as no solitary bee could live. So it is with the state and its citizens, as Aristotle makes plain, not only in all his state-planning, but also in explicit statements concerning the distinctive character of political life as compared with the lives of its economic and other units, and the distinctive degree of goodness attainable in it and nowhere else.

But it is a corollary of this aspect of an organic unit that its component members receive from the whole a stamp and character that could only come from it, and fulfil in the whole a purpose altogether surpassing their purposes as separate individuals. From this it is arguable from the pagan point of view (which has no grasp of the eternal, and therefore altogether transcendent, purpose for which each individual man was created) that the lives of the citizens owe all that is best in them to the state and, indeed, would have little or no meaning outside the state, so that they should be completely at the disposal of the state, to serve its purposes, far higher than their own. We have already quoted Aristotle to this effect.

It is here, indeed, that the metaphor manifests its double edge. When it was used to show that the component members all have their own lives and distinctive functions, it seemed to support the citizen against the excessive claims of the state; but the insistence on the subordination of the members to the whole is a stand-by of totalitarianism and moral absolutism. Aristotle can, as we have said, be quoted on either side; but at least he was not in either case committing the elementary blunder of arguing from a metaphor.

Finally, the state like all organisms, contains within itself its own behaviour-pattern, or law of its own being, manifested in those innate propensities that on the animal level we call instincts. Moreover, in organic communities, the propensities born in individual members are so correlated with those of all other members as to form a single pattern or law of corporate behaviour, as in a swarm of bees. And, because the units composing a state are rational beings, they will be conscious of these laws of the state's life, and their own, and formulate them in political terms as political rights and duties, recognizing them as implied in the relationships in which they find themselves to have been born and to be instinctively living. They will also regard them as carrying moral obligations, because all the practical precepts of the natural reason carry moral obligations; and thus we arrive by another road at the sovereignty of law. All this, again, is the purest Aristotelianism.

Such is the philosophy of the organic state, set out in terminology unknown in Aristotle's day but finding, point for point, its counterpart in Aristotle and in a very large measure derived from the Aristotelian tradition. Indeed, it may be said that the developments in biological science that in comparatively recent times made this terminology possible and popular, gave a new lease of life to Aristotle's influence, because in Aristotle was found the only great political thinking that would fit the conceptions of the latest biological science.

If, in face of such a revival of a scientist who taught more than two thousand years ago, we must still speak of the limitation of his political observation and ideals to the little Greek world, then, instead of mocking at it, we would be better employed in marvelling at the intellectual power and insight that could reach such majestic and enduring generalizations from such restricted and ephemeral data.

To political insight and intellectual power, we ought to add, as part of the explanation of the wonder, Aristotle's philosophical technique. The essentials of it he owed to Plato, but he transposed Plato's theory of "ideas" into a doctrine of "informing" patterns and receptive material, whose mutual interactions he interpreted in terms of purpose, so as to connect the shapes and development of things with the purposes they appeared to serve. Thereby he provided himself with the best possible terminology for a philosophy of the organic. For the biological organism clearly is what it is in virtue of the fact that it is animated by a distinctive behaviour-pattern that guides its activities towards ends discernible by rational observers of its life.

It is no mere coincidence, therefore, that the profoundest political teachings of Aristotle have been most appreciated when his metaphysical technique has been generally accepted, and have been disregarded or disparaged when that technique has been derided. It was conspicuously during his eclipse as a philosopher, after the Renaissance, and largely in consequence of that eclipse, that artificial contractual theories of the state and atomistic individualism had their feverish day. Correspondingly, it was largely owing to the adoption of the Aristotelian philosophical technique in her official philosophy in the thirteenth century that the Catholic Church has preserved a continuous tradition of the organic state (under other names) in her political thinking from that time till now.

But both the reaction against Aristotelian politics and the continuation of them are embodied in books that are themselves among the decisive books of history. Between them, indeed, these books constitute an appreciable proportion of the latter part of our list. That is in itself some measure of the decisiveness of the book they superseded. And indeed, in the *Politics*, for all its inconsistencies—we may almost say, because of them —was epitomized for all time the best political thinking of antiquity. For Plato attempted what is given only to the angels; but Aristotle stood firm upon all the wisdom attainable by fallen and pre-Christian man.

INDEX OF NAMES

[In the following Index of Names of persons, places and institutions, the arabic numerals refer to pages, and the large and small roman numerals to chapters and chapter-sections respectively.]